JOIN, OR DIE

DIGITAL ADVERTISING IN THE AGE OF AUTOMATION

PATRICK GILBERT

MILL CITY PRESS

Mill City Press, Inc.
2301 Lucien Way #415
Maitland, FL 32751
407.339.4217
www.millcitypress.net

Cover Design: Teddi Black
Interior Design: Megan McCullough

Printed in the United States of America

Paperback ISBN-13: 978-1-6322-1768-4
Dust Jacket ISBN-13: 978-1-6322-1888-9
Ebook ISBN-13: 978-1-6322-1889-6

Contents

Foreword: David Sable & Isaac Rudansky

I first met Patrick and the AdVenture Media team for dinner in 2018. Over good food and a few bottles of wine, we discussed life... work...Google and Facebook...spirituality...family time....and have continued on those topics and more since.

What attracted me to them and the company was their ethics...work and personal...the modest and humble way they approach their business dealings and clients. They knew that the advertising industry was in need of a cultural change...or maybe an attitude adjustment... and they wanted to be the drivers of that change...specifically related to the automated technology they were bringing to bear for their clients.

Many years ago, I coined the phrase DIGIBABBLE to reference companies and people who pontificated and opined on technology being the all-in solution for everything. As if there could be a Harry Potter magic wand that would solve all problems.

Modern tech firms and marketing agencies are prime spewers of Machine Learning and AI DIGIBABBLE...preaching the Gospel of end to end technology solutions. Yet, the truth is, technology, any technology...as efficient as it might be...is only as powerful as the human experts who know how best to leverage its full potential.

AdVenture Media embraced automation, long before many, but they have the human intel of it baked into their DNA. They have learned, the hard way, that it is necessary to have a deep understanding of how and when to use technology to unlock the best outcomes, resulting in more meaningful and profitable engagements. They've put in the work, and they're now willing to share their secrets with the world.

Patrick has been burning the midnight oil on this wonderful book for over 18 months. It won't take long to read, but those that choose to really study and learn from it will reap benefits that will last a lifetime. These principles are core to whatever new technology will emerge… and they will…sooner than you think.

Their *People First* approach has enabled them to thrive in the Pandemic of 2020…when other, bigger; smaller; newer; older companies fell by the wayside.

They hate smug complacency and are generous in their offering us all an opportunity to learn from their success.

I love learning…this book fulfills….

Use it well,

David Sable
Senior Advisor, WPP; Former Global CEO, Young & Rubicam

Dear Reader,

I'm miserly with praise. Not so much with criticism. It's a regrettable dimension of my character.

But I may not be in such bad company. David Ogilvy, at twenty-two, took a job as a chef at the acclaimed Hotel Majestic in Paris. Ogilvy's thirty-seven man brigade was run by the supreme, spellbinding head-chef Monsieur Pitard.

> "M. Pitard praised very seldom, but when he did, we were exalted to the skies...On one of these memorable occasions, I was covering frogs' legs with a white chaud-froid sauce, decorating each little thigh with an ornate leaf of chervil. Suddenly, I became aware that M. Pitard was standing beside me, watching. I was so frightened that my knees knocked together and my hands trembled. He took the pencil from his starched toque and waved it in the air, his signal for the whole brigade to gather. Then he pointed at my frogs' legs and said, very slowly and very quietly, *"That's how to do it."*

So come, reader, gather round. Look closely.

The book you hold in your hands is an experience, if you allow it to be. And like ogres and onions, experiences have layers.

The top layer: Knowledge!

Join or Die is a digital advertising masterclass. Marketers have no shortage of information, but there exists an unfortunate dearth of knowledge … what propels your career, the matter of the intellect, the substance from which competence blooms.

Patrick's got it, and here he's offering it to you.

Take it. Follow this roadmap, and you'll be a better marketer. In *Join or Die*, Patrick teaches the curious reader how to think about complex problems; how to brush away the topsoil and inspect what lies beneath the surface.

The knowledge Patrick imparts in *Join or Die* is accessible. And it's no small thing to take a complex algorithm, break it down, and present it so a marketer unfamiliar with machine learning can understand, appreciate and actually implement. Patrick spent untold hours writing, sure, but he spent as many or more hours thinking about the writing.

The hard work paid off. For you, primarily, reader. Armed with the knowledge, techniques and understanding found in *Join or Die*, you will have an unfair advantage over your co-workers; your colleagues; competing agencies.

What a damn thing.

Onwards, to the next layer down.

Patrick recounts his first interview with AdVenture Media, so I need not recall it here. There was a lot of sawdust.

I met Patrick six years ago. We were a company of three in 185 square feet of office space. It was tight. I called Patrick back for a second interview only as a formality; I wanted to hire him halfway through the first. What stood out to me was his character.

Patrick had (and still has) an insatiable desire to grow, an immutable thirst for knowledge and an otherworldly ambition to master his craft. But it's Patrick's consistent head-to-the-ground, no-excuses work ethic which puts his character in motion.

You have a front row seat to what several years of hard work looks like. Pay attention, because it's inspirational. Patrick took no shortcuts. His accomplishments are a credit to his perseverance, positivity and sense of divine discontent.

Join or Die is the best of Patrick's wisdom, inspiration, knowledge, and training. It's authentic. It's what he teaches at AdVenture Media. And it's delivered with the utmost respect for the reader; with an implicit belief in *your own* capability to achieve mastery.

And finally, on a *personal* level, writing this foreword and seeing this book near publication gives me an enormous sense of satisfaction. The satisfaction that calms your nerves and warms you up. That things are working out, that they'll be alright. That hard work does pay off. That relationships are worth investing in. That life is moving forward. Up and down, surely, but forward nonetheless.

So this is as much a note to Patrick as it is to you, reader.

The publication of Join or Die is in no trivial way a validation of my own life, ambitions, desires. To surround myself with great people, capable of great things; to orchestrate an environment where greatness can be manifest. It's a blessing.

What both Patrick and you (and me) don't know about digital marketing can fill libraries. But Patrick's library is smaller than yours (and mine). Don't take his word as gospel (don't do that with anyone). If Patrick says "Jump," don't ask, "How high?"

But assume there's a good enough reason to jump. Work hard to understand his perspective… Then decide.

If I were the great Monsieur Pitard, and I had a pencil in my pocket, I'd wave it in the air, signaling you to gather. To draw close to me.

And I'd say, "This is how it's done."

With much gratitude,

Isaac Rudansky
Founder and CEO, AdVenture Media

Introduction

As I write these words, my team and I are attempting to steer our agency through the height of the COVID-19 pandemic. This period, which will go down as the largest economic disruption since the Great Depression, has had a profound effect on the world as we know it.

Confirmed cases of the Coronavirus continue to rise each day, particularly across the greater NYC area where we are all based. For some, these changes have been relatively minor, such as adjusting to remote work or navigating the difficulties and loneliness of life in isolation. For others, these changes have meant loss of income, security, and even life. In the last week, I've had several interactions with devastated clients who are being forced to close their doors and carry the weight of having had to lay off employees.

If not for the massive cultural and technological shift that we embraced years ago, my agency might have been in the same position. We would not be as efficient, nor would we have attracted and retained the high caliber of employees whom we have trusted to manage our client accounts during these turbulent times.

I am confident that our agency will make it through this pandemic with little more than a few bruises. In fact, I expect us to be stronger than we were before, and the principles that make up the following chapters reflect that determined optimism.

Here's how we got there:

I grew up surrounded by retail. My father has had a long career serving various IT roles, developing loyalty programs, inventory management systems, and point-of-sale solutions for companies like Duane Reade, Walgreens, and Vineyard Vines. He will strike up a conversation with anybody and has been known to badger the occasional grocery store clerk with questions about the POS system on the cash register. Concepts of customer service, sales techniques, and retail technology were omnipresent throughout my childhood.

When I was fourteen, I got a job working for a small appliance store in my hometown. The owners wanted to advertise their spring BBQ sale and needed someone who was willing to stand up on top of a truck, dressed as a BBQ chef while waving to drivers coming down the town's main road. It was hilarious and a bit humiliating, but it paid well.

Moreover, it worked. Jay's Appliances sold more BBQs that year than ever before. It was the first—and probably the most successful—ad campaign of my career. I spent the next six years at Jay's Appliances, spending time in nearly every role and learning the inner workings of a small business in a competitive industry.

I went on to study marketing and economics at Penn State. My college career was filled with extracurriculars, from case studies with the American Marketing Association to club lacrosse. But the experience that left the largest impact on my future was with the Penn State Dance Marathon (THON), a year-long student philanthropy that raises money for childhood cancer care and research.

Through THON, I learned what felt like to work alongside highly intelligent, passionate, and altogether wonderful people. It was all-encompassing, energizing, and extremely rewarding work in service of a phenomenal cause. My time there has had a massive impact on my current definition of success.

In his book, *Principles,* Ray Dalio claims that the concept of success is subjective and generally determined by personal values. These values fall somewhere on a spectrum with *Savor Life* at one end and *Make An Impact* at the other. Most people live their lives somewhere in the middle.

According to Dalio:

> Some people want to change the world and others want to operate in simple harmony with it and savor life. Neither is better… The question isn't just how much of each to go after, but how hard to work to get as much as possible. I wanted crazy amounts of each and was thrilled to work hard to get as much of both as possible. I soon found that they could be one and the same, and mutually reinforcing.[1]

He ultimately concludes that true success is earned as a result of the *meaningful work* you produce and the *meaningful relationships* you develop throughout your career. These are equally important and self-reinforcing.

I held several retail internships throughout college, and the start of my post-graduate career was spent meandering between nonprofits and Wall Street. I would eventually pursue a career with a digital agency and conclude that I needed to find an agency where I could have access to meaningful work and meaningful relationships.

I stumbled upon AdVenture Media Group in the spring of 2015. The company was based on the south shore of Long Island in a town called Cedarhurst, about a mile from JFK airport.

On a humid Friday morning, I met Isaac Rudansky at the tiny office that we now refer to as *AdVenture Media 1.0*. The night before my interview, a construction crew was converting a storage closet into a small conference room, and the whole place was filthy. Isaac and I arrived at the same time, and upon unlocking the door, he casually wiped a thick layer of sawdust from the couches so that we could sit down and talk.

He joked that he started the company by accident in 2012. He was an artist, making a living selling paintings at Long Island art shows. He launched a website in hopes of selling his art online and turned to Google AdWords to drive traffic to his website. In classic Isaac fashion, he became obsessed with this topic. He read every Google AdWords article and book he could get his hands on and started running campaigns for friends and family members who owned small businesses.

He eventually recorded an hour-long training video that quickly became the top result for *Google AdWords Tutorial* on YouTube. It wasn't long before people started calling to ask for his help in managing their own campaigns. Isaac shrugged his shoulders and thought, *I guess I have a PPC business now.*

Call it fate or coincidence but owning a PPC business turned out to be a pretty good fit for his personality and skill set.

Isaac invited me back for a second interview the following week, a meeting that was more of a formality. We mostly spoke about the Dave Matthews Band and how he planned on working from the beach at least once a week that summer.* He introduced me to the other two team members, Danny Tawil and Ari Pirutinsky, and I immediately sensed that there was something unique about this group of people.

Danny brought a long career in digital advertising to the table—literally, a table—as he and Isaac spent the first few months working from Isaac's kitchen. Ari joined the team a few weeks before me and has been my counterpart throughout this entire journey.

Joining AdVenture Media was going to be a significant risk, and any concerns I had were certainly amplified on my first day. When I arrived, Isaac told me that we'd take a trip to Best Buy later that afternoon to pick out a laptop,

> But first, we have to stop at Hofstra University. I'm getting a master's in Industrial Psychology, and I have an exam this afternoon, so you'll have to come with me and just hang out while I do that.

Oh, OK. That's totally normal, Isaac.

Those first few months were crazy. Ari and I immediately had full workloads and much to learn. Isaac hired a consultant to train us, three nights a week for six months. We'd order food from the same burger

---

* *AdVenture Media Beach Wednesdays* were crucial in helping us develop the relationships that have carried us this far. They were short-lived, but we've continued to ensure that we create an environment for these sorts of interpersonal bonds to flourish as we grow the team.

place up the street almost every night, and Isaac would graciously pick up the tab. We were unbelievably unhealthy, spending twelve to fifteen hours per day cramped in a small office and eating burgers almost every night. But it was glorious. The photos from the original *Beach Wednesdays,* however, are not glorious.

Our hard work quickly began to pay off, and we doubled in size every year across four consecutive years. We moved into a larger office in 2017, and then again in 2019. AdVenture Media currently has twenty employees working out of our new office in Woodmere.

I've since taken on the role of executive director, managing the team and day-to-day client services so that Isaac can dedicate the majority of his time to projects that will help us continue to grow long term. Danny now manages an SMB consulting arm of the company, and Ari heads our enterprise sales efforts. The team has grown substantially over the last few years and is now filled with an eclectic mix of account strategists, data scientists, CRO analysts, content specialists, and business development associates.

During this period of quarantine and social distancing, this project has brought me a great deal of comfort. It has forced me to reflect on the meaningful work and meaningful relationships that I've been blessed with over the last five years. I'm excited for what is to come as well as the opportunity to provide a blueprint for other marketers, agencies, and future AdVenture Media employees who wish to survive in the age of automation.

Who Is This Book For?

This book is for both marketing agencies and their clients, but specifically for the leaders in those organizations who are responsible for establishing goals, setting expectations, and developing the culture in which their marketing teams operate. The lessons that fill the following pages are geared toward decision-makers who are interested in taking their organizations into the modern world, where machine learning and artificial intelligence are driving success in all marketing and advertising activities.

Unfortunately, many individuals in these decision-making roles are too stubborn to read this book. Even if they were to receive a copy, they would likely just skim through, skipping sections that they are certain they're already experts in.

Therefore, I have really written this book for the next generation: the open-minded, optimistic marketers of the future, who aspire to be decision-makers in their organizations. If you are early in your marketing career or looking to take the next step, these pages will be instrumental in helping you frame your perspective and will prevent you from developing outdated habits.

This book isn't exclusively geared toward those who work with Google Ad campaigns. While Google is the central platform referenced throughout, the concepts translate cross-platform and will help you make intelligent marketing decisions on all advertising channels.

This book is filled with essential, foundational knowledge that will empower you to drive your own success. It is filled with best practices that will work well in a vacuum. That said, I would advise you not to let the idea of a best practice lead to complacency. You should always be willing to challenge best practices, given the unique characteristics of your business.

Just as there are no guarantees in life, there are no guarantees in marketing. There's no perfect algorithm that can anticipate the likelihood of a conversion with 100 percent accuracy. The algorithm's goal is never to become *perfect;* that's impossible. Its goal is to reduce the gap between expected outcome and actual outcome. With more data, the algorithm increases its confidence and can reduce the size of that gap, increasing the likelihood of success. This is your goal, as well.

The foundational knowledge in this book will lay the groundwork that will allow you to work alongside automated technology to unlock success now and in the future.

Why Does This Book Exist?

There has long been tension between Google and the PPC managers that run ads on Google's platform. First is the idea that Google could automate so much of the platform that agencies become obsolete. But above that, there is often a distinct gap between the performance expectations that Google sets and the reality of what PPC managers actually experience.

I sit in the middle of this tension. I see both sides, and I want to tell you how it really is.

On the one hand, I have great relationships with several product specialists, agency development managers, and account strategists at Google. They've been instrumental in our agency's growth. Without their guidance over the last few years, this book wouldn't exist.

On the other hand, I am on the ground floor of an agency that sees these campaigns at play, and I am held responsible for the budgets spent on advertising. We are the ones who must answer to clients when things go haywire, and we've experienced instances where the boilerplate Google response is both frustrating and unhelpful.

There are times when we believe that Google's recommended best practices would be more effective for a given campaign in the long term, but short-term goals or other events might force us to stray from those recommendations. Additionally, clients often have expectations, or demands, that are far from what would be considered a Google best practice, so concessions need to be made on our end for the good of the relationship.

A good agency will sit in the middle, consider both sides, and make decisions that are in the best interest of the client. A bad agency will blame Google every time something goes wrong.

Agencies aren't alone in their contentious feelings toward Google. Marketing executives across industries have either had bad experiences themselves or been brainwashed by their PPC agencies into thinking Google is evil.

Many agencies have earned client trust by painting Google as the villain. We've all heard the battle cry: *automation is just Google's way to trick you into spending more of your money!* When an agency says that to a client, the client is given the impression that the agency is on their team and looking out for their best interests. It's a sales tactic—one I have utilized in conversation with clients when I was younger, and a bit naive.

Google Ads remains atop the list of profit-generating advertising channels for many of our clients. It is our responsibility as an agency to adapt. I am very pro-Google, but I have no problem calling attention to the imperfections within the Google Ads platform or their broader service offerings.

The message to embrace automation has largely fallen on deaf ears. So here I am, an agency leader myself, to tell you: *Join or Die.*

The Motivation Behind It All

I was frustrated with a client.

In 2018, one of our clients outright refused to allow our team to adopt automated strategies, despite the data inside their own account that proved its viability. I began drafting an email to their management team, outlining the benefits of automation and the looming threats that existed if we sat back and allowed our competitors to integrate automation before we did.

As I wrote, it became clear that this attempt was in vain. There was no way I could change this client's mind, and I didn't want to sully the relationship. So, I never sent that email. We carried out our marching orders and did the best we could, given the parameters set by the client.

That moment was a catalyst. I realized then that I needed to help change the conversation around automation. So I pasted that unsent email into a Google Doc and began writing a blog that was eventually titled: *Join or Die: It's Time to Embrace Google Automation.*

Much of the article was written from a wobbly table at the Charleston International Airport. I was flying home after a long wedding weekend, and as I sat adjacent to a fast-service pizza counter, I noticed a man sitting nearby with a massive calf tattoo of the *Join or Die* snake. The snake is a symbol from the American Revolution, used by Benjamin Franklin to inspire the US colonies to join together in the fight against the British Empire.

I realized then that the tone of my article needed to accurately reflect the stakes at hand. I now had a title and a new tone that would inspire my writing for the next two years. My goal was to use this article to help prime clients understand our attitude toward automation. I dreamed of a world where clients would stumble upon our site and think: *Wow! These people get it!*

That didn't happen, but in December of 2018, I received a LinkedIn message from someone named Adam with the title of *Regional Product Lead (Automation) at Google.* The message read:

> Dude, your Join or Die article def got some buzz internally. Would love to chat more on this as it's pretty much the same theme I've baked into our positioning. Let me know if you're free for a call this week!

I spoke to Adam and a few of his colleagues later that week. After our conversation, they invited me to host a Q&A session at an internal training summit, where agency development managers, product specialists, and account strategists from around the country gathered at Google's NYC headquarters to discuss how they could aid partner agencies more effectively in the coming year.

My session was centered around how AdVenture Media had embraced automation, and I provided advice to the Googlers in attendance about how they could coach their agencies through the same process. We discussed managing client expectations, making hiring decisions, and the myriad ways in which day-to-day operations have changed for agencies as they've struggled to adapt to the fast pace of automation.

I was then introduced to Richie, a Google product lead based in Ireland, and Suzanne, the director of agency solutions for the UK market. They invited me to speak at the Google Innovation Summit in 2019 and then to deliver a keynote at the Global Google Premier Partner Awards in 2019.

The theme of all these conversations: Join or die.*

Despite all of this, there are plenty of agencies, clients, and marketing executives who have not yet embraced automation or remain focused on the wrong PPC KPIs. Too many people are underutilizing this incredible technology. What's worse: those who use it are often doing so incorrectly. I'm hoping to change that.

Here are my steps to achieving digital advertising success in the age of automation:

1. Embrace change. Automation is a necessary component to achieving marketing success, now and in the future. Embrace that fact. Even if you have decades of experience in PPC, there is still plenty to learn about the modern digital advertising landscape.
2. Learn everything there is to know about automated technology and how it can be manipulated to achieve your marketing goals.
3. Use this knowledge to find creative solutions to complex problems, both in your advertising campaigns and within your organization. Think differently about how to hire, how to manage your team, and what value you provide to your clients. Find comfort in the fact that everything you do will continue to change every year or so.

I've been so proud of the creative solutions that our team has developed over the last two years. Solutions that use automation in unique ways to solve complex problems. You'd be astonished at what can be achieved when you surround yourself with smart people—individuals who understand the tech and are constantly thinking up new ways to use it.

I want you to experience these victories. My goal is for the global PPC community to reach a point where we are all sharing ideas, building upon them, and challenging one another to continue growing.

---

* Funnily enough, the name of my presentation was accidentally changed to *Automate or Die* before I gave one of these talks in London. In hindsight I was lucky, as it wouldn't have been great for me to be on stage in London specifically referencing anti-British propaganda from the American Revolution.

What started as an emotionally charged email to a client has been rearranged in countless iterations—from a blog post, to several blog posts, to a few speaking arrangements, and countless conversations. And now, a book.

I set out to change the conversation around automation. What I learned along the way is that *real* change has to be a team effort.

It is on all of us in the industry—agencies, clients, and even Google—to change the conversation around automation. To learn all that we can and become informed participants in the conversation about how to best use this technology to drive success in our campaigns.

Before I accepted the offer to join AdVenture Media in 2015, I sent a long email to a mentor of mine in which I outlined my concerns, as well as what I found appealing about the opportunity. One concern was that I feared I might not "have the opportunity to play a role in strategy and partake in content creation for both the agency and for clients" and might instead be trapped "tooling around with keywords all day hoping to improve Quality Score."

I recently rediscovered this email thread and showed it to Isaac. He laughed and said, "And here we are, all these years later, *still* churning out content that tells people to stop spending their time tooling around with keywords, hoping to improve Quality Score."

Perhaps this book will get the message across, once and for all.

Section 1

Join or Die

"It's incredibly important for anyone in business to have one foot in the present and one foot in the future.

"[Roone Arledge] was the first person I ever worked for who embraced technological advancements to revolutionize what we did and how we did it … He wanted to try every new gadget and break every stale format.

"Roone taught me the dictum that has guided me in every job I've held since: *Innovate or die, and there's no innovation if you operate out of fear of the new or untested.*"

Bob Iger, CEO, The Walt Disney Company

1 Automation Insecurities

I've always had a weird relationship with automation. I began working in PPC at a time where manual optimization was more effective than Google's nascent automated campaigns, at least for the SMB sized budgets that I was working with at the time.

I didn't mind manual optimizations. I took pride in building massive campaigns with single keyword ad groups (SKAGs), nuanced audience segmentation, and keywords covering all four match types. I loved exporting massive datasets into Excel and using complicated formulas to uncover hidden search term gems that could be added as exact match keywords with an aggressive bid. It was monotonous but satisfying work. I felt important. I was providing value and helping my clients grow.

I pushed back against automation for a long time. Many of the PPC thought leaders that I'd subscribed to had made the claim that automation was evil. Our agency published quite a bit of content that devalued automation in hopes of convincing prospective clients that manual bidding, managed by an agency, was the only way to go. I wrote some of that content.

Even as the value of automation began to outweigh manual campaigns, my stance against it remained strong. I continued to steer clients away and used every opportunity that I had to take a jab at Google for pushing it down our throats.

Despite all of that, there were still plenty of times when I included automation as part of my campaign strategy. However, more often than not, it failed.

"*Well—the results of the Automated Bidding tests are in, and all it seemed to do was increase our CPCs. It looks like Manual Bidding is the way to go for this campaign.*"

I've emailed a variation of that sentence to dozens of clients.

Looking back on that time, I feel a mixture of embarrassment and humility.

Of course, it failed. I had been rooting against it all along because I'd wanted to believe that I was better than the algorithms. I would constantly ignore suggestions from Google that could have increased the success of the automated strategies because I really wanted to be able to go back to the client and report that my manual campaigns had once again outperformed the machine. I was biased, so I never gave it a chance.

It's obvious to me now that the stubborn anti-automation stance that I, and so many of my colleagues, believed in was rooted in fear.

I was convinced that automation would put me out of a job, so I pushed back every time Google introduced a new feature that would automate part of my work.

While my over segmented manual campaigns were impressive to look at, they generally missed the mark at achieving one thing: profitable growth.

It became clear that our inability to drive profitable growth for clients on a consistent basis was a much larger threat to our agency than the machines.

What's more, it wasn't just that our clients weren't growing. Our agency wasn't growing either.

How to Grow an Agency

There are three ways a marketing agency can grow revenues:

1. Acquiring new business
2. Improving retention rates
3. Growing existing clients

Five years ago, the last of these was essentially off the table. It was rare that we'd grow a client to the point where we could charge them a higher management fee on a consistent basis. Sure, it happened from time to time, but it wasn't common enough for us to rely on as a realistic means to grow to the agency we wanted to become.

New Business

We've been blessed with plenty of new business opportunities that have helped us grow over the years. In 2015, Isaac Rudansky, our CEO, published a 15-hour Google AdWords course on the learning platform Udemy.com. For three months, Isaac worked 20 hours a day to complete this course, converting the living room in his one-bedroom apartment into a full production studio.*

The agency was just four people at the time, including Isaac. During this time, I would go entire weeks without seeing him, and it drove me crazy. It was a huge risk, but it was a good bet to make.

The Udemy course was a huge success. At the time of writing, it has more than 140K students worldwide. Isaac went on to publish three more courses: one course on retargeting, one on conversion rate optimization, and one on Facebook messenger bots (co-branded and supported by Larry Kim, founder of Wordstream and MobileMonkey).

Isaac has since gone on to develop *Isaac Rudansky's Agency Overdrive,* an online training library to help freelancers and digital agency owners.

---

* Isaac's wife, Frayde, is the unsung hero of this story for having agreed to this and the other wild things Isaac has done over the years.

Now, Isaac is often recognized as the *marketing guy in the green beanie.* One night after a client meeting, Isaac and I were grabbing dinner at a cramped burger bar in Soho when a young couple, clearly on an awkward first date, sat down at the table next to us. As our bill arrived, the man saw his window of opportunity closing and gestured for our attention.

"Excuse me, but are you Isaac Rudansky?"

To this day, I feel bad for the young lady who sat there silently watching her food get cold as Isaac's fan of the year continued to ask for tips on how to sell guitar lessons online. It was excruciating to witness and finally ended when I cut in to remind Isaac that we had a train to catch.

The Udemy course became our primary driver of inbound leads, including the likes of *Forbes* magazine, AMC Networks, Hearst Media, and TaxJar.

Retention

By the end of 2015, the Udemy course helped fuel revenue growth in terms of new business. Unfortunately, new business isn't nearly as profitable as client retention. We offered month-to-month contracts at the time, and clients occasionally chose to opt out shortly after coming on board. Sure, even a short-term relationship contributes to revenue growth, but in the long term, it would often be unprofitable for us.

What's more, we needed to hire new team members to work on all the great new accounts we were signing, but we couldn't afford to do so if we didn't first find a way to improve client retention. We needed stability.

I made it my personal mission to solve our retention problem and found that there were three main reasons why good clients left:

1. Misaligned expectations

   Misaligned expectations could be remedied with better communication and transparency. In the last five years, we've overhauled our sales and onboarding process three or four times with the intention of setting better expectations, outlining more definitive deliverables, and establishing trust early in the relationship.

2. Poor performance

   The second downfall to retention, poor performance, can't just be solved after a few creative brainstorming sessions. We've had many clients whom we've worked our asses off for, but we just couldn't drive the necessary performance. It was awful being unable to deliver results for clients whom you enjoyed working with, but it was the unfortunate reality.

   We needed to challenge ourselves to do better: to hire the best talent, break old habits, not be afraid to make mistakes, and exercise extreme self-awareness at all times. We needed to constantly be learning and growing.

3. Decreased value-added by the agency over time

   A client will leave if they feel that the value your agency provides has declined over time. Campaign performance might be strong—phenomenal even—but if your perceived value has declined, the client will choose to terminate the relationship in search of a more proactive agency, or decide to bring the efforts in-house.

   This one hurts the most because it's completely avoidable. When an agency becomes complacent and stops bringing new ideas to the table, the client will inevitably realize that their investment is better spent elsewhere. Don't take them for granted; *these are the clients that you should be focused on growing.*

I'm proud to say that our retention rates are better than ever. We've changed our processes so that we can set clearer, more realistic expectations with our clients, and overall campaign performance is better than ever. We have developed much stronger relationships with our clients, to the extent that even when performance dips, they maintain trust in our abilities and dedication.

Client Growth

Thanks in large part to automation, we have added to our service offerings and are able to spend more time working on client projects outside of the specific ad platforms. Our clients used to view us as their PPC agency (or simply, their *Google Ads agency*). Now, they view us as their partners or marketing consultants.

We now have dedicated team members who are tasked with identifying clients with growth opportunities in order to ensure that the relationship stays active. A growth officer can focus on the long term, while the rest of the account management team is free to manage the day-to-day operations and focus on short-term performance goals. These roles would never have fit into our organization five years ago.

After much speculation about how our agency would grow and where technology fit into that plan, I eventually realized that, while automation would change my job, it wouldn't necessarily replace me.

In fact, if the last two years have taught me anything, it's that *thanks to automation, the opportunity to provide value to clients is now greater than ever before.*

Basic Machine Learning Principles

Pedro Domingos, author of *The Master Algorithm: How the Quest for the Ultimate Learning Machine Will Remake Our World,* claims that we've reached a point with machine learning where there is too much at stake. Our fates, individually and collectively, will be determined by machine learning. Therefore, the layperson needs to increase their understanding of the technology in order to thrive.[2]

It's like driving a car. Only the engineers and mechanics need to know the details about how the engine works, but everyone needs to know where the steering wheel and pedals are in order to get on the road.

This chapter includes the baseline information you need to know in order to properly operate a machine learning engine.

What to do with Ubiquitous Data

I've been playing fantasy football for about 15 years. When I was starting out, fantasy analysis was hard to come by. My friends would show up to our fantasy football drafts with information that they'd curated from various sources.

Nowadays, there's *too much* fantasy football coverage. Even the laziest owners will hear about the sleeper prospects that would have won you your league in 2005. There are few secrets or surprises that come up during a fantasy draft. The data is ubiquitous.

Similarly, there are few keyword secrets in the modern digital advertising ecosystem that your competitors don't know about. In 2016, AdVenture Media started working with a company called ProShotCase, makers of a smartphone case that essentially turns your iPhone into a GoPro camera. The case was completely waterproof and had a fish-eye lens attached that enhanced photo and video capabilities.

When building a keyword list for this product, one might assume that *waterproof iPhone case* would be considered a *bottom-funnel* (BOF) keyword. However, you would be wrong.*

Most people searching for *waterproof iPhone case* are looking for an $80 to $100 solution that will protect their phone if they happen to drop it in the toilet. They're not looking for a protective case that will allow them to take their phones on a scuba diving excursion 100 feet below sea level.

We determined that a slight adjustment to the search query made the world of difference. If someone was searching for *waterproof iPhone case,* they were not in our target market. However, if they searched for *underwater iPhone case,* they were.

The simple adjustment from *waterproof* to *underwater* told us that this person was looking for a case that would allow them to *intentionally* bring their phones into the water with them. This small change was the hidden gem that initiated a period of exponential sales growth for ProShotCase.

Not only did those search terms yield a high conversion rate, but they were also significantly cheaper due to less competition. CPCs on these keyword auctions ranged from $1.50—$2.50, whereas CPCs on *waterproof* auctions would range between $4 and $5. The *underwater* keyword was our golden ticket.

---

* When we say *bottom-funnel,* we are referring to keywords that are so closely related to our product that, when a search is performed, the searcher is almost guaranteed to be in the market for the product/service we offer.

Today, the secret is out. ProShotCase's competitors have since learned this information, in the same way that everyone in my fantasy football circle was aware that Lamar Jackson (QB of the Baltimore Ravens) was likely to have a huge year in 2019. Today, a search for *underwater iPhone case* will yield tons of relevant results, and the CPCs are significantly higher than they were a few years ago.

At this point in the game, your competitors have the same basic knowledge as you do. You've all read the same PPC blogs, worked with some of the same agencies, and probably even watched Isaac's Udemy course. Imagine that you were a human algorithm who needed to take all this knowledge (data) and translate it into a strategy. How would you create your own set of rules to test and refine over time?

It's not about *who* has the best data anymore. It's about how you *use* that data.

"All Models Are Wrong, but Some Are Useful"

George Box, a British statistician, coined this phrase in 1976 and elaborated on the concept throughout his career. In 1997, he wrote:

> All models are wrong but some models are useful. In other words, any model is at best a useful fiction—there never was, or ever will be, an exactly normal distribution or an exact linear relationship. Nevertheless, enormous progress has been made by entertaining such fictions and using them as approximations … So the question you need to ask is not 'Is the model true?' but 'Is the model good enough for this particular application?'[3]

As Box suggests, it is absurd to believe that complex physical, biological, or sociological systems can be exactly explained by a formula. However, like Peter McCullagh and John Nelder wrote in their 1983 book, *Generalized Linear Models:*

> Some principles do exist, however, to guide the modeller. The first is that all models are wrong; some, though, are

> better than others *and we can search for the better ones.* At the same time we must recognize that eternal truth is not within our grasp.[4]

The search for better modeling is the reason that the machine learning industry exists. We start with one model, then run a simulation to gather data. Then we use that data to evolve the model.

A model can be used to make a prediction about an outcome. For example: *What is the probability that this ad click, given the information we know about the user and the search being performed, will result in a conversion?*

When we accept the fact that the model cannot accurately predict the outcome 100 percent of the time, we can then instruct the model to attempt to improve its decision-making process.

The goal of a machine learning algorithm is *not* to establish a reliable model that predicts an outcome with 100 percent certainty; rather, the algorithm will constantly rework its imperfect decision-making processes over time, with the goal of reducing the gap between *expected outcome* and *actual outcome.*

An Incomplete Fantasy Football Learning Algorithm

My fantasy football league consists of ten owners, of which I am one. Our teams are made up of NFL players in different positions and on various teams throughout the NFL.

Individual players score points based on their actual gameplay: if Saquon Barkley, a running back for the NY Giants, was on my fantasy team and scored a touchdown, my team would earn 6 points.

A fantasy football draft is an event that determines which players end up on which teams. A lot of strategy goes into a draft, and countless books, articles, and podcasts have covered draft strategy alone.

My friends and I scheduled our 2016 fantasy draft for the night of August 27th. With just a few minutes to go before the draft officially started, no one had heard from our buddy Chris. He was spending the weekend with his wife's family and planned on drafting from the ESPN app on his phone. But when the draft began, he was stuck on a clamming boat in the middle of the Long Island Sound and out of reach of phone service.

When a team owner is unable to make a draft, *auto-draft* is enabled. That is, when it becomes that owners' turn to make a player selection, they are automatically given the highest-rated available player—as determined by ESPN's player ranking model.

Given the fact that all models are wrong, you don't want your team to be auto-drafted. Auto-draft is the fantasy football equivalent of a Google Ads script. It operates under a given set of rules with no added learnings to be had with each subsequent pick. Auto-draft does not have *real-time* data. It will not consider outside variables such as player bye-weeks or the risks involved with taking multiple players from the same NFL team. It does not factor in aspects of *game theory* that are often at play during a fantasy football draft. It is as simple as the *Bid to Position script*, which we will discuss later.

The outcome of Chris's 2016 fantasy draft was an excellent example of how auto-draft, or any script for that matter, could go horribly wrong. His entire team was composed of questionable selections. Worst of all, ESPN's statistical model would only end up selecting one quarterback for his roster: Tony Romo.

This wouldn't have been much of an issue if this draft had taken place during any of the previous ten years. Unfortunately, it had been announced *earlier that day* that Tony Romo was going to miss the season and likely retire as a result of a back injury that he had just sustained during a preseason game. This news had not yet been reflected in ESPN's player ranking model, which was only updated once a day. The auto-draft model had no way of knowing that Romo would be out for the year. Because of this, Chris missed the opportunity to draft a competent QB to his roster. Consequently, he didn't do well that year.

We can see how auto-draft can lose you a season in the same way that a Google Ads script can inhibit your ability to profitably grow on the platform. The only way to drive real success is by operating in real time, learning, and adjusting your strategy as you navigate throughout the process.

Fantasy football owners are algorithmic learners, even if they don't realize it. The team owners in a league essentially have access to the same data, so the difference is in how players use, or ignore, the data signals at their fingertips. For example, when deciding between two similar players in a draft, one might tend to choose the player that Matthew Berry, fantasy analyst for ESPN, recommends. Whereas I might choose the player that Jeff Radcliffe, of Pro Football Focus, recommends. Over time, we gather more data and adjust our decision-making models accordingly.

My 2019 fantasy football season was terrible, but it was a learning experience that will improve my decision-making model forever. To prepare for the draft, I ran a series of simulations that ranked player values based on our league's unique scoring settings. My simulations suggested that Travis Kelce, a tight end for the Kansas City Chiefs, provided more value than David Johnson, a running back for the Arizona Cardinals. I had the 5th pick in my draft, and although my model suggested that Kelce was the better choice, I selected Johnson. It was an emotional decision; choosing a tight end instead of a running back with my first pick would be considered asinine. I feared the ridicule I'd face, week after week, if I turned out to be wrong.

David Johnson went on to have a terrible season, finishing outside the top 20 at his position. Travis Kelce was drafted shortly thereafter by another team—the one that would ultimately win the league championship. So, it goes.

The question is, what do I do now? How can I learn from this mistake and improve my process for next year? I knew that I shouldn't throw away my original model, as those principles have often helped me draft reliable early-round players. I just need to adjust it. I needed to increase my confidence, with more data, in the simulations I ran that had correctly suggested that Kelce provided more value. I needed my model to factor the risk involved in selecting players from bad teams (the Cardinals were abysmal in 2019). Finally, I needed to grow a thicker skin and stop making decisions based on whether my buddies would taunt me.

I am confident that I will do better in next year's draft. Unfortunately, a year is a long time to wait to see the results of my new and improved model. A real machine learning algorithm would have learned all this information a decade ago and would never have made a decision based on emotional insecurities. But you just wait, next year will be my year!

The Automation of Automation

In the first era of the information age, we needed to program the computers ourselves. When programmed correctly, computers could play chess, file our taxes, and create Pixar movies. In each case, a human programmer had to tell the computer what to do, step-by-step in painstaking detail. It was a slow and inefficient process, which ultimately inhibited progress.

If you'd wanted to teach a computer to play chess, you would need to write each move that the computer could or should make. A machine learning algorithm, however, could be dropped into a game of chess with no background knowledge whatsoever and become a grandmaster in no time.

In 2017, Google's DeepMind team developed a software program called AlphaZero, an AI that self-learned chess from scratch by playing against itself, without any input regarding the rules. In four hours, the program had mastered the game and was able to defeat *Stockfish 8*, the world's chess computer champion of 2016.[5]

In *Outliers,* Malcolm Gladwell coined the 10,000-hour rule. This rule asserts that it takes a person 10,000 hours of practice (three hours/day for ten years) to achieve mastery in any given subject.[6] Machine learners can blow past this level of proficiency in minutes. What's more, traditional programming required a unique algorithm for each task you wanted to complete; a program trained to play chess could never generate a medical diagnosis. However, this would be possible for a machine learner to achieve if it were given access to the correct data.

We are now in the second era of computer programming. Computers can now teach themselves with data that is presented to them. It is the automation of automation.

In the final chapters of *Harry Potter and the Sorcerer's Stone,* Harry, Ron, and Hermione chase the antagonist through a trapdoor in hopes of preventing him from stealing the Sorcerer's Stone. They are met with a series of challenges that must be overcome to advance to the next room. The challenges included retrieving a flying key, winning a game of chess, and developing the antidote to a poisonous potion.[7]

Imagine what would have happened if they sent a machine learning algorithm after Quirrell, the antagonist, instead of going themselves.

Harry, Ron, and Hermione each brought a unique set of skills to the table, in the same way that a traditional simple program would. Harry was an expert on a broom, Ron was an experienced chess player, and Hermione had actually paid attention in potions class all year. Each of them could complete one task, but no individual character could have completed all three.

A machine learner would have provided a single solution. If the goal of a machine learning algorithm were to capture the Sorcerer's Stone, the machine would have first learned to fly a broom in order to capture the key. In the second room, the machine would have quickly learned the rules of wizard's chess and beat its opponent. Then, in the final room, it would have studied up on potions and concocted the antidote required to advance to the stone.

Harry, Ron, and Hermione could have safely stayed behind and watched the much more efficient problem solver save the day.

The Learning Phase

The learning phase is the period during which a machine learning algorithm is gathering data from initial tests. When a significant change has been presented to an algorithm, the machine must test these new variables until it learns about predicted outcomes with statistical significance.

Google's DeepMind documented the process of a learning phase by recording an instance where a machine learned how to play and master Brickbreaker on Atari. The machine was not given the rules of the game. It was simply instructed to find a way to break all the bricks.

The paddle moved randomly at first, but eventually, the machine learned that the pixilated ball would remain in play if it made contact with the paddle, increasing the likelihood that more bricks would be broken. After just two hours of learning, the machine mastered the game.

Most digital advertisers are familiar with this concept, but many don't realize that a portion of their campaign budget (for any smart campaign) will always be dedicated to learning, even after you've exited the original learning phase.

Many digital advertisers mistakenly believe that the learning phase is a bad thing. I've had many discussions with clients where we have outlined our strategy for changes to a Facebook campaign, but the client pushes back because those changes *will send the campaign back into the learning phase.*

You should not fear the learning phase. In fact, we have seen many instances where campaigns perform better when they are actively learning. The Always-Be-Learning construct is a fundamental principle of machine learning and is essential to continued improvement and optimization.

Confidence vs. Accuracy

In a learning algorithm, confidence refers to the probability of an event. Accuracy, on the other hand, represents the skill of the algorithm to predict accurately.

For example, a learning algorithm might predict that the probability of an event is 50 percent, but it's unclear if the probability is 0.5 because no examples have been provided or if its 0.5 because enough examples have been provided that the event has been proven to actually be 50 percent.

We refer to a **confident** algorithm as one that has run enough tests in the learning phase to accumulate statistically significant confidence intervals regarding its hypothesis. However, just because a machine is confident does not mean the machine is *accurate.*

For decades, fitness experts believed that running under a four-minute mile was physically impossible. They were confident that a 4:01 mile was possible and that a 3:59 mile was impossible. That changed when Roger Bannister proved them wrong in 1954. We have now learned that this is possible.[8] More than 1,400 athletes since have clocked a sub-four-minute mile as well.[9]

It's often necessary to hit the reset button on a learning algorithm so that it erases its previously confident hypotheses and can relearn based on new tests. That is, some overly confident algorithms need to be humbled back to reality.

Consider the impact that incorrect conversion tracking might have on a learning algorithm, such as placing your conversion pixel on the *view cart* page, as opposed to the page that a customer lands on after they've successfully completed checkout. The algorithm would be confident, and possibly even accurate, at acquiring traffic that would navigate to the *view cart* page. However, it would have no historic data about which kinds of users were more likely to complete checkout.

In this case, the historic data used to confidently drive conversions would need to be completely erased. You would need to send the algorithm into a new learning phase if you wanted to retrain it to learn how to confidently acquire *actual* customers.

3 The Dawn of a New PPC Era

The pre-Smart Bidding era was a simpler time. You could write a script to do most Google AdWords optimizations for you. Clients could easily understand the work that you were doing on a day-to-day basis because that work mostly involved making physical changes to the account structure, all of which was logged and timestamped in the *change history* tool.

However, this era had many limitations. It was much more challenging to profitably scale a campaign beyond a core group of bottom-funnel keywords. The technology that we remember from the original Google AdWords platform was not advanced enough to give advertisers the ability to profitably scale.

That era is behind us.

You are no longer a Google AdWords account manager. This role has been replaced by *algorithm jockeys,* with automation serving as your loyal steed. Your primary responsibility now is to have a deep understanding of how platform algorithms work and to guide the machine in achieving your client's goals.

Your job is to find creative solutions to complex problems, specifically within the realm of the broader digital advertising space. Your value can no longer be logged into a *change history* tool.

Here's an example of an account we inherited in the spring of 2017:

There were nearly 20K changes logged over a 14-month period—nearly 300 changes per week. *That is what this client was paying their previous agency for.*

The graph, however, indicates that no growth was realized in revenue or profitability. The client admitted that they stuck around because the agency celebrated improvements in Quality Score and decreases in cost per click. So the client, wrongfully, assumed that actual revenue growth would soon follow.

When it didn't, they jumped ship.

I still see too many marketing decision-makers (clients) who are asking the kinds of account-structure questions that make it clear that they care more about Quality Score, Ad Group structure, and logged changes than they do about finding creative ways to drive profitable growth. That must change.

Contextual vs. Behavioral Targeting

All advertising campaigns include either *contextual* or *behavioral* targeting, and the best campaigns leverage both.

Contextual advertisements are ad placements that are targeted based on the context of the advertising medium. The primary factor is the *where*, meaning the physical environment in which the advertisement is being served.

For example, Geico heavily invests in billboards because people who see billboards are driving in cars. Drivers likely have, or need, car insurance. Similarly, Rolex believes that its upper-class target market is likely to be interested in golf. As a result, viewers of professional golf events are bombarded with Rolex watch commercials.

I am not currently in the market for car insurance, but I still see a lot of Geico ads. I watch a lot of golf, but I'm definitely not Rolex's target customer. Contextual targeting is what traditional advertising was built upon, but obviously, it has its flaws.

Behavioral targeting has less to do with the medium and, instead, relies on customer behavior to determine the timing, placement, and audience of an ad. This placement favors the *who.*

L.L. Bean uses behavioral targeting when they send their catalogs to all previous customers, regardless of their physical location. The behavior, in this example, is that the person previously purchased a pair of *Bean Boots.*

Manual CPC Google Search advertising primarily relies on contextual targeting. The *context* here is a search query that the user has typed. A search engine result page (SERP) is the digital equivalent of a billboard.

This is one of the fundamental misinterpretations of the modern digital advertising ecosystem. Let's revisit the ProShotCase example from Chapter 2. One might think that a Google Search Ad served as the result of a search for *waterproof iPhone case* is behavioral targeting because the person performing the search is in the market for your product. However, that is not definitively true. A Google search does not guarantee that a customer is in the market for whatever they searched for. There isn't enough confident data to prove that.

Sure, certain signals can tell you that there is a greater likelihood of that happening, but a data scientist would never say that the predicted outcome for a given event is 1.0—or guaranteed.

Instead, you are choosing to serve that ad because you believe that people who are viewing that specific Google SERP page are *likely* to be in the market for your product. You believe that www.google.com/search?q=waterproof+iphone+case is a great *place* to serve an ad for ProShotCase. This is no different from a Geico billboard on the highway, or a Rolex commercial during the U.S. Open. The emphasis remains on *where*.

A search query is still an incredible place to start! If I had to choose between including *search query* as a bidding signal or ignoring it altogether, I would almost certainly include it. However, just like every wasteful Rolex ad that I've had to endure when I turned on the Golf Channel, this contextual targeting method is far from perfect.

Instead, we can increase our likelihood of serving the perfect ad if we combine the context of the search query with additional behavioral signals.

For ProShotCase, we determined that if the average person searches for *waterproof iPhone case,* they are not likely to be in the market for our product. It wouldn't be profitable for us to bid aggressively on this keyword, because the majority of this audience will never become our customers.

That's the problem with averages. There are certainly instances where the user performing this search might be interested in our product, but *on the average*, a bid here wouldn't make economic sense.

However, what if we also knew that this person frequently participated in action sports, like skiing and surfing? Or that they'd just planned a trip to Hawaii and were searching for scuba diving lessons? Or that just one minute ago they'd searched Google for *GoPro Alternatives?*

If we use automation to factor in this behavioral data, the conversion probability on this user's search for *waterproof iPhone case* increases exponentially. It might just be economically viable to place a bid in that individual auction.

Failure to leverage valuable behavioral signals as part of your bidding strategy limits your ability to accurately predict conversion rates for individual auctions, which in turn limits your ability to profitably scale.

Limitations of Manual CPC

Imagine you are a licensed retailer for my favorite NFL football team: the Buffalo Bills. The Bills have had some mild success over the last few years, thanks to their exciting young quarterback Josh Allen. Bills fans love him, and all this attention has been great for your business.

I'd bet that your ecommerce store would be profitable if you were to bid on long-tail, *bottom-funnel* keywords such as *Buy Josh Allen Jersey Online*. That is, of course, exactly what you sell, and there are only a handful of competitors selling Josh Allen jerseys online.

If you only cared about reaching the handful of potential customers who *specifically searched for this exact term,* then a manual CPC Search campaign would suffice. To be profitable, you would have to determine your average conversion rate for this keyword, which we'll say is 5 percent in this scenario. You'd then factor in your average order value (AOV) and gross margin to determine your max CPC bid. On a $100 jersey with 35 percent gross margins, you'd have $35 in wiggle room to spend on advertising and remain profitable. A 5 percent conversion rate would mean that one out of every twenty clicks results in a conversion. Therefore, we can afford to pay up to $1.75 a click for this keyword search.

Before we proceed, it's helpful to consider *why* these types of bottom-funnel keywords are so attractive in the first place. Typically, it just means that there is little question that the user performing the search is *in the market* for your product. In this case, we can be confident that a user searching for *Buy Josh Allen Jersey Online* is a Buffalo Bills fan and is willing to buy a jersey from us online.

Unfortunately, only a fraction of your target market is actively searching for something this specific. You'd have to broaden your targeting if you wished to increase company revenues.

Then, we would introduce a plan to launch campaigns that focus on utilizing *middle* and *top-funnel* keywords, and we'd put a system in place to ensure that we could be profitable in the process.

We'd start with the keyword: *NFL Jersey,* which is surely has a high search volume. However, the Bills are one of thirty-two NFL franchises. We lose our confidence with these keywords because we cannot know for certain that a person performing this search is even a Bills fan.

It would be ill-advised for us to assume that our 5 percent conversion rate would remain consistent across this audience. The conversion rate would likely be lower. However, if a given user has an expected conversion rate greater than zero, then we should still be willing to bid on their search. We'd just need to calculate what the user is *worth* to us, based on their actual expected conversion rate.

That is, a user with a 0.01 percent conversion rate might still be worth a penny to us.

If we assumed that one out of every thirty-two NFL fans was a Buffalo Bills fan, then we could assume that our predicted conversion rate on a search for *NFL Jersey* would be 1/32 of our average conversion rate, which we stated earlier was 5 percent.

Using the same math that helped us determine that our Max CPC Bid for *Buy Josh Allen Jersey Online* should be $1.75, we can determine that our Max CPC Bid for *NFL Jerseys* should just be $0.05.

Before our agency embraced automation in 2017, this seemed to be the proper way to manage an account. Looking back, it's clear to me that this method is completely asinine. While five cents might be mathematically correct, it is rarely *actually* the correct bid for any individual auction. It's just an *average*. Your customers are not statistics.

If a Dallas Cowboys fan performed a search for *NFL Jersey,* there is nothing you could do to convince them to buy something from your Buffalo Bills store—nothing! The expected conversion rate for this audience and for the fan-bases of thirty-one other NFL franchises is zero; therefore, we should do our best to not bid on their search at all—even if it was just a five-cent throwaway!

PPC Traditionalists (i.e., fans of manual bidding) would argue that you need to be willing to pay five cents for the *NFL Jerseys* keyword because there are, of course, Bills fans who will be performing this search. However, when a Bills fan does a search for *NFL Jerseys,* is five cents the correct bid for that auction? No!

We have already determined that a user searching for *Buy Josh Allen Jersey Online* is worth $1.75 to us, due to their expected 5 percent conversion rate. Remember, we landed on a 5 percent conversion rate because we can confidently say that the person performing that search is, in fact, a Bills fan who would be willing to buy something from our store. It ultimately has nothing to do with the query itself, but everything to do with the individual performing the search.

If an individual searched for *NFL Jersey,* and if we were confident that they were both a Bills fan *and also* willing to buy something from our store, we should assume that their conversion rate would be 5 percent; and therefore, we should bid $1.75 in that auction. Five cents was never the correct bid, regardless of how you approached it.

Traditionalist PPC managers fail to wrap their heads around this concept because they are stuck on the *averages.* If an automated bidding solution can correctly pick out the Buffalo Bills fans from the Dallas Cowboy fans and accurately set bids based on their value, then you'd think that PPC managers and their clients would embrace that option, right? Unfortunately, no. They generally lack an understanding of how the system works on the backend. Instead, they see their Average CPCs increase and panic. They incorrectly assume that automated bidding is just a way for Google to charge more per click.

Then, they resort to strategies that rely almost exclusively on bottom-funnel keywords. The million-dollar question that PPC Traditionalists have looked to solve over the last decade is: *How can we expand beyond bottom-funnel keywords but still remain profitable?*

The collective PPC community has agreed that this can be achieved by layering bid adjustments. We would start by making adjustments for variables like geographic location, search device, and time the day (called **dayparting**).

For your Buffalo Bills ecommerce store, a Traditionalist PPC manager might recommend that you broaden your keyword targeting in the geographic areas with the highest concentration of Bills fans. They'd launch new campaigns targeting keywords like *NFL Jersey* in the greater Buffalo area.

Of course, this is limited in scale. Bills fans exist all over the country! So, the only choice that the Traditionalist PPC manager has at this point is to tell you that they are going to optimize for *Quality Score*. An improved Quality Score would theoretically allow you to bid more aggressively and enter more ad auctions while keeping your CPCs relatively stable.

This is great in theory, but it doesn't solve the problem that we identified with our conversion rate averages.

For the *NFL Jersey* keyword, let's say that we improved our Quality Score by 50 percent. Going from a six to a nine (which is no easy feat, ask any PPC veteran). Given that, we should be able to raise our bids by 50 percent and increase the auctions we enter by 50 percent—all while staying profitable.

Our $0.05 bid then becomes $0.08. Is this *ever* the correct bid for a search for *NFL Jerseys*? No! We've already determined that if a Bills fan is searching for *NFL Jerseys,* it's worth $1.75, but if that search is being performed by the fan of any other NFL team, we should not enter the auction at all.

An improved Quality Score is nice, but it won't help your ecommerce store profitable scale because it ignores the fact that every search and every customer is unique. Therefore, a Smart Bidding campaign, which has the freedom to pick out the Bills fans from the Cowboys fans, is the best method for you to lengthen your reach.

Manual CPC search campaigns were filled with restrictions: match type restrictions, geographic restrictions, negative keywords, device bid adjustments, and more. Although they were put in place to ensure that your campaigns remained profitable, each restriction put up a barrier that excluded a different audience from seeing your ads. Those users *could* have become your customers.

Automation removes those barriers and treats people the way they should be treated: as individuals with unique preferences, quirks, and predicted conversion rates.

What if Google knew that I had a long history of watching Buffalo Bills highlights on YouTube, that I'd just booked a flight from NYC to Buffalo, and that I had been performing Google searches, spanning several days, for hotels and restaurants in the Buffalo area? Shouldn't you be willing to bid at least $1.75 in an ad auction when I almost inevitably search for *NFL Jerseys,* despite being outside of the region when I performed the search?

None of these variables would have been factored in a Traditionalist's bid adjustments.

To take it one step further: What if Google also knew that sports fans traveling out of town for a game tend to spend twice as much, with a higher overall conversion rate than local fans? I have no proof to suggest that this statistic is true, but if it was, Google would certainly know about it.

If I was executing this search, you would want to bid *much more* than $1.75. The lifetime value that I'd contribute to your business would be well worth an aggressive bid. However, if your campaign were set up by a Traditionalist PPC manager, you and I would have never virtually met. I would have never heard about your ecommerce store, and I would have had to buy my Josh Allen jersey from Amazon—an outcome that neither of us would have preferred.

Marketers need to stop being satisfied with averages—average ROAS targets, average CPCs, and average click-through-rates. Traditionalist Manual CPC campaigns that rely on averages restrict you from appealing to your most valuable customers.

It is time to raise the bar.

Liquidity and the Micro-Moment

4

In 2006, NASA engineers attempted to clearly define the roles that should be reserved for a human and those that should be left to automation, while operating an aircraft. In the paper that describes their final recommendations, they drew on the following analogy:

> Imagine you were riding your bicycle through a park with trees and people. You are late for an appointment so you're in a hurry. You're trying to avoid hitting anything and also get to your appointment on time, but you're not familiar with this park, and you need to keep referring to your map. The problem is that it's very difficult to steer a bike and read a map at the same time. So you are forced to stop.
>
> As the time for your appointment draws nearer, you keep thinking to yourself— *Is there a way to move through an environment with obstacles without having to stop every time you need to do something else?*

How about a Horse?![10]

If you were on horseback, you'd be free to read your map while confident that you wouldn't hit any trees or people. A horse would instinctively avoid such obstacles. Through haptic feedback (touch, feel, and other kinesthetic cues), you'd be aware of what your horse was doing even if your attention were elsewhere. Any change in direction or speed would be obvious immediately. So, you could safely read your map and offer additional instructions to your horse as they became necessary.

The NASA engineers refer to this analogy as the *H-Metaphor,* which can be described as such: the humans chart the course, then rely on machines to manage the real-time calibrations.[11]

Traditional advertisers and media buyers are fixated on finding the best way to ride their bicycles. A modern advertiser knows that a well-trained algorithm can operate as a horse. It is able to adapt to sudden changes in audience targeting, market fluctuations, creative executions, and placements options.

To elaborate on the park example, consider the ways in which you might convey your goals to a horse: *I want to reach the other side of the park in the fastest amount of time, without hitting any trees or people.*

The trees and people are added restrictions that the horse, which either instinctively or as a result of your input, must consider as it navigates throughout the park. In a restriction-free environment, like an empty park with no trees, the horse would help you reach your goal with even better results.

PPC managers are prone to adding unnecessary restrictions to their digital advertising campaigns that, if removed, would improve overall performance. Restrictions generally include limited budgets, conservative ROAS/CPA goals, audience and placement exclusions, and exact match keywords.

The opposite of a restrictive environment is a *liquid* environment.

A paper published by the *International Advertising Bureau (IAB)* defines liquidity as such:

> In a fluid marketplace, machine learning helps to identify the most valuable impressions. When every dollar is allowed to flow to the most valuable impression, we call

> this condition "liquidity," and it is made possible when humans take their hands off the controls and allow the system to read the terrain.[12]

The four dimensions of liquidity are as follows:

Placement liquidity refers to the medium in which the advertisement is being served. A negative mobile bid adjustment on Google is a restriction that limits placement liquidity, as does a Facebook campaign that has not opted into *Automatic Placements.*

Audience liquidity is the act of showing your ad to the broadest possible audience. For example, you can increase audience liquidity on your LinkedIn ads by enabling the *Audience Expansion* option or by choosing broad match keywords in your Google Ads campaigns.

Budget liquidity includes removing restrictions of your budget. This does not necessarily suggest that you need an unlimited budget; rather, PPC managers instinctively set budget restrictions, often without even realizing (segmented campaigns with individual budgets, for example). PPC managers can increase budget liquidity by consolidating campaign structures, using shared budgets, and using *Campaign Budget Optimization* in their Facebook Ad campaigns.

Creative liquidity is achieved when you allow the system to test and choose the best performing creative assets. A Google Ad's ad group that has two Expanded Text Ads and at least one Responsive Search Ad that is optimized for creative liquidity.

The IAB paper also highlights the importance of leaving machines room to run:

> Media planners accustomed to creating very detailed maps for client campaigns might be tempted to specify who to target, where and with what creative. But planners can also use machine learning to surface insights and spark new ideas. To do so, they need to allow the system to explore as many opportunities to find value as possible, by setting broad parameters whenever they can.

After the campaign runs, advertisers can then use the system's reporting tools to retrieve insights. This allows learnings from campaign performance to be surfaced without having to run many experiments manually.

In many cases, machine learning within automated systems can bring planners closer to success. Campaigns aiming for wide reach can run across large audiences and platforms, allowing more choice and accessing valuable and efficient impressions at scale. When aiming for specific outcomes, marketers who choose broad audience parameters and an agnostic approach to platforms can produce more efficient conversions.

In every case, allowing machine learning algorithms to process as much data as possible improves liquidity. By removing restrictions on a campaign, media teams can test more opportunities simultaneously—including creative iterations, placements, audiences and more—and ensure budgets are applied to find the right people and produce the most cost-efficient results.[13]

The Value of Liquidity

An increase in liquidity should result in an increase in reach, conversions, or a combination of the two as the system finds more or better opportunities to show the ad for the same cost. When done at scale, this usually drives lower cost per outcome.

While different advertising platforms present different choices during campaign setup, these four dimensions (placement, audience, budget, creative) are often nodes where planners and buyers must choose whether to restrict opportunities considered for delivery during the campaign. Setting as few restrictions as possible, thereby increasing liquidity on as many dimensions as possible, should confer the greatest benefit.

In 2016, Facebook's *Marketing Science* team set out to prove the value of liquidity by conducting a comprehensive study that included advertisers from various industries and multiple countries. The study aimed to prove the value of *Automatic Placements* (placement liquidity) and *Campaign Budget Optimization* (budget liquidity). The hypothesis was that a liquid budget with fewer placement restrictions would result in more reach and better overall results.

> While advertisers and agencies can manually allocate budgets across platforms to account for these changes, [automatic] placement optimization leverages Facebook's ad delivery system to dynamically seek out the lowest cost per outcome at any given point in time wherever it's available, whether it be on Facebook or Instagram. As a result, running ads across multiple placements should provide lower cost per outcome than advertising on a single platform or even trying to manually allocate budgets across platforms.[14]

These trials proved that campaigns with more liquidity experienced a 4.1 percent increase in reach, a 5.2 percent lower cost per impression (CPM), and between 10 percent and 27 percent lower CPA.

Micro-Moments

In *Commercial Communication in the Digital Age,* Andrew McStay writes that, while traditional advertising objectives included long-term branding and stimulating desire, modern digital advertising platforms took a different approach.[15]

> Modern techniques aim to *interact* with individuals in moments when they appear on the verge of acting, clicking, or purchasing.
>
> [Modern digital advertising platforms] promise advertisers the capacity to offer the right message, to the right person, at the right time. This means being able to reach across device types, apps, websites and platforms to reach people with videos, rich media, static and native ads, and even promoted tweets.

> Whereas advertising deals once took days or even weeks to negotiate, and media had to be bought several days if not weeks upfront, [modern platforms] allow this haggling and buying to take place in the time it takes to load a webpage.[16]

This is how advertising platforms identify *micro-moments.*

In 2015, Google's Senior VP of Advertising and Commerce, Sridhar Ramaswamy, introduced the concept of micro-moments in a blog post titled "How Micro-Moments Are Changing the Rules."

> There are the other moments—the I want-to-know moments, I want-to-go moments, I want-to-do moments, and I want-to-buy moments—that really matter. We call these "micro-moments," and they're game changers for both consumers and brands.
>
> Micro-moments occur when people reflexively turn to a device—increasingly a smartphone—to act on a need to learn something, do something, discover something, watch something, or buy something. They are intent-rich moments when decisions are made and preferences shaped. In these moments, consumers' expectations are higher than ever. The powerful computers we carry in our pockets have trained us to expect brands to immediately deliver exactly what we are looking for when we are looking. We want things right, and we want things right away.[17]

McStay writes that the introduction of the micro-moment represents something truly unique. Modern digital advertisers do not seek to simply understand our preferences or interests. Rather, they seek to identify *moments.* Then, at the moment of identification, *interact.*[18]

Micro-moments can only be achieved in liquid environments. For every restriction that is added to your campaigns, another opportunity for valuable micro-moment interactions is removed.

It is no longer adequate to simply *identify* your target audience. You must also have the ability to interact with them as they navigate throughout their lives, patiently waiting for the right moment to engage with them, and ensuring that you're available to do so.

McStay emphasizes this point by comparing the modern digital advertising landscape to finance and the stock market, suggesting that similar real-time factors that determine the price of a barrel of oil are being leveraged to determine the value of an ad click.[19]

What's more, the market value of an ad click on Google is just as volatile as the price of oil. Thankfully, machine learning and Smart Bidding can be used to calculate this at scale, identifying those micro-moments and ad auctions with the most value.

The Bones of the Google Ads Platform

5

Google Ads, formerly Google AdWords, continues to evolve. However, the foundational technology of the platform remains intact. New technology has simply been layered on top of that foundation, as well as new strategies that advertisers might implement to leverage that technology to grow their businesses profitably.

Isaac published the first variation of his fifteen-hour Google AdWords training course on the Udemy learning platform in 2015. A lot has changed since then, but the fundamentals of Google advertising have not. The course has been updated several times, including a massive update published in 2019 that includes a lot of content regarding automation. Even since that update, many new ad formats and features have changed on the platform. Most students recognize that the core principles being taught in any given lecture remain current. However, there are those who get stuck on these nuances and miss the broader point.

Ad formats change constantly. As of this writing, Expanded Text Ads (ETAs) now feature three headlines, whereas a year ago they only featured two. A year from now, Responsive Search Ads (RSAs) may completely replace Expanded Text Ads. Despite these changes, the principles of writing effective ad copy remain intact.

In short: the layered technology and the strategies evolve over time, but the foundation of the platforms does not.

A keyword is and will always be a keyword, as is the same for a search term. There are many fundamental, evergreen topics that require mastery, should you expect to thrive in the modern era.

If anyone in your organization is making strategic decisions regarding PPC strategy or budgets without maintaining an understanding of how the Google Ads auction system works, how CPC is determined, the value of various audience segments, and the true role of Quality Score, the entire organization is at risk. Thankfully, this information is readily available in the Google Ads support documentation library. Those documents are updated frequently and provide a ton of insight regarding technical functionality and policies.

Did you know, for example, that Quality Score is not actually used at auction time to determine Ad Rank?[20] Most people don't.

Before my agency embraced automation, we were often guilty of falling behind on new policies and best practices. Today, I dedicate a significant portion of time each month to reviewing the training material that Google releases, even for the most basic topics. I always learn something new, or at the very least, am given a new perspective on a concept that I can use in conversation with team members or clients.

This chapter will provide a *back-to-basics* review of the platform so that in later chapters, we can more effectively cover additional technologies that have been layered on top of this foundation.

The Basics of Search Advertising

A *search query* is the entirety of what an individual physically types into Google. A *search term* is a specific word or phrase within the larger query. These two terms are often used synonymously, and we typically use *search term* by default when describing what a user searched for.

A keyword is a word or phrase that matches or is similar to a user's search term. When building Google Ads Search Campaigns, advertisers select keywords that they believe are relevant to their business. Different keywords might reflect varying levels of a user's intent to buy a product or service that the advertiser is offering.

Google Search advertising can be summarized as such: Users visit Google to find answers to questions or solutions to problems, and companies can use search advertising as a means to engage with those people regarding their products and services.

Users have varying degrees of *buyer intent.* Intent can be expressed within a search query (by including phrases such as *buy online),* or with other signals. It is generally accepted that if a search query expresses higher intent, then it is more valuable to the advertiser and worthy of a *more aggressive bid.* Advertisers will be willing to raise their bids to increase the likelihood that they will win an impression and a more favorable position on the Google Search Results Page (SERP), *even if* that means they will have to realize a higher cost-per-click.

The Google Ads Auction

When a search is performed on Google, the Google Ads system finds all ads whose keywords match that search. From those ads, the system ignores any that aren't eligible, like ads that target a different country or are disapproved based on a policy violation. Of the remaining ads, only those with a sufficiently high Ad Rank may show.[21]

When discussing the auction, we often use Search campaigns as the primary example because they're the simplest to explain. However, the core elements that make up a Search ad auction are at play for auctions on the display network, YouTube, and elsewhere. When a user opens a YouTube video and a fifteen-second bumper ad is set to serve before the video begins, the auction that takes place here is identical to the one that would have occurred had that same user performed a search on Google.com. At auction time, Google identifies all advertisers with eligible video ads that are bidding on that placement and evaluates which ad will serve based on Ad Rank.

This also happens for the display ads, or banner ads, that appear on publisher websites who've opted into the Google Display Network (GDN). When a user visits a GDN publisher site (*The New York Times* website, for example), the webpage is embedded with code that signals individual ad auctions for different pixel sizes. The top of a NYT article might reserve a rectangle 728 x 90 pixels of space, and when that page loads, an auction takes place where eligible advertisers are able to bid on that placement. The advertiser with the highest ad rank wins the impression.

This process is repeated for Gmail Ads, Google Shopping ads, ads that are served inside mobile apps, and so on. The Facebook Ad auction follows a similar process, as do auctions on other digital advertising platforms.

Ad Rank and Actual CPC

Ad Rank has become more dynamic over time, but the fundamentals and utilization remain the same.

For a detailed description on how Ad Rank and Actual CPC were traditionally calculated, please see the supplemental material at www.joinordiebook.com.

The modern Google Ads auction has evolved to become much more complex. While Google was previously transparent about how both Ad Rank and Actual CPC were calculated, these formulas can no longer be found throughout the Google Support Documentation library. We can, therefore, assume that these calculations have evolved over time.

Despite these changes, the fundamental ideas and takeaways from the original calculations are still relevant today. Specifically:

- You will only be charged what's minimally required to clear the Ad Rank thresholds and beat the Ad Rank of the competitor immediately below you.[22]
- Improving your ad quality can help you enter more auctions, by way of increasing your Ad Rank, in addition to lowering your Actual Cost-Per-Click.

Below is an updated definition of Ad Rank, as per Google support documentation:

> Ad Rank is calculated using your bid amount, your auction-time ad quality (including expected clickthrough rate, ad relevance, and landing page experience), the Ad Rank thresholds, the competitiveness of an auction, the context of the person's search (for example, the person's location, device, time of search, the nature of the search terms, the other ads and search results that show on the page, and other user signals and attributes), and the expected impact of extensions and other ad formats.[23]

These variables are used to determine Ad Rank regardless of your bid strategy. If you are using Manual CPC bidding, advanced signals are still being used to determine aspects of the auction, including your Actual CPC.

Ad Rank Thresholds

Ad Rank Thresholds represent the reserve price of your ad. If your bid is lower than the threshold, your ad won't show. If none of your competitors are eligible to show, the threshold is the price you pay for a click.[24]

Ad Rank Thresholds help protect Google from advertisers colluding and deciding that, for a group of keywords, all advertisers will lower their bids to one penny. It also decreases the chances that individual advertisers will uncover a keyword that no one else is bidding on, therefore allowing them to buy that traffic at a fractional cost of what the market rate should be.

For example, *mesothelioma lawyer* is an expensive keyword that costs between $100 and $1,000 per click. If a law firm discovered that none of their competitors were bidding on the exact match keyword *mesothelioma lawyer free consultation new york city,* it would allow Google to charge a rate for that click that is equitable to its value.

This might seem unfair, but keep in mind, we are advertising on Google because this is the best traffic that money can buy. It's completely within their rights to be paid a just amount for that traffic.

Thresholds are determined dynamically at the time of each auction based on a variety of factors, including:

- Your ad quality: To help maintain a high-quality ad experience for consumers, lower-quality ads have higher thresholds.
- Ad position: Ads that appear higher on the search results page have higher thresholds than ads that appear lower on the page. That way, people are more likely to see higher quality ads higher on the page.
- User signals and attributes such as location and device type: Thresholds can vary based on user attributes, including the location of the user and the device that the user is on (mobile versus desktop).
- The topic and nature of the search: Thresholds can vary based on the nature of the user's search terms. For example, thresholds for wedding-related searches may be different than those for basket-weaving class searches.
- Related Auctions: Thresholds can also depend on the auctions for related queries. For example, Ad Rank thresholds for the search term [car insurance] could be informed by auctions for the search terms [auto insurance] and [collision insurance].

These factors ensure that, when it comes to the ads users see and the price advertisers pay, the right consideration is given to the quality of the user experience, advertiser bids, and the value advertisers place on users' engagement.

Quality Score

I would have loved to publish a book on Google Ads and found a way to not mention Quality Score once. Alas, it's relevant to understanding the broader platform.

Here's my disclaimer: Too much time has been spent thinking about, talking about, and optimizing for Quality Score. It is not a key performance indicator (KPI), nor is it representative of your PPC manager's abilities. Overanalyzing this metric in search of lower CPCs is essentially futile. That said, a broad understanding of this topic will help shape your perspective of the Google Ads auction.

Google's support documentation makes it clear that your *auction-time ad quality* is factored into your Ad Rank; however, it should be noted that *auction-time ad quality* and Quality Score are two different things. Many PPC advertisers make the mistake of believing that these two are the same.

At auction time, Google uses real-time signals to determine the relevance of your ad to the individuals who'll interact with them. Each time your ad is entered into the auction, new considerations are made, and your relative scores could vary drastically.

Per Google:

> **Important:** Your Quality Score is not used at auction time to determine Ad Rank.

Quality Score, then, is a diagnostic metric that helps advertisers get a sense of the overall quality of their ads. It's based on historical performance. The number that you see represented in your Quality Score column is an *estimated average* of how your ads have been graded by various quality considerations in past auctions that you've entered.[25]

The factors that make up ad quality are not specifically outlined by Google, but all considerations generally fall under three categories:

- Ad relevance
- Landing page experience
- Expected click-through-rate (CTR)

Ad Relevance is the simplest of these to understand. It represents how appropriate the ad is to the keyword being targeted. If Geico were to place an ad for car insurance on a search for *dishwasher repairman,* they would score very low on the ad relevance spectrum. Google will leverage landing page content as part of ad relevance.

Landing Page Experience is an estimate of how useful your landing pages will be for users. According to Google, "You should make sure your landing page is clear and useful to customers, and that it is related to your keyword and what customers are searching for." [26]

Ease of navigation, page-load speed, mobile responsiveness, and clarity of page copy are all factors that makeup landing page experience. Your conversion rate is a good proxy for this component of ad quality, even though conversion rate itself is not considered. You should always do whatever possible to increase conversion rate on your site, and when that happens, it is often as a result of improved landing page experience.

Advertisers have over-interpreted Google's stance on landing page experience and often attempt to game the system by keyword-stuffing client's landing pages. Google has addressed this tactic directly:

> The word-for-word phrase from a query doesn't need to be on your landing page. A query for "South Chicago Chihuahua-friendly budget hotels" doesn't need to lead to a landing page with the headline "South Chicago Chihuahua-friendly budget hotels."
>
> In fact, we advise that you not try to "keyword stuff" your landing pages in an attempt to increase landing page relevance. Instead, we urge all advertisers to focus on creating great experiences that deliver what a user is looking for. Our scoring is merely an attempt to measure that—to measure, you might say, user delight. [27]

Expected CTR is an estimate of how often Google thinks your ad will be clicked, given a variety of considerations. As per the Google support documentation:

> A keyword status that measures how likely it is that your ads will get clicked when shown for that keyword, irrespective of your ad's position, extensions, and other ad formats that may affect the prominence and visibility of your ads.

> This status predicts whether your keyword is likely to lead to a click on your ads. Google Ads takes into account how well your keyword has performed in the past, based on your ad's position. The expected clickthrough rate (CTR) that Google Ads provides for a keyword in your account is an estimate based on the assumption that the search term will match that keyword exactly. At auction time, when someone's search terms triggers one of your ads, Google Ads calculates a more accurate expected CTR based on the search terms, type of device, and other auction-time factors.[28]

Keep in mind that many Google searches don't result in a click. In fact, Rand Fishkin, founder of Moz and current CEO of SparkToro, reported in 2019 that we have reached a point where more than 50 percent of Google searches don't lead to a click on an organic or paid link.[29]

There are many reasons why people don't click on links after performing a search. If someone is dissatisfied with the results, they might refine their query and perform a second search. Often, they'll find their answer directly on the SERP without clicking into a website. Perform a search *sunrise tomorrow* or *boiling point Fahrenheit* and see for yourself.

With less than 50 percent of searches resulting in a click, it is pointless to ask questions like, *What is a good benchmark CTR for my industry?*

A few years ago, a rumor spread throughout the marketing universe that all Google AdWords accounts averaged a 2 percent CTR. That's ludicrous. In some accounts, a CTR for certain keywords above 2 percent is natural. In others, not so much. A higher CTR is generally an indication that your account has more bottom-funnel keywords. It's not an indicator of actual performance or profitability.

Historically, Expected CTR was thought to be the most influential aspect of ad quality, due to the fact that CTR is a specific measurement whereby individuals are voting on better ads with their clicks. This is opposed to Ad Relevance and Landing Page Experience, which are more reliant on algorithmic page analysis and, therefore, not as reliable as a measuring stick.

However, we have seen time and again that poor Landing Page Experience will significantly lower your overall ceiling. You can work day and night to improve CTR and Ad Relevance, but you'll never be able to make progress with a below-average site experience.

Quality Score should be used as a diagnostic tool. It is not something that you should be optimizing for. If I wanted to impress my client with a high Quality Score, there are a number of provisions I could take to inflate the scores that are reported in the dashboard, keeping in mind that this number is a predicted *average* of the Quality Scores you've received in recent auctions.

For example, many websites are optimized better for a desktop viewing experience than they are for a mobile one. As a result, it is likely that they'd receive higher scores in desktop-based auctions and lower scores when the user is searching on mobile.

A client might see a 5/10 in the Quality Score column and request that we do whatever possible to increase those scores. They might feel that we are losing a competitive advantage because they are paying more per click than they would be if they had a 10/10 Quality Score.

But this isn't necessarily true. In most accounts that I've seen, desktop traffic costs significantly more than mobile traffic. This is due to supply and demand. Many websites are set up in a way that leads to a higher conversion rate on desktop. Therefore, advertisers are willing to pay more for desktop traffic, thus increasing the market rate for that click.

If the client was adamant about increasing their Quality Score, I might suggest that we stop bidding in auctions where the user is searching from a mobile device. If we were to exclude ourselves from those auctions where we are receiving a lower Quality Score, we could naturally expect an increase in the Quality Score column.

This would be a morally corrupt way to manage an ad campaign and a client relationship. Your client might be thrilled to see an increase in Quality Score, but you've probably left a lot of business on the table by excluding mobile traffic. What's more, your actual CPC may have *increased* as a result of cutting out the less-expensive traffic.

When asked about Quality Score, PPC Managers should make it clear that Quality Score is not a KPI, and optimizing for this metric alone could have a negative impact on overall performance.

In comparing Google Ads to the stock market, Quality Score is the equivalent of a *dividend.* Dividends are nice to have, as they marginally increase your profit and/or rate of returns. However, you don't become Warren Buffet by focusing on stocks that pay great dividends. You become Warren Buffet by investing in Coca-Cola in 1987, a move that resulted in returns of more than 1,600 percent.

Sure, when you invest in great companies like Coca-Cola, you are likely to also see a handful of dividends over the years. That's certainly a benefit, but it's not the reason you bought shares in the company. When you have a great product that people want to buy, as well as engaging ads and a website that delivers a superior user experience, you will see the marginal benefits that come with a better Quality Score. But don't let the score itself distract you from what really matters.

Traditional Search Strategy

Google AdWords became so popular because of the idea that anyone with any budget had an opportunity to buy premium traffic. Many advertisers, especially those with budgets of less than 10K, relied on conservative keyword strategies to ensure that their budgets were spent as judiciously as possible.

For more information on keywords, search terms, and keyword match types, please see the supplemental material at www.joinordiebook.com.

If you were running Google advertising campaigns on behalf of an ecommerce store that exclusively sold Buffalo Bills apparel, you would be better off dedicating a majority of your budget to Bottom-Funnel (BOF) keywords such as *josh allen jersey* compared to more Top-Funnel (TOF) keywords such as *gifts for a football fan.*

In fact, if there was enough search volume for BOF search terms, then many PPC Traditionalists would advise you to spend 100 percent of your budget on those keywords. We would assume that a search for *josh allen jersey* would have a higher conversion rate than a search for *gifts for a football fan*. If that's the case, a dollar spent acquiring the former click is more valuable than a dollar spent on the latter.

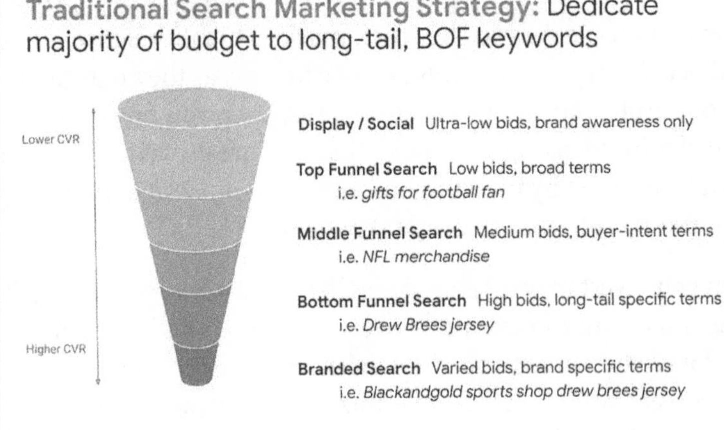
Traditional Search Marketing Strategy: Dedicate majority of budget to long-tail, BOF keywords
Lower CVR
Higher CVR
Display / Social Ultra-low bids, brand awareness only
Top Funnel Search Low bids, broad terms
i.e. gifts for football fan
Middle Funnel Search Medium bids, buyer-intent terms
i.e. NFL merchandise
Bottom Funnel Search High bids, long-tail specific terms
i.e. Drew Brees jersey
Branded Search Varied bids, brand specific terms
i.e. Blackandgold sports shop drew brees jersey

As we discussed in Chapter 3, automation has changed all of this. We should no longer assume that bottom-funnel search terms are more valuable than top of funnel search terms. However, this traditional approach is still useful for many accounts.

Negative Keywords

Negative keywords allow you to exclude search terms from your campaigns in order to focus on keywords that matter to your customers. They can be added at the ad group level, the campaign level, or across multiple campaigns through *Negative Keyword Lists.*

Negative keywords, particularly as they relate to negative keyword match types, are a source of confusion among many PPC managers. For more information on Negative Keywords, please see the supplemental material at www.joinordiebook.com.

Negative keywords are becoming less of a factor in the age of automation. Smart campaigns—including Smart Shopping, Discovery, and Universal App Campaigns—do not allow advertisers to add negative keywords, for reasons that will be addressed later. However, so long as traditional search campaigns are available, negative keywords will remain a crucial aspect of your PPC strategy.

Campaign Types

6

Campaign Type Overview

Google Ads offers a large stack of campaign options and attempts to simplify the campaign creation process has resulted in Google grouping campaign options by *Goals,* including:

- Sales
- Leads
- Website traffic
- Product & brand consideration
- Brand awareness & reach
- App promotion

This is a filtering system through which you can narrow your choices between campaign options. When *Sales* is selected, all seven options remain, whereas a selection of *Product & Brand Consideration* will filter into just *Video campaigns* and *Display campaigns.*

This might be helpful for small business owners who are setting up their account, but most experienced PPC managers see this as an unnecessary step and quickly select the option to manually select their campaign option of choice.

The seven campaign types currently available in the Google Ads UI are:

- Search
- Shopping
- Display
- Video (YouTube)
- App
- Smart
- Discovery

We won't go in depth for each of these, as the guiding principles are similar throughout. Once you fully grasp Smart Shopping, for example, Discovery Campaigns will be a breeze.

It's important to recognize that the full suite of traffic which can be acquired through the Google Ads platform covers many channels. Too often, we think of Google traffic as users who come directly from a Google Search Results Page (SERP).

In the age of automation, the channel that your traffic is acquired from is less important than it used to be. As a result, campaign types are evolving to automatically include more crossover between various placements.

In addition to Google Search, your ads may be eligible to show within:

- Google Shopping
- Google Maps
- Google Images
- The Google Play Store

- Gmail
- YouTube
- The Google App Discovery Tab
- Any website that has a YouTube video embedded on it
- Google Search Partner Sites (>100 non-Google search engines)
- The Google Display Network (2M websites and apps that opt into Google's AdSense program)

The breadth of available placements often intimidates advertisers. Instead of keeping an open mind and continuing to test new placement options, we mentally discard them as *crap traffic* and exclude them from our accounts.

If you possess these habits, I strongly encourage you to reconsider.

There are advantages to opting into nontraditional placements. The first is reach. Obviously, you can reach a larger audience if you are willing to show your ads on more placements. The second is the value. A click on a Search Partner site will *almost always* be cheaper than a click acquired through a traditional Google Search.

If a given ad auction has a predicted conversion rate above 0.00 percent, then it is, in theory, *worth* bidding on. In the age of automation, we can use machine learning to calculate these variables in real-time and determine whether we should enter a specific auction.

Even if a click earned from a Search Partner site is 75 percent *less likely* to convert than the same click acquired from a Google search, we should still trust the automation to adjust our bid, in real-time, to -75 percent. For example, if the same keyword typically costs $1 on Google Search, you should be willing to pay up to $0.25 to acquire the same click, if that click is 75 percent less likely to convert via this placement.

The cherry on top, in terms of added value, is that so many PPC managers continue to opt out of this traffic, thereby decreasing competition and lowering the actual cost of that traffic *below market value!*

In the example above, it is likely that you will be able to acquire the Search Partner click at a discount—possibly even less than the $0.25 that you should be willing to spend—because the competition is significantly lower. That is an opportunity you should always consider.

Search Campaigns

The cornerstone of the Google Ads product suite, Search campaigns, allow advertisers to show an ad when someone performs a search on Google or one of Google's Search Partners.

Ads can appear above or below search results on Google Search. They can appear beside, above, or below search results on Google Play, Google Shopping, Google Images, and Google Maps—including the Maps app.

For Search Partner sites, ads might appear as search results themselves, or as part of a related search or link unit.

Types of Ads on the Search Network

The most common kinds of ads on the Search Network include Text ads, Dynamic Search Ads, and Call-Only Ads. The Google SERP will often contain Shopping ads, although these ads do not fall under the same umbrella as *search*.

Traditional Text Ad Campaigns (Non-Dynamic) operate based on the keyword/auction bidding model that was outlined in Chapter 3. The advertiser chooses the keywords that will match to various search terms and have a variety of text ad options to serve on the search results page.

As for ad formats, advertisers can choose between Expanded Text Ads (ETAs) and Responsive Search Ads (RSAs).

Expanded Text Ads are a modern, updated variation of the original Google Text Ad format, where the advertiser writes the headlines and descriptions and will typically A/B split test multiple variations against one another.

Responsive Search Ads are considered *Smart Creative* and will likely replace Expanded Text Ads in the near future. RSAs are an automation-driven creative solution. The advertiser inputs multiple variations of headlines and descriptions, and Google will use machine learning to mix and match various combinations of these ad assets to deliver the best possible ad in any given auction.

It is currently recommended to have at least two ETAs and one RSA per ad group. RSA implementation is a must, as certain auctions are specifically reserved for RSA creative solutions.[30]

As of this writing, ETAs and RSAs are shown in different auctions, so it is not necessary or helpful to grade these ads against one another. You should not shut off your RSAs if they have a lower CTR than your ETAs. To maximize coverage, ensure that each ad group has variations of all available ad formats.

In addition to the traditional text ad formats, Google is currently testing a new variation of Search Ads called *Gallery Ads* that will allow you to add imagery to your traditional text ads that will appear on the Google Search Results Page.[31]

Dynamic Search Ads

As opposed to the traditional Search campaign targeting, wherein advertisers specifically choose the keywords that they feel best match their products and services, *Dynamic Search Ads* place search term control in the hands of Google. Google's bots will crawl your landing pages and use automation to determine which sorts of search queries match with your product or service.

Dynamic Search Ads provide excellent coverage at scale but only for websites that are optimized to leverage such technology.

When Google determines that a search matches the content of a landing page, an ad will enter the auction with a dynamically generated headline. The headline can be completely customized using machine learning to deliver the most relevant experience to the user. The advertiser is still required to write the description lines of the text ad.

This is extremely valuable. It simplifies account structure by reducing the number of keywords that are necessary to reach your audience. It's also a proactive approach to traffic acquisition. Given the fact that 15 percent of all Google searches are completely unique, it would be impossible to account for all the variations of searches that your target audience might perform.

Google estimates that 86 percent of Dynamic Search clicks are incremental, meaning they would not have been triggered by existing keywords in an account.

Though they can be valuable, Dynamic Search Ads are also risky. If your website is not set up in such a way that Google's bots can correctly determine your target audience, then Dynamic Search ads could have disastrous effects.

I don't claim to be an SEO expert, but if I see an account that struggles with Dynamic Search, it is usually an indication that there is something wrong with their SEO efforts. Several years ago, we worked with a SaaS client who offered marketing software. For reasons I still cannot explain, they were only able to trigger Dynamic Search ads for searches related to *coloring books.* This was extremely helpful information for the client, as it illuminated serious issues with the backend of the site. Despite all of this, Dynamic Search is an incredible product that allows you to easily scale your reach and win incremental traffic that you would not have otherwise been eligible to serve ads to.

It's also a helpful marketing research tool. The broad nature of Dynamic Search allows you more insight into the specific terminologies that your customers are using, and it's a great place to discover new competitors that have entered your space. We often find Dynamic Search Ads matching with competitor queries, but this isn't necessarily a bad thing.

One of my favorite use-cases for Dynamic Search Ads is for clients who have high-quality FAQ pages or blog content. In those instances, we can use Dynamic Search Ads to reach a broader, top-funnel audience that is seeking information in the early stages of their decision-making process. We can use this information to help prioritize our conversion rate optimization efforts on the most popular content and to provide guidance on new content opportunities.

Display Campaigns

Display Overview

The Google Display Network (GDN) is a network of more than 2 million websites, apps, and video placements where your ads can appear. According to Google, their Display Network allows you to reach more than 90 percent of the internet's users worldwide.[32]

Often referred to as *programmatic display* or *banner ads,* display advertising allows you to maximize your reach with potential customers. This compared to Search advertising, which only allows you to serve ads to users who are actively performing searches on Google.

As we'll discuss later, in our chapter on audiences, all advertising falls into one of two buckets—*Prospecting* or *Retargeting.* The former is the act of appealing to new users, who may not be familiar with your products or brand. The latter refers to the act of reengaging with previous website visitors or customers, with the goal of bringing them back to your site to convert.

Display campaigns fit into both strategies, and it is becoming less common to split these efforts into their own campaigns. If your overall goal is to *increase profitable revenue,* then it might be unnecessary to segment your campaigns based on whether an individual has recently visited your site. This is another restriction that can be removed in the age of automation, often leading to better overall performance.

The success of a well-placed Display advertisement is dependent on two factors. The first factor is whether your ad is being served to the correct person. We refer to this as *audience validation*. The second factor is dependent on a combination of timing and placement. Even if you've determined the perfect audience, your ads will fail to make an impact if they aren't correctly timed. Expecting parents might be the perfect audience for an ad promoting a diaper-delivery service, but it won't make a difference if that ad is served over the car radio while they're en route to the hospital.

Google Display Campaign's targeting options include a mix of contextual and behavioral targeting opportunities. This is the best way to ensure that you are finding the right audience at the right time. For a detailed description of the various targeting options, including the differences between *Managed Placements, Topics, Audience Targeting,* and more, please see the supplemental material at www.joinordiebook.com.

Advanced, Automation-Driven Display Options

When setting up Display campaigns, advertisers are given the option to select *Targeting Expansion.* This setting allows Google to serve ads to users who might not be on your targeted audience lists, or viewing ads on the selected placements and topics, but would likely convert at a similar CPA.

The next frontier of Display campaigns includes fully automated *Smart Display Campaigns*—a display ad format that automates bidding, targeting, and the actual creative content that is served to your audiences.

Smart Display campaigns use target CPA, focusing on conversions as opposed to clicks or viewable impressions. Your Smart campaign optimizes to bid most aggressively when performance data suggests the highest likelihood of conversions and to bid significantly less when data suggests that there is a low likelihood of conversion. After a necessary learning period, within two weeks or after having generated about fifty conversions, your campaign should begin to optimize.

As per Google:

> Smart Display campaigns combine two targeting methods: automatic remarketing to people who have visited your website and also automatic targeting, which excels at catching customers "mid-funnel"—that is, much earlier in the buying process.
>
> For example, say you sell sparkling water. Ordinarily, you may not have thought to include "office supplies" as a targeting keyword for your sparkling water campaign. But if there are

> strong associations between "office supplies" and sparkling water sales, automatic targeting will work to get you sales with that targeting. This is just one example of one keyword. Smart Display campaigns can find many such keywords, using machine intelligence and browser data to target signals that you couldn't have anticipated on your own.
>
> Don't worry if you already have other campaigns using remarketing—a Smart Display campaign tends not to shift customers away from those unless you choose to combine them. When you have multiple campaigns serving ads to the same audience, we'll always use the ad that's most relevant.[33]

Dynamic Prospecting is one way to extend the power of feed-based dynamic remarketing to reach new users with your high-performing products. Unlike dynamic remarketing, which is focused on getting the most value out of your existing customers, Dynamic Prospecting is used to acquire new users. This difference makes Dynamic Prospecting a preferable method if you're a new advertiser or if you're targeting an audience different from your own first-party data—including your remarketing lists.

You can also choose to pay for conversions instead of clicks on Smart Display campaigns that use Target CPA bidding.

If you set your Target CPA to $100, Google will serve your ads *for free* until you reach a conversion. At that point, the account will be billed $100 for the conversion. That in of itself is pretty amazing. It shows that Google is willing to bet on themselves, and you'll only be charged if they drive results.

A Smart Display Case Study

When we first received beta access to the Smart Display Pay for Conversions feature in 2017, we were ecstatic. This was a low-risk, high-reward option that *should have* allowed us to quickly scale client campaigns.

The first set of clients that received access to this beta fell under the category of *Lead Gen,* where the conversion actions we were optimizing for were generally just a contact form. We activated these campaigns and sat back in amazement as our new campaigns began serving ads *for free!*

One by one, these campaigns started to drive leads, and the campaigns worked just as advertised—The *Cost* column was now factored by multiplying the *Conversions* column and the Target CPA, and it had nothing to do with clicks or impressions.

What followed was an extremely humbling moment in our journey with automation.

Campaign spending skyrocketed, but we didn't sound the alarm as lead counts were reaching record highs.

I don't remember if it was a few days or a week, but it wasn't long before clients were calling us in a panic. There is no worse feeling than picking up the phone and expecting praise, only to be met with an irate client on the other end, especially when the client was completely justified in being so.

The leads were junk. Every one of them. In every account we tested.

I'm not here to discuss bot traffic or ad fraud. Those topics warrant books unto themselves. Google attempts to police both occurrences, but they still exist. Especially when it comes to traffic acquired via the GDN. It's frustrating, but it's a reality of the business. I personally don't think it's significant enough to avoid advertising on the GDN or other programmatic platforms. Bot traffic exists everywhere; it is not exclusive to the GDN. Once you accept that reality and become cognizant of the risks, you can proceed in a manner that allows you to drive positive performance.

A few lessons from my first experience with Smart Display campaigns:

1. Put a damn Captcha on all forms on your site.

2. If you are optimizing for leads, you need to have a CRM integration in place, or some other means to regulate the quality of leads coming through. You should only fire a conversion for these campaigns when a *quality* lead comes through. This

is a rule that goes beyond Smart Display campaigns, but it's extremely important here.

Imagine you're a SaaS company that collects leads through a contact form. Once a salesperson successfully reaches out to a lead, they are marked off in the CRM system as a *marketing qualified lead (MQL).*

You can track both events for reporting purposes. That is, you can have multiple conversion actions set in your account. However, be mindful of which conversion actions are included in the *conversion's column*—the setting that tells Google which conversion actions you want to optimize for.

In this instance, you will only want to optimize for and count your MQL event as a conversion for your Smart Display campaign.

This will ensure that you don't fill your pipeline with junk leads, while training the system to specifically serve ads to users who are more likely to become MQLs. Everybody wins.

3. Ecommerce sites have a built-in defense system, so long as the only conversion action in the account is *Purchase.* Thankfully, it's not common for bot traffic to successfully submit an order on an ecommerce site, wouldn't be able to pass the step in the checkout process where a valid credit card is needed.

4. When Google is unable to drive the necessary results under the Pay for Conversion model, your impressions will slow over time and eventually stop showing altogether. This shouldn't be surprising, considering Google is betting on themselves and willing to serve your ads for free until they generate conversions.

   If they're unable to drive MQL leads or ecommerce sales from Smart Display efforts, they will eventually cut their losses. This is not a bad thing. It's a failed test, but it didn't cost your client any money. This outcome is preferable to filling your client's pipeline with junk leads.

5. If you failed once, try again under a different set of parameters. This attitude is key for advertisers in the age of automation.

   I'll be honest: it took me a long time to activate another Smart Display campaign after that initial massacre, but I eventually accepted my share of the blame and learned from the experience. We mustered up the courage to try again, even within accounts where initial tests went haywire. We entered new tests under strict variables and were able to achieve results which were positive and legitimate.

   We also trust that the machine has become smarter and more reliable over time, which it has and continues to do.

By and large, we've seen success with Smart Display campaigns for at least a year now. Bear in mind that every strategy doesn't work for every business. We work on an individual basis to test new ideas and ad formats until we find something that drives results.

Regarding the Display Network Ad Auction

Google ad auctions act on the same principles outlined in Chapter 3; regarding Ad Rank, Max Bid, and Quality Score. However, the auction for Display campaigns is more complicated, as individual advertisers have the opportunity to win multiple ad placements on the same webpage.

Few PPC managers have a complete understanding of the nuances of the Display Auction or an understanding of *incremental clicks.*

Shopping Campaigns

Google Shopping Overview

I recently had the opportunity to have coffee with a former Google engineer who helped build the original Google Shopping product nearly fifteen years ago. After initial pleasantries I got right the point and asked a question I've had for six years:

Why the hell did you base everything off a data feed, which requires the help of a developer, and not on keywords, which marketers can manage on their own?

He laughed, and then paused before answering, as if he were questioning whether or not his response would offend me:

"We built Shopping for large retailers. It needed to be a scalable solution that could get the Walmarts of the world up on Google Shopping, and we weren't really conscious of the fact that small retailers or marketers would have any issues."

He went on to explain that large retailers, the earliest Google Shopping customers, generally have an IT department that included in-house developers. These developers could speak directly to his team at Google and work through any implementation issues. He continued to explain:

> We were developers, not marketers. It's easier, and more efficient, for a Google developer to send instructions to a client-side developer, than it would be for us to translate through several marketing people. It cuts out the middleman.
>
> Many retailers at the time didn't have a team of PPC specialists within the marketing department that would be our points of contact. Google AdWords management was an afterthought, as most marketing budgets were still held up in traditional media. It wasn't typical at the time to have one person in charge of paid search, but there was always a specific person in the IT department that handled the product data, so we built the product for them.
>
> It's ironic, actually. A lot of those jobs probably aren't needed anymore, since platforms like Magento and Shopify come with these solutions built-in. It's almost too easy to set up a feed nowadays.

I couldn't agree more. In the early AdVenture Media days, we worked with a lot of clients who didn't have in-house development teams. I used to spend entire days trying to set up feeds for clients, so it is no surprise that Google has invested in simplifying this process for PPC managers.

While it is easier than ever to set up a Google Shopping campaign, many PPC managers are left scratching their heads with questions about how to optimize them. Once you set up a Smart Shopping campaign, for example, there doesn't appear to be much left to do.

In the pre-automation era, we relied on a strategy referred to as *Query Level Bidding*

(we called it "The Catch and Bid" strategy around the office). This strategy is no longer relevant, so PPC Managers have been forced to rethink Shopping campaigns and how to optimize them for performance.

Google Shopping was the first campaign type to become almost entirely automated with the introduction of Smart Shopping. This is likely to continue for other campaign types, so it's important that we start to think now about how to properly optimize, improve, and evaluate Smart Shopping.

Our primary focus within Smart Shopping campaigns has shifted to the data that the campaigns are exposed to. The act of optimizing your conversion data has replaced the optimization of product-level bids.

The Google Merchant Center

Unlike most ad formats that are physically constructed inside the Google Ads platform, Google Shopping Ads are physically manufactured through the Google Merchant Center. The Merchant Center is an intermediary between your website and your Google Ads account, which turns your product data into Shopping Ads. The Merchant Center is used to host your feeds, allow you to troubleshoot issues with your product data, and contains crucial information related to the taxes you collect on sales, your shipping policies, and any promotions that you want to feature in your Google Shopping Ads.

For more information on Shopping Feeds, including best practices, shopping feed optimization, and use of custom labels, please see the supplemental material at www.joinordiebook.com.

Shopping Feed Quality Score

As with keywords in a Search campaign, products listed in a Shopping feed have their own variation of Quality Score that is used to help determine Ad Rank. The original components of Quality Score, including CTR, Landing Page Experience and Relevance still apply. Relevance is a bit more complicated in this regard, as it is dependent on the information in your product data feed.

There are several Google policies in place regarding Shopping feed data that would impact your product Quality Scores as well. The Google Merchant Center has a complete *Diagnostics* tool, providing details on why certain products are disapproved or at risk of being disapproved. You should take these recommendations seriously and rectify as many issues as you are able.

If you continually violate these policies, your Merchant Center is at risk of suspension.

Not all policy violations will result in a product being disapproved in the feed. These issues don't always draw your immediate attention and, therefore, could be even more disastrous than if a product were outright disapproved. **What's more, not all policy violations will even show up as warnings in the merchant center.**

We recently had an issue where a client updated their product titles on their website to include certain percent-off promotional text. The titles went from *XYZ Widget* to *XYZ Widget | 15% Off.* We were using a *Content API* feed solution, so these titles were automatically updated in our feeds.

It's a violation of Google Policy to feature promotional text in your product titles; however, it doesn't always result in a product disapproval.[34] The punishment comes in the form of lower Quality Scores.

The client didn't think of this as a major update to their site, nor did they think that it would impact our campaigns, so they didn't communicate this change with our team (I don't blame them, either. We couldn't have expected them to know the nuances of this often-ignored Google policy).

Many PPC managers would see this and think, "Good for you! You pushed the boundaries of Google's policies and you're getting away with it!" **Don't think this way.** You're not getting away with it.

A day or two after the product titles were updated to include the promotional text, we started to see a slight increase in our Shopping campaign CPCs. Unaware of the root issue, we assumed that new competition entered the arena or that some external market force was driving up our costs.

Approximately ten days went by before we discovered that the titles had been updated. There was no change in the Merchant Center Diagnostic Report, as this policy is so obscure that it doesn't even trip up a yellow *warning* signal. We almost discovered it by accident, as a team member was performing Google searches in hopes to find changes to the way our competitors' ads were showing on the search results. Thankfully, they were served an ad for our client's products, and we determined that the policy violation was impacting our Quality Score.

We used feed management software to correct the issue, and the CPCs gradually fell back down over the next week.

Smart Shopping Campaigns

Introduced as a beta feature in 2018, Smart Shopping has become one of the most polarizing topics in the PPC space. Those in favor of the campaign type enjoy the simplicity and believe in the scalable performance that can be earned through Smart Shopping. Critics are skeptical over Smart Shopping's lack of data transparency and lack of optimization levers that can be pulled by the PPC manager.

Regardless of your current opinion on Smart Shopping, one thing is for certain: it is not going away. In fact, several Googlers have mentioned to me that the product team has stopped posting updates to the Standard Shopping campaign type altogether.

We all have that friend or distant relative who has refused to update the operating system on their iPhone. The reasoning spans from the logical ("I don't like change!") to the extreme ("It's a conspiracy!"). The conspiracy theorists are just too naive to understand that innovation naturally creates more powerful software, which is not compatible with older hardware.

The same is true for Standard Shopping campaigns. This campaign type is outdated hardware that cannot support the powerful machine-learning capabilities of the modern Google Ads ecosystem. They might be *fine* for the time being, but I'm betting that these campaigns will be replaced altogether before 2022, and I don't recommend you being the last person at the party. If you wait for all your competitors to adapt to this new technology before you are absolutely forced to, you'll be at such a disadvantage that you might never be able to catch up.

Join or Die.

On the surface, Smart Shopping campaigns are incredibly simple. Once you have your feed setup and your Merchant Center account linked to your Google Ads account, you simply select this campaign option, select the country you are targeting, input some basic creative assets that can be used (headlines, cover imagery, etc.), and voila! You are off to the races.

Your bidding options currently include *Maximize Revenue* and *Target ROAS*. The distribution of your ads will be completely automated, using machine learning to determine the optimal assets that have the greatest likelihood of generating revenue from each auction.

For Smart Shopping to work properly, you need a few things in place:

- Conversion tracking (obviously) via the Global Site Tag.
- Dynamic Remarketing tag properly installed on your site.
- Remarketing lists with at least 100 active users. Currently, new accounts need to wait for their remarketing lists to populate or start off with Standard Shopping before activating Smart Shopping. However, it is likely that by the time this book goes to print, that restriction will have been removed altogether.

The next logical question, as I so often get from new team members, is, *Now what?* The optimization process starts with a full understanding of how the campaign operates and the recommended best practices.

Smart Shopping campaigns feature product shopping ads, local inventory ads, and display ads (including dynamic remarketing and dynamic prospecting), which are eligible to appear on the Google Search Network, Display Network, YouTube, and Gmail.

So basically, everywhere. Your ads will be served everywhere. This is the most overlooked feature for first-time users. If you activate Smart Shopping and are confused as to why you are now seeing your client's ads as Gmail promotions, you now know why.

Automated ad creation and placement means that your ads will appear in the ad spaces where they're relevant and that your bids will be set to maximize your conversion value.

You will notice that the Average CPCs on Smart Shopping campaigns are typically cheaper than traditional Search or Shopping clicks. This is due to the variety of *liquid* ad placements and auctions that your Shopping ads will now be eligible for, and the *average* is brought down by lower-priced auctions. You might still be paying $4 for a Smart Shopping click on *shopping.google.com,* but just $1 each for two clicks on Smart Shopping ads served on the Display Network. At the end of the day, your Average CPC will show $2 for these three clicks.

It is often the case that as the machine becomes less confident, advertisers see their Average CPCs rise. You should consider the possibility that a rising CPC might be a result of Google showing a smaller percentage of your impressions on the Display Network and other lower-cost placements. If in the example above, Google throttled your impressions on the Display Network and you only received one click on the Display Network plus the one click on *shopping.google.com,* your Average CPC will "rise" 25 percent to $2.50.

If this happens, it doesn't necessarily mean that you are paying more per click. You are just *averaging* a higher CPC. Your actual CPC for these auctions may have remained the same. When viewed through this perspective, you'll realize that the machine is making this change to successfully meet your ROAS targets. This is why it is crucial to set clear expectations with clients about CPCs—how it is not an indicator of success—and not to sound the fire alarm when CPCs rise.

Of course, you should consider all possibilities, including any changes to the feed that might be impacting your Quality Score (such as my example above) or new competition.

There is no search term report or placement report associated with Smart Shopping campaigns. This is a bummer, but the lack of search term data is not enough of a reason to shy away from this campaign type.

You can, however, see predefined reports segmented by specific product attributes, such as category, product type, and custom label by clicking the reporting icon at the top of the page and selecting Predefined Reports (Dimensions), then Shopping. Conversion data (revenue, ROAS, etc.) is readily available, as are typical performance metrics, including clicks and impressions.

You also cannot add negative keywords to Smart Shopping campaigns. If you have been running Standard Shopping campaigns over the last several years and have accumulated massive negative keyword lists, it is likely that your Smart Shopping campaigns will take slightly longer to optimize and drive a profitable ROAS. The system will not factor your negative keyword lists into its learning process and will test all variations of relevant search queries. The machine will decide if a search query or display ad placement is relevant or not.

Optimizations for a Smart Shopping campaign fall under two categories: feed optimization and attempts to *guide the machine*. The former ensures baseline performance, and the latter is what enables your campaigns to scale successfully over time. For example, one of Google's best practices mentioned in their support documentation is to *take outside factors into account*. If you have a handful of products that drive a significant amount of revenue when they are in stock but frequently go out of stock, this could be impacting the machine's ability to make confident decisions. You should consider what measures, if any, could be put in place to ensure stability for the other, less volatile products.

Early adoption of Smart Shopping was one of the most profitable decisions that our agency has ever made on behalf of our ecommerce clients. The benefits and value remain consistent today, and I expect this campaign type to become even more powerful over time.

YouTube Campaigns

The Value of Video

In February of 2020, Google's parent company Alphabet made global headlines after their Q4 earnings report.

This was not a typical earnings report storyline that highlighted overall revenue, growth, or a new product (in fact, they fell short of their Q4 revenue projections, causing their stock price to fall 4 percent that day). Rather, the financial media was obsessing over the fact that Alphabet had reported earnings from YouTube for the very first time in history (a fiduciary loophole allowed them to get around this until now).

YouTube advertising contributed $8.2B in revenue in 2017, $11.2B in 2018, and $15.1B in 2019—35 percent and 37 percent annual growth rate, respectively.

And yet, YouTube revenues only accounted for approximately 10 percent of Alphabet's overall revenue in 2019. To put this in perspective, YouTube ad revenue was approximately 1/5th the size of Facebook's.

In my opinion, that is *low!* YouTube is the second most popular search engine on the internet, and depending on your source, falls within the top five most trafficked sites on the web (Alphabet does not report on active monthly users).

YouTube has the traffic, but advertisers have been slow to meet them there. The lack of adoption has two reasons: Many advertisers have not yet bought into the concept of video, and of those that have, many don't have resources to create video content.

Currently, YouTube advertising costs are *below* market value. Average Costs-Per-Interaction range between $0.10 and $0.20, when they *should* cost much more than that.

On their February 7th, 2020 episode of the *Snacks Daily* investing podcast, hosts Jack Kramer and Nick Martel compared ad revenues between YouTube and Facebook and concluded that YouTube is more *generous* to its advertisers than Facebook. They charge advertisers less. While I enjoy this podcast and have a great deal of respect for the hosts, Kramer and Martel's assertion fails to consider the impact of real-time bidding on ad auction prices. They've assumed that the platforms, YouTube and Facebook, are setting the price per impression. YouTube is not more generous; their ad auctions are just less competitive.

Competition on Facebook is fiercer than YouTube for two reasons:

1. Facebook is not just a video advertising platform. Advertisers can display static images in almost all ad placements, allowing greater access for those who do not have video assets readily available. YouTube, however, only serves video ads. If an advertiser does not have video assets readily available, they cannot compete for that ad placement.

2. Facebook now has a built in video creation tool, where advertisers can create video assets directly inside the platform. YouTube does not currently have anything like this.

The lack of competition on YouTube is so dramatic that advertisers are currently receiving a discount on YouTube ad impressions. If you're not conveying this message to your clients (or your CFO) and urging them to invest in this opportunity, you are doing them a disservice.

What's more, video is much more powerful in delivering *ad recall* than any other ad format available through the Google Ads suite. Consider the potential impact of a YouTube ad, even one that is skipped after five seconds, compared to a Search ad impression or Display ad impression. As consumers, we are mostly blind to the latter two ads if we are not actively clicking on them.

Also, the way in which advertisers are charged for YouTube ads drastically increases their value. Advertisers are charged if a user *interacts* with the YouTube ad, and an interaction is defined by either:

1. A user clicking on the ad, which directs them to a landing page.

2. A user watching at least 30 seconds of an ad that is longer than 30 seconds.

3. A user watching the entire ad, for ads that are shorter than 30 seconds.

The concept is referred to as *TrueView,* where the user is in control of which ads they want to see and interact with.[35]

I see a ton of YouTube ads for the project management tool *Monday.com*, and I've skipped every one of them. I'm not currently in the market for a new project management tool, but if that were to change, *Monday.com* would certainly be on my short list of choices.

Why? I honestly have no idea. I've only seen their ads in five-second increments and have no clue if the platform would be useful to me. I would still check them out early on because they are *top of mind.* If someone were to ask me to list project management tools, I'd likely name *Monday.com* before I name their competitors - even ones that I have actually used! If I ever became a customer of theirs, the acquisition cost for me would literally be zero.

It is likely that ad recall on YouTube skips is so powerful because, in order for a user to skip the ad, they have to actively engage with it. They have to be conscious of the fact that they are being served an ad, hover over the small *Skip* button with their cursor, and then actively click it. It is a different experience from display ads because they are almost impossible to ignore.

Put simply—I love YouTube advertising. Not only does it leverage the extreme power of Google's automation to help find the right audience and determine the correct value of your bids at the right time, it's also incredibly cost-efficient!

Other Campaign Types

Campaign formats will continue to evolve over time. The goal of this chapter was to deliver an outline of the various campaign types and channels at play, providing a flexible foundation that can adapt to changes in the platform.

As of this writing, several other campaign types exist on the platform and are valuable in their own ways. Most of these campaign types include a blend of the principles learned from these core four campaign types. For example:

- The fundamentals of the **Search Campaign** ad auction remain consistent throughout all ad formats. Marketers benefit from using Search to understand customer psychology and evaluate buyer intent.

  While the traditional strategies of buyer intent based solely on the context of the search query are now becoming outdated, the practice of evaluating intent across new signals remains consistent as campaign types evolve.

- The targeting options first made available through **Display Campaigns** are now used for YouTube campaigns, Discovery campaigns, and other campaign types that will evolve over time. The concepts of *contextual* and *behavioral* targeting will always be relevant and should be consciously considered for any type of ad placement served through any platform.

  Nuanced segmentation of remarketing audiences is becoming less important in the age of automation. In fact, we will soon reach a point where it is unnecessary to segment your remarketing campaigns from your prospecting campaigns, as Google automation is becoming powerful enough to properly factor in these variables when predicting conversion rates, setting appropriate bids, and ultimately finding ways to meet your revenue and ROAS goals.

  Regarding ad assets, Responsive Display Ads were our introduction to the dynamic creative ad format, which is now used across all campaign types and has essentially replaced the need for ongoing A/B split testing of ad copy.

- The evolution of **Smart Shopping** is one of the most important topics for PPC managers to currently study, as this is likely the first wave of campaign types that are fully automated and used at scale. Universal App Campaigns were a fully-automated solution that preceded Smart Shopping, but it was not as widely used as Smart Shopping. Discovery campaigns, for example, are a variation of Smart Shopping that can be used by all, including non-ecommerce stores. If you work for a Lead Gen company and chose to skip the section on Shopping, I advise you to return to that section.

What's more, the original principles of shopping, including the *Catch & Bid strategy* and the act of evaluating the messaging of our product titles and descriptions, are beneficial to consider as we evaluate campaign performance and customer psychology over time.

- The current below-market value of **YouTube ads** is not something that will last forever. Strategic advertisers will use this perspective to evaluate future opportunities that might follow suit. They will benefit from understanding the impact of brand recall and considering the instances in which a free ad impression is worth its weight in gold.

  Video is the future, and regardless of the medium, advertisers need to become more comfortable with video advertising and understanding what creates a quality video ad.

7

Audiences

Isaac is a bit obsessive over certain things. When he and I started working together, he used to drink 10 or 12 Diet Cokes per day (plus four or five coffees). It was both terrifying and impressive to witness.

A Whole30 cleanse in 2017 convinced him to stop drinking Diet Coke and transfer his obsession to seltzer water. After meandering through several brands, he eventually committed to Spindrift.

Now he drinks an ungodly amount of Spindrift seltzer every day and is *constantly* in the market for more. Not just for a few cans, or even a few packs. He is constantly in the market for bulk orders. We often joke that we might need to move into a larger office, just so that we can have space for the pallets of seltzer he has delivered each week.

A few months back, a colleague of ours forwarded him an email that a beverage barn in Brooklyn was going out of business and liquidating their entire inventory. The sender assured Isaac that he often shopped there and had taken note of a massive Spindrift display.

It was around 11 a.m. on a Tuesday when Isaac shut off the lights in his office and fumbled around for his car keys. He informed me of the journey on which he was about to embark, the first step which required him to drive home to swap cars with his wife. If he was driving into the depths of Brooklyn, he was going to maximize his trunk space.

He returned several hours later, defeated and toting three measly packs of seltzer. As it turns out, thirsty New Yorkers had ransacked this liquidation sale long before Isaac arrived.

The humiliation he endured thereafter was significant enough to alter his buying habits forever. From that point on, he would only order Spindrift from trusted retailers with large inventories and fast delivery. By only ordering Spindrift online, he personally initiated a massive change in the online advertising market for retailers selling that bubbly beverage.

This traumatizing experience affected his other buying habits as well. He is now more likely to order something online, from a trusted supplier, than others who might consider a trip to their local grocery store or mall. He is more concerned with ease of purchase and is less price sensitive. If a product that he uses frequently goes on sale, he is likely to make a bulk order and stock up. As I write this, an entire closet in our office is dedicated to 15 jars of Costco mixed nuts that went on sale a few months back.

Isaac's buying habits are different from mine, which are also different from yours. You, me, and Isaac might all search the same query: *buy Spindrift online,* but each auction would represent significantly different value to an advertiser. Not only would there be a difference in our *predicted conversion rate*, the chance that any of us buys anything at all, but there would also be a difference in *predicted conversion value,* as Isaac is likely to purchase two or three times as many cases than you or I would in that micro-moment.

Both Isaac and I might have the same predicted conversion rate, but if he is likely to buy twice as much product, an advertiser should be willing to bid twice as much to win his click.

Audience Overview

Audience targeting allows you to target users based on who they are: what their interests and habits are, what they are actively researching, or how they have interacted with your business. A modern Google

Ads auction, particularly as it relates to automated campaigns, leans heavily on audience data to make predictions on expected outcomes.

Audience data not only provides insight to Google regarding *intent to buy* but also regarding certain consumer tendencies and preferences. Two advertisers might be nearly identical, but Google could identify certain trends that suggest that *Green Living Enthusiasts* would prefer Advertiser A over Advertiser B.

This aspect of competition benefits all advertisers entering an auction. If a user is significantly *more* likely to buy from my competitor, then I personally want my bid to reflect that by lowering. I am not willing to pay as much for that click, as it is *less* likely that that user will choose to buy from me.

Audience targeting allows advertisers and algorithms the opportunity to make more intelligent decisions and ensure that their budgets are dedicated toward the users most likely to convert on their individual site.

Remarketing

Every ad interaction falls into one of two categories: *Prospecting* or *Remarketing*. Prospecting involves serving ads to new users who are likely unfamiliar with your brand or have never been to your website before. Remarketing is the act of serving ads to previous website visitors, app users, or customers. The goal is to reengage with users who are still in the decision-making journey and to motivate them to return to your site and convert.

Remarketing and *retargeting* mean the same thing. Google refers to it as remarketing, whereas most other ad platforms will refer to this as retargeting.

Nonmarketers like to say that remarketing is creepy, and while I won't disagree with that, there is no denying the overwhelming amount of data that suggests that it works. It works really well. Due to its effectiveness, it's become a key component in nearly all online advertising initiatives.

Humans are complex creatures. The decision-making process is multilayered and nonlinear; it doesn't follow the same path every time.

An entrepreneur performing a Google search for *best CRM for small business* is unlikely to convert into a customer after just one ad click. Advertisers attempting to sell CRM software licenses would benefit from nurturing this entrepreneur with well-timed remarketing ads over time. Reengaging with the entrepreneur using messages which highlight the benefits of their CRM software, then prompting the entrepreneur to come back to the site and convert into a lead.

Remarketing is often thought of in the context of display advertising, but it's much broader than that. Anytime you make a marketing decision regarding an audience that is familiar with your brand, you are constructing your remarketing strategy.

Advertisers should take a global approach to their remarketing efforts. Email marketing plays a similar role as remarketing, and we recommend integrating your email marketing initiatives with your PPC remarketing strategy.

Remarketing Lists in Search Ads (RLSA)

Remarketing Lists in Search Ads (RLSA) should be added to every search campaign in your Google Ads account. Often, previous website visitors and customers will convert at a higher percentage than cold traffic.

When assigning RLSA audiences to your search campaigns, you will need to choose between two targeting options: *Targeting* and *Observation Mode.*

When *Targeting* is selected, you are telling Google that you *only* want to bid in auctions where the user performing the search is in your remarketing audience. *Targeting* mode makes your campaign eligibility exclusive to your remarketing audiences.

The second option is *Observation Mode,* which allows you to assign the remarketing list to your search campaign and potentially alter your bid for these audiences. However, with *this option*, your ads are still eligible to show for users who are not on your remarketing lists.

Targeting is generally used when there is a specific reason to exclude non-remarketing traffic. You might choose *Targeting* if you wanted your ad copy to include a promo code, but only for users who were listed on your *Cart Abandoner* audience.

In all other instances, *Observation* audiences should be used. *Observation* audiences provide useful reporting insights, whereby you can see the percentage of your traffic that fits into these remarketing audiences and the associated performance metrics (conversion rate) that are associated with those users.

Remarketing data is first-party data. Therefore, it is extremely valuable information that you have but that is not accessible to your competitors. Google will not use your remarketing data unless you give them permission; hence, the need to assign these audiences to your campaigns.

Creating Remarketing Lists

Historically, we preferred to manage our client's remarketing lists through their Google Analytics accounts. The Google Analytics Solutions Gallery includes a library of premade remarketing packs that can be easily added to your account. However, we have chosen to move away from this for three reasons:

1. Automation has made it less necessary for us to aggressively segment our remarketing lists. Instead of manually placing a value on previous website visitors, we trust automation to make predictive conversion rate analysis and assign a proper bid in real-time.

2. The Google Ads audience manager has improved over the years. It is now easy and effective to manage your remarketing audiences through this tool.

We've recently learned that the Google Ads remarketing pixel is faster and more accurate than Google Analytics when adding users to audience lists. I've tested this myself and can confirm that Google Ads audiences will receive between 4 and 6 percent more active users than Google Analytics audiences with the same targeting parameters.

What Time Duration Should I Use for My Remarketing Lists?

We used to create multiple variations of the same remarketing list, but with different time durations. For example, we would have a remarketing list for all users who have visited the site within the last 24 hours, and then another for the last 7 days, the last 30 days, the last 90 days, and the last 540 days. 540 days was the maximum time-frame allowed by audiences created within Google.

This would quickly become messy. We'd end up with dozens of overlapping remarketing lists.

The following screenshot is pulled from a now paused, legacy campaign inside one of our client accounts:

Audience	Bid adj.	Targeting setting	↓ Impr.	Clicks	Conversions	Cost / conv.	Conv. rate
All visitors	+20%	Observation	1,103	92	4.15	$27.46	4.52%
[Engagement Pack] Visited last 540 days	+20%	Observation	584	133	8.33	$21.44	6.26%
[Engagement Pack] Visited last 180 days	+20%	Observation	499	95	9.34	$11.73	9.83%
[Engagement Pack] Visited last 360 days	+5%	Observation	407	68	4.00	$20.32	5.88%
[Engagement Pack] Visited last 7 days	+20%	Observation	304	41	2.50	$20.17	6.10%
[Engagement Pack] Visited last 14 days	+5%	Observation	269	35	2.00	$25.93	5.71%
[Engagement Pack] Conversions > 0	+15%	Observation	265	82	13.58	$8.26	16.57%

Thankfully, there is no longer a need for this.

When using automation, remarketing lists are time-weighted. Google's algorithms are factoring in signals such as *Time Lag*, which is how long it takes for a user to convert after they interact with your ads and other data regarding the buying journey. This helps to determine the value of each individual within your remarketing lists.

Therefore, for remarketing lists that are added to Search campaigns, always opt for 540 days. For display, it is still time-weighted, but you'll likely want to limit your display remarketing lists to a shorter time period.

Similar Audiences

Your remarketing lists and customer match lists (lists created by uploading your customer email lists which Google will match with individual users) are considered first-party-data. You own this data, and your competitors do not have access to it.

Similar Audiences can be created from your remarketing and customer match lists, expanding upon the potential value earned from leveraging your first-party data.

The concept of Similar Audiences is much more popular in Facebook Advertising, where *Lookalike Audiences* are the cornerstone of just about every ad strategy.

How Similar Audiences Work:

> Google Ads looks at the recent search activity of the visitors in your remarketing list to help aggregate search behavior of the visitors in your list. Based on this information, the system finds new potential customers whose search behavior is like that of people in your remarketing list.
>
> Say you've created a remarketing list of people who bought running shoes from your sporting goods site. Instead of helping you reach broad groups of people interested in *running*, similar audiences will identify that people on this list tended to search for *triathlon training* and *buy lightweight running shoes* before coming to your site and making a purchase. Based on this, similar audiences will then find other people with similar search behavior, such as people who searched for *buy lightweight running shoes.*
>
> Your similar audience lists will automatically get updated as the original list evolves and people change their search activity. So, you don't need to update the similar audience list after it gets created. [36]

Advertisers are still required to manually create and assign these audiences to campaigns if they wish to leverage this data via automation. As Smart Campaigns become more ubiquitous, it is likely that advertisers will simply need to create the audiences at the top level of the account, and Google will do the rest.

Affinity Audiences

Affinity Audiences provide a holistic picture of users' lifestyles, passions, and habits. Affinity audiences have demonstrated qualified passions in each given topic, allowing advertisers to reach the people who matter most with their products.

Anyone with a Google Analytics account can see performance data based on Affinity Audience categories by navigating to *Audience > Interests > Affinity Categories.*

If you do not see data in these reports in Google Analytics, enable them by navigating to *Admin > Property Settings > Enable Demographics and Interest Reports.*

One of our clients sells fitness-enabled office furniture: stand-up desks, treadmills, etc. These are premium products that appeal to many, but only specific groups of consumers will actually convert into customers.

When evaluating audience reports, it's important to differentiate between *size* and *value.* There are many more *Movie Lovers* on the planet than photography hobbyists (referred to as *Shutterbugs).* Relative conversion rates are much more valuable here. *Avid Investors* have the highest conversion rates of this group, despite being a smaller overall audience than *Value Shoppers.* Therefore, we should be willing to bid more aggressively on a search performed by an *Avid Investor.*

In Market Audiences

Like Affinity Audiences, In-Market Audiences can both be seen in Google Analytics and used for targeting purposes inside your Google Ad campaigns.

Google buckets these audiences based on people who are in the market for various goods and services, which means that they are researching products and are actively considering a purchase decision.

The key differentiating factor between Affinity Audiences and In-Market Audiences is that a user drops out of In-Market Audiences once they are no longer in the market for that product or service. However, a *movie lover* is likely to remain so for the long term.

Affinity Audience and In-Market Audience data provide valuable insight about your website traffic, but you won't be using this data to shape strategy in a significant way. This data is automatically factored into Google's bidding process.

Affinity and In-Market Audience data provides valuable insight about your website traffic. However, it will rarely impact your keyword strategy or campaign structure. This audience belongs to Google and is automatically factored into your automated bids, regardless of whether you assign it to your campaigns. That said, it is useful from a reporting standpoint. This data can be used when making broader decisions around messaging, landing pages, and other strategic marketing initiatives.

Custom Intent Audiences

Custom Intent audiences allow you to leverage the power of Google search inside your Display and YouTube efforts. This feature allows you to select keywords that you would normally bid on in Search, and Google will match those keywords with users who searched for similar keywords within the last twenty-four to seventy-two hours.

As per Google Support Documentation:

> **Custom Intent: Display**
>
> Custom intent audiences allow you to define and reach the ideal audience for your Display campaigns. You can use custom intent audiences to segment your ad groups for a specific vertical or landing page. You can use auto-created segments or define your own audience by entering in-market keywords, URLs, and apps related to products and services that your ideal customer is researching across sites and apps.

Custom Intent: YouTube Campaigns

Custom intent audiences can help you reach new customers on YouTube based on the terms they use to search for your products or services on Google.com. You can select from 300 to 500 keywords that your ideal audience would most likely use in a search. Focus on general keywords to reach as many people as possible. For example, if you own a sporting goods store, you might want to choose keywords like "basketball shoes" instead of more specific keywords like "discount blue high-top basketball shoes."[37]

Cross-Platform Audience Data

In my opinion, the most valuable audience data that can be gleaned from any ad platform comes from the LinkedIn Insights Tag. This can be leveraged even if you are not actively running LinkedIn ad campaigns.

LinkedIn has cleaner data than any of the other ad platforms. For example, Google and Facebook use a variety of signals to establish, with relatively strong confidence, assumptions about individual interests and behavioral characteristics. However, it's not perfect.

Very few people list their accurate job title and company name on their Facebook profiles, and even fewer list information related to their skills and education.

LinkedIn users, on the other hand, will provide accurate information nearly all the time. LinkedIn doesn't need to rely on signal data to determine that you work for a marketing agency with fifteen to twenty people, that you have proficiency with Photoshop, Google Analytics, Microsoft Excel, and negotiation skills, or that you have twelve years of experience in your field. They don't have to assume anything because you've willingly given all that information directly to them!

This is the primary reason why LinkedIn advertising is a premium solution. It costs much more per click to advertise on LinkedIn, but you can tailor your ad impressions to the highest quality audiences that you'll find on the internet.

The downside is that LinkedIn can't measure buyer intent like Google or Facebook can. A cross-platform strategy would include using LinkedIn to validate your audience (to ensure that you are reaching the *right* people) and then craft advanced Google search strategies, leveraging RLSAs (outlined above) to aggressively bid on that audience when they express intent to buy.

8

Attribution

Attribution Overview

Customers often perform multiple searches and interact with many ads on their path to conversion. Attribution Modeling is the practice of assigning value to each of those interactions and using the data to better understand your customers' conversion paths.

It's the act of assigning credit for a job well done and assigning responsibility for lackluster results. This confusing topic often creates friction, as various business units within one organization will often attempt to use attribution models that will overattribute positive results to their own efforts, while passing off the blame to others.

Attribution can be used at the micro-level inside a Google Ad account to determine the value of one campaign or keyword against another, but it can also be used at the global level as well.

One of the worst mistakes we've seen clients make is allowing a decision maker who doesn't have a complete understanding of attribution to influence the way in which attribution is modeled across campaigns and across channels.

We've also seen instances where clients will hire multiple agencies and ask them to compete against one another, oftentimes within the same

Google Ads account. Do not do this, as you create an attribution war where each agency is going to be more concerned with earning credit and less concerned with driving profitable growth for your business. It's like when a politician is more concerned with gerrymandering district lines to ensure reelection, as opposed to actually driving the positive change that would benefit the district they were elected to serve.

Google Ads attribution works in a way that credits conversion data to the ad click, on the day that the ad click took place, *not when the conversion takes place.*

For example, if a user clicks on an ad on Monday, but completes checkout and actually buys a product on Tuesday, the Google Ad account will *attribute* that conversion to the ad click that took place on Monday (even though the business did not earn that revenue until Tuesday).

Therefore, if your POC (client-side point of contact) receives a weekly report, including performance that is attributed to the previous week's ad spend, it is oftentimes doing more harm than good.

If the account experiences a significant *Time Lag* (the time it takes for an ad click to result in a conversion), then the conversion data for a recent snapshot will be incomplete. It is the responsibility of the agency to help educate their clients about attribution and provide realistic expectations as to how to evaluate performance.

My intention for writing this book was to clear the air about topics that cause tension between marketers and provide information that can lead to effective collaboration. For attribution, though, the lack of knowledge is much more dangerous. Too many marketing executives are making strategic decisions with an outdated perspective on concepts like cross-channel attribution models or branded search and complete ignorance on topics like Time-Lag.

As an industry, we need to speak about attribution in a more sophisticated way and use every interaction with clients as an opportunity to educate them about this complicated topic.

I hope the content of this chapter helps initiate some of those conversations.

Revisiting Accounting 211

Most digital ad platforms, including Google Ads, base attribution on the *accrual method,* a concept borrowed from the accounting world. *Accrual Accounting* is a commonly used accounting principle whereby revenues or expenses are recorded in the books *in the absence of* an actual cash transaction.

When you pay your Verizon phone bill for December on January 1st, Verizon is crediting that income, via the accrual method, to December's books—even though they didn't receive the cash payment until January.

The reporting data gleaned from digital advertising platforms is also a form of accounting. Advertisers make investments in various channels and use basic accounting principles to *attribute* revenue earned to the various investments they have made. It is, therefore, necessary to understand the basics of these principles if you ever wish to wrap your head around complex, cross-channel attribution modeling.

Entrepreneur.com offers the following definition of accrual accounting:

> Most businesses typically use one of two basic accounting methods in their bookkeeping systems: cash basis or accrual basis.
>
> The cash method is the simplest in that the books are kept based on the actual flow of cash in and out of the business. Income is recorded when it's received, and expenses are reported when they're actually paid. The cash method is used by many sole proprietors and businesses with no inventory.
>
> With the accrual method, income and expenses are recorded as they occur, regardless of whether cash has actually changed hands. An excellent example is a sale on credit. The sale is entered into the books when the invoice is generated rather than when the cash is collected. Likewise, an expense occurs when materials are ordered or when a workday has been logged in by an employee, not when the check is written.[38]

Digital advertising platforms prefer to base attribution on an accrual method, as this credits more revenue to their platform's ad spend over time.

For example, let's say you are preparing for a Black Friday sale on November 29th. To build awareness, you invest 100K into YouTube advertising between November 15th and November 28th. This investment is not going to turn into actual revenue earned until November 29th; however, you will still need to use an attribution model that determines the true value of that 100K investment. An accrual-based system allows you to find the individual YouTube ads that ran between November 15th and November 28th that helped contribute to the actual sales that took place on Black Friday.

A cash method would have attributed that revenue to the day that cash is received. In this example, a cash method would make it seem as if the Black Friday revenue appeared out of thin air (and would likely be attributed as *Direct* revenue in Google Analytics), thus misrepresenting the impact of your advertising investment.

Google Ads and other ad platforms including Facebook Ads, use the accrual method. Google Analytics uses a cash method, which is helpful for perspective.

We can best understand the differences between Google Ads reporting (accrual) and Google Analytics reporting (cash) by comparing the reports for one of our ecommerce clients.

The following screenshot is from Google Analytics, outlining revenue earned during the Black Friday season of 2019. You can see the significant spike in revenue that occurred on Black Friday (Nov 29), as this is where many of the actual sales took place.

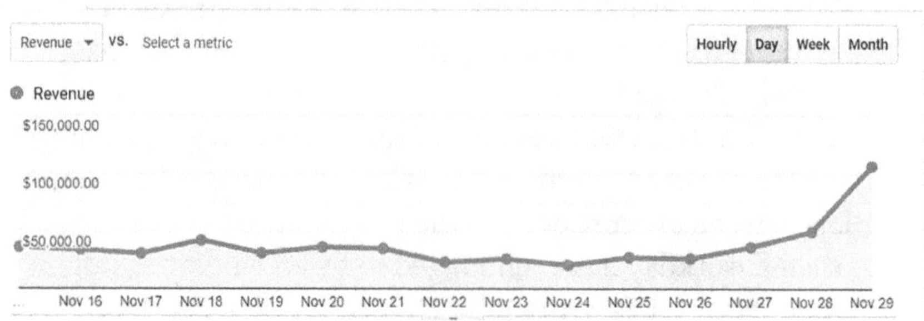

However, when we pull a report showing *attributed conversion value* from the Google Ads account for the same period, the revenue is spread out more evenly across the month.

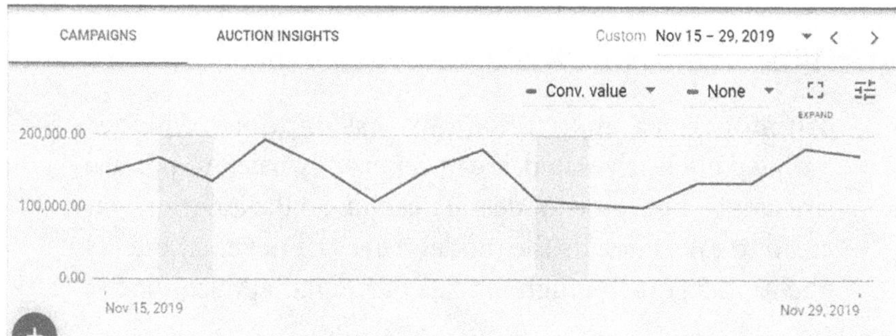

This is due to the accrual method *attributing* revenue earned to ad spend that was invested earlier in the month. We invested in advertising across Search, Shopping, Display, and YouTube in the weeks leading up to Black Friday, but those users didn't convert into customers—thus resulting in the cash exchange outlined in the Google Analytics report—until Black Friday hit.

Is either of these reporting methods *better?* Of course not. It's important to see all angles and use the various reports to solve various business problems. Yes, the Google Ads accrual method accurately reflects the impact of your advertising investments, but without the Google Analytics cash method report, the strategic decision-makers would not have a complete understanding of the marketing mix.

For example, a naive retail executive might conclude that, since the Google Ads reporting shows that attributed revenue is evenly distributed throughout the month, perhaps they shouldn't wait until Black Friday to introduce their sales. They might look at this data and think that their customers are unaffected by the Black Friday sales craze, and it would be a competitive advantage for them to jump ahead and attempt to capture the market earlier in the holiday season.

This would be a bad idea, as we can confidently say that this business is significantly impacted by Black Friday demand, and thankfully we have the Google Analytics data (along with other attribution data that we'll cover shortly) to defend that statement.

Therefore, the key lesson in relation to attribution: The question should not be, "What is the ideal attribution model?" Rather, the question is, "Which attribution model should I use at this moment to answer a specific question?"

To revisit George Box, the British statistician mentioned in Chapter 2:

> All models are approximations. Assumptions, whether implied or clearly stated, are never exactly true. All models are wrong, but some models are useful. So the question you need to ask is not "Is the model true?" (it never is) but "Is the model good enough for this particular application?"[39]

Understanding the various attribution models and tools will give you a 360-degree view of your performance and allow you to answer this question with confidence.

Non-Last Click (NLC) Attribution Models

Most digital ad platforms have historically relied on *Last Click* conversion attribution. This would not be an issue if we lived in a world where a user's conversion journey only required one ad interaction.

However, nearly every account I've worked on averages *at least* 1.5 ad interactions per conversion—for every conversion that only required a single ad interaction, there was a second conversion that required two ad interactions. Most accounts, especially in the ecommerce or SaaS space, require many more than two ad interactions.

Last-Click attribution assigns all conversion credit to the last ad click that took place before converting. If multiple ad interactions take place on the conversion path, none of the interactions aside from the final ad click will receive credit for contributing to that conversion.

Consider the following conversion journey:

1. Prospecting Display Ad Click
2. Middle Funnel Keyword Search Ad Click

3. Remarketing Display Ad Click
4. Branded Search Ad Click

Shortly after clicking on the Branded Search ad, the user converts, purchasing a product worth $100 in revenue.

In *Last Click* attribution, that conversion and its $100 in revenue will be solely credited to the Branded Search click. Your reports will not reflect the impact that the other three ad interactions had as part of this conversion journey, and worse, a machine-learning algorithm that is determining your bids, placements, and ad formats in an automated campaign will not receive that feedback either.

Without properly attributing conversion data to various ad interactions, your naive algorithms will be trained to think that the only ad interactions that contribute to earned revenue are clicks on branded searches. This is no way to treat an algorithm, nor is it a way to achieve profitable growth in your account. You, therefore, need to work with a more advanced attribution model that assigns conversion credit in a way that more accurately reflects the value of the various ad interactions your customers take.*

First Click attribution is nearly as dangerous as *Last Click*, as it would reward 100 percent of the conversion credit to the first ad-interaction (which, in the example above, would be the Prospecting Display Click). Both *First Click* and *Last Click* should only be used when attempting to find answers to a specific question and should never be used to evaluate overall performance.

Linear attribution would evenly distribute conversion credit across all ad interactions. If a conversion required two ad interactions, each interaction would receive 50 percent of the credit. If there were three interactions, each would receive 33.3 percent.

---

* The Google Analytics platform uses *Last Click* attribution by default but is not an issue. Google Analytics provides a single, uniform perspective of our reporting, and the data that are reported through this system are not used (or at least, should not be used) to feed a bidding algorithm. Smart marketers will keep the *Last-Click* model in mind as they analyze Google Analytics data, cognizant of the fact that this model is useful to answer some questions, but not all.

Your total sum of conversions (shown in the conversion column) will always add up to a whole number. As a result, you might see fractional conversions attributed in your account. This is not an error; rather, it is the result of your attribution model.

In our example above, *Linear* attribution would assign the following credit:

- Prospecting Display Ad Click—0.25 conversions, $25 in revenue
- MOF Keyword Search Ad Click—0.25 conversions, $25 in revenue
- Remarketing Display Ad Click—0.25 conversions, $25 in revenue
- Branded Search Ad Click—0.25 conversions, $25 in revenue

*Total conversions across the account equal 1, and total conversion value (revenue) accurately reflect the $100 earned.

While *Linear* is certainly a better option for reporting (and for training an algorithm) compared to *First Click* or *Last Click*, it's still not perfect.

Position-Based is a more advanced variation of *Linear* attribution, which places more emphasis on the first and last interactions. This attribution follows a simple calculation, whereby 40 percent of the conversion credit is assigned to the first ad interaction, 40 percent of the credit assigned to the last ad interaction, and the remaining 20 percent is evenly distributed across any other ad interactions that took place in the middle.

For example:

- Prospecting Display Ad Click—0.40 conversions, $40 in revenue
- MOF Keyword Search Ad Click—0.10 conversions, $10 in revenue
- Remarketing Display Ad Click—0.10 conversions, $10 in revenue
- Branded Search Ad Click—0.40 conversions, $40 in revenue

However, this still is not perfect. What if, for example, our Prospecting Display Ad Click took place on January 1st, but the other three ad interactions all took place between February 13th and February 15th? Is it rational to say that the first ad interaction that took place more than a month ago was 40 percent of the reason that this user converted in the end?

A pessimist could argue that the user likely *doesn't even remember* clicking on that first display ad forty-six days prior to their conversion, and that ad, therefore, had no impact on their conversion journey or purchase decision. It would be preposterous and irresponsible to assign 40 percent of the conversion credit to this ad click and dangerous to train an algorithm to think this way!

Therefore, Position-Based attribution can certainly be useful. However, it definitely isn't perfect.

Time Decay attribution is a slightly more advanced model as it uses a combination of factors to determine how credit is distributed among ad interactions. This model will place most of the weight toward the later clicks in a conversion journey.

The formula to calculate *Time Decay* distribution is much more complicated than *Position-Based,* but a simplified example of *Time Decay* might include the following conversion distribution:

- Prospecting Display Ad Click—0.05 conversions, $5 in revenue
- MOF Keyword Search Ad Click—0.15 conversions, $15 in revenue
- Remarketing Display Ad Click—0.30 conversions, $30 in revenue
- Branded Search Ad Click—0.50 conversions, $40 in revenue

This is an estimation and would vary, depending on the timing of each of the ad clicks. However, you can see that *Time Decay* skews more weight toward the final interactions that took place before the conversion.

Of the five traditional attribution models, *Last-Click, First-Click, Linear, Position-Based* and *Time Decay,* it is generally accepted that the latter two, *Position-Based,* and *Time Decay* are the only two that should be used within a Google Ads account. But how do you choose?

Colleagues of mine at Google have recommended that clients with a growth mindset and/or long-term focus should opt for *Position-Based,* whereas clients who prioritize short-term profitability and are willing to temporarily sacrifice growth should opt for *Time-Decay.*

Think of it this way: Given your current marketing goals, how would you personally value the four ad interactions that have been used as an example throughout this chapter? If new customer acquisition is your goal, then you would likely prefer *Position-Based* attribution, which will train your algorithms to place more weight on interactions such as the Prospecting Display click.

However, if you are taking a conservative approach and willing to sacrifice total revenue for efficiency, then you might want to go with *Time Decay.*

Current marketing goals are not the only factors you should consider. You should also be practical about your business and use your own experience to determine your default attribution model. For example, if most of your leads convert within one day after learning about your business, you should choose *Time Decay.*

In contrast, if your customer conversion cycle (also referred to as your *Time Lag*) is longer than most businesses, you should opt for *Position-Based.* Real estate agents and CRM software providers should use *Position-Based* attribution, as these are purchase decisions that can take several weeks or months.

As most of our clients have a growth mindset, I tend to prefer *Position-Based* attribution to *Time Decay,* unless the latter is the logically better solution. But that is merely a matter of preference.

And when possible, we opt for *Data-Driven.*

Data-Driven

The future of attribution models—*Data-Driven* is a machine-learning-based model that creates a unique attribution model for your account. As per Google:

> *Data-Driven* attribution is different from the other attribution models, in that it uses your conversion data to

> calculate the actual contribution of each keyword across the conversion path. Each data-driven model is specific to each advertiser.
>
> Google Ads looks at all the clicks on your Google Search ads. By comparing the click paths of customers who convert to the paths of customers who don't, the model identifies patterns among those clicks that lead to conversions. There may be certain steps along the way that have a higher probability of leading a customer to complete a conversion. The model then gives more credit to those valuable clicks on the customer's path.[40]

This model, in theory, should account for the flaws in both the *Time Decay* model and the *Position-Based* model. Unfortunately, Google does not provide advertisers with their given *Data-Driven* models, so we have no way of understanding how our conversion data is distributed and essentially have to trust Google to make this model work for us.

Most Google Ads accounts do not currently have access to Data-Driven attribution, as there are conversion and click minimums that must be met and maintained for this model to be available.

As of this writing, advertisers must have at least 15,000 Search ad clicks and 600 conversions within the last 30 days to become eligible for Data-Driven attribution. At this point, Google will attempt to create a statistically significant model that can be used, but this doesn't happen immediately.

This model is unique to each conversion action, so these conversion count minimums are related to the action in which you will be using Data-Driven attribution. That is, 600 conversions spread across multiple conversion actions in your account will not qualify. If your account drops below 10,000 Search clicks and/or 400 conversions for this action, this model will no longer be available. It is likely that these minimums will decrease or be removed altogether in the future when Google's systems are able to confidently create models with less data.

Data-Driven attribution is the future, but it already has its critics. Much of the PPC community is of the opinion that, given the lack of transparency that advertisers receive about their individual Data-Driven models, Google would likely "game the system" to create models that serve their agenda. For example, if Google was eager to convince advertisers to invest more in Display and Video, they *could* skew the data in a way that rewards more conversion credit to these ad interactions and less to Branded Search or BOF Search.

I personally don't believe that this is true. Even if it was, it is the responsibility of the advertiser and their agency to maintain a 360-degree view of their return on ad spend. If you are naive enough to let any attribution model convince you to make destructive decisions regarding your digital strategy, that is your fault alone.

The purpose of an attribution model, as it pertains to your Google Ads account, is to train an algorithm to make intelligent decisions on your behalf. For you to understand the real return on your ad spend, you should be comparing the results that you see inside Google to other analytics tools within your marketing suite.

In the age of automation, a 360-degree understanding of attribution is one of the primary value-adds that an agency provide to their clients.

Members of the PPC community who critique automation and *Data-Driven* attribution have stated that "You should always test which attribution model works best for your account!" This is a lazy perspective and a colossal waste of resources. It would be nearly impossible to run a true blind test that provides statistically significant, conclusive data about which of two models provides better results. Especially given that your *Data-Driven* model will evolve over time and improve with more data.

Even if you *could* run this test, it's so trivial. There are dozens of other's you should be running instead, many of which we will cover in later chapters. If you are paying an agency to manage your account, and they report that they are currently running a test on *Data-Driven* vs. *Time Decay,* I would advise you to seek out a new agency.

Embrace *Data-Driven* if it is available and start thinking about the next move that will improve your account.

Time Lag

As mentioned, *Time Lag* is the amount of time that passes between a user engaging with an ad, and when they ultimately convert. Much of the AdVenture Media team likes to poke fun about how much I seem to love the *Time Lag* report, but I passionately believe that it is the most overlooked and misunderstood concept in all of PPC advertising.

Below is a screenshot from the Time Lag report from one of our client's accounts, showing that their customers take ten days, on average, to convert. That is, from the time someone first clicks on an ad, it takes an average of ten days for them to convert (or for us to realize the revenue).

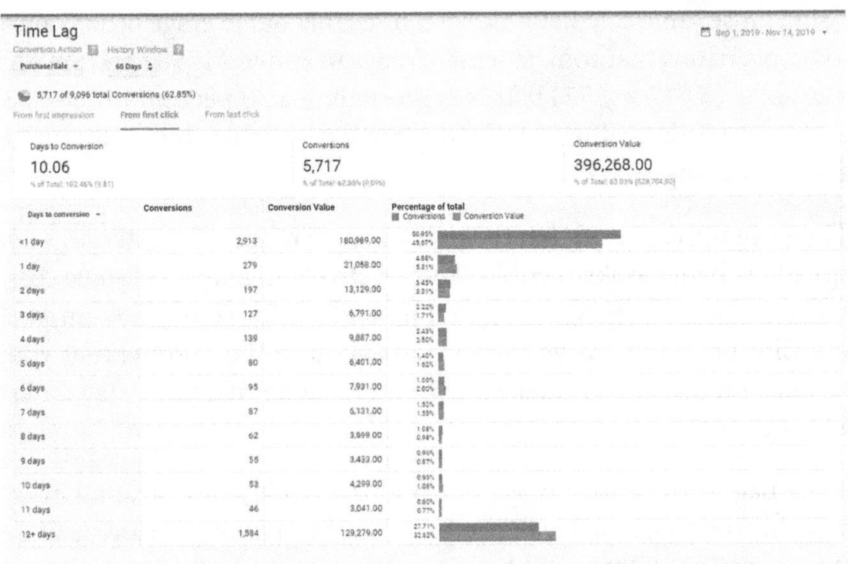

Time Lag

Sep 1, 2019 - Nov 14, 2019

Conversion Action: Purchase/Sale | History Window: 60 Days

5,717 of 9,096 total Conversions (62.85%)

From first impression | From first click | From last click

Days to Conversion: 10.06 (% of Total: 102.46% (9.81))

Conversions: 5,717 (% of Total: 62.85% (9,096))

Conversion Value: 396,268.00 (% of Total: 63.03% (628,704.00))

Days to conversion	Conversions	Conversion Value	Percentage of total (Conversions / Conversion Value)
<1 day	2,913	180,989.00	50.95% / 45.67%
1 day	279	21,058.00	4.88% / 5.31%
2 days	197	13,129.00	3.45% / 3.31%
3 days	127	6,791.00	2.22% / 1.71%
4 days	139	9,887.00	2.43% / 2.50%
5 days	80	6,401.00	1.40% / 1.62%
6 days	95	7,931.00	1.66% / 2.00%
7 days	87	6,131.00	1.52% / 1.55%
8 days	62	3,899.00	1.08% / 0.98%
9 days	55	3,433.00	0.96% / 0.87%
10 days	53	4,299.00	0.93% / 1.08%
11 days	46	3,041.00	0.80% / 0.77%
12+ days	1,584	129,279.00	27.71% / 32.62%

However, averages are skewed by outliers. In this instance, we can see that while 45 percent of revenue is earned within the first day of clicking on an ad, **nearly 33 percent of revenue takes at least twelve days to be realized.**

Is it totally fair, then, to say that our typical customer takes ten days to convert? Maybe, maybe not. However, there are other takeaways from this report. For example, this data shows that larger purchases take longer to convert. This is reflected by the ratio of Conversions vs. Conversion

Value throughout, with Conversion Value under-pacing Conversion Count at the top of the chart and over-pacing it towards the bottom.

The key values at the top of the report show that this data reflects 5,717 conversions worth $396K in revenue. Therefore, our average order value across this time period is $69.31.

Additionally, the average order value varies, depending on how long it took for a user to convert. For *same-day* conversions, the first row of our Time Lag report, we can see that the conversion count is 2,913 (50.95 percent of 5,717 = 2,913), and our conversion value is $180,975 (45.67 percent of $396,268). Our average order value for customers who convert within one day of first clicking on an ad is $62.12 ($181K / 2,919).

Using those same calculations, we can see that our average order value for conversions that took at least 12 days to convert is $81.60 ($396K x .3262) / (5,717 x .2771). This is more than a 30 percent difference in average order value (AOV), depending on what the customer is actually buying.

Time Lag is the reason that the performance report for yesterday's ad spend probably looks terrible. If you actively manage a Google Ads account, I encourage you to pull it up and see for yourself. Compare the CPA or ROAS for yesterday's ad spend to the average that you saw last month or last quarter. I would imagine that yesterday looks a lot worse.

Time Lag is the reason why just about all weekly reports, and even monthly reports, look bleak compared to the previous period or year. If you or your clients don't have an understanding of Time Lag, you might start to panic and make changes that are not necessary. Changes which might inflict damage on your account.

While the concept of Time Lag certainly complicates the reporting process, we can use the Time Lag report to draw speculative projections about overall revenue. For example, the data above shows that, on average, 45 percent of our revenue is earned *within one day* of someone first clicking on an ad. On the other end, 33 percent of your revenue takes at least twelve days to come in.

Let's say we spent $1,000 in advertising yesterday and the account is currently attributing $2,000 in revenue to that spend. We would therefore be currently showing a 2.0x ROAS for yesterday's ad spend.

However, based on this report, we can assume that this $2,000 is just 45 percent of what the total amount of attributed revenue will be, once Time Lag runs its course. Try thinking this way: we invested advertising dollars in customers yesterday that have not converted, but will likely convert in the future.

Therefore, we can project that the *adjusted* attributed revenue to yesterday's ad spend will be $4,445—2K is 45 percent of $4,445. The extra $2,445 is projected incremental revenue.

The projected ROAS for yesterday's ad spend would be 4.45x.

While arduous, we have used full-scope Time Lag projections to help visualize this concept with clients and validate the Time Lag data over time.

For more information on making PPC projections while factoring in Time Lag and other attribution variables, please see the supplemental material at www.joinordiebook.com.

9 Changing Perspectives on Automation

In February 2016, Isaac and I took a trip to Costco to discuss the future of my career. Our entire office at the time was the size of one of our conference rooms today, and private conversations were hard to come by. The Costco on Rockaway Turnpike wasn't the best location for this type of conversation either, but with the rate at which we were going through Diet Coke, K-Cups, and peanut butter pretzels at the time, we figured we'd kill two birds with one stone.

As we added a half palette of Diet Coke to our wagons, I asked Isaac what I would need to do to increase my value to the agency. We were all strong account managers, but there was a unanimous feeling in our office that none of us wanted to spend the rest of our careers muddling around in Google AdWords. We were passionate about finding innovative solutions to complex problems, but more specifically, to solutions that helped our client's businesses grow. We loved the relationships we formed with our clients and experienced immense pride when we had even a small part in helping them advance their careers.

None of us have ever jumped out of bed in the morning because we couldn't wait to get to the office to optimize keyword bids or to write new text ad headlines. However, these monotonous tasks were important pieces that, when united, allowed us to deliver the results that we were actually passionate about, problem-solving and relationship building.

Isaac felt that, in the future, we'd become an agency where Google AdWords and Facebook Ads were just two small line items on our client meeting agendas. He speculated that the majority of our meeting agendas would center around broader marketing problems and that we'd embrace a consultancy role, oriented around guiding our client's through the ever-changing digital landscape.

To get there, we needed to develop new skills and gain experience outside of the ad platforms that we worked in so that we could increase the value that we delivered to clients. We would also need to ensure that we drastically increased our ability to drive profitable growth inside Google Ad accounts but to do so in a way that was more efficient for our agency.

The two of us reminisced on our successes and failures up to that point. We made a few great hires and a few bad ones. We made some great investments, including the first Udemy course. We also made some bad ones. Earlier that year, it became clear that we needed to move into a larger office. After a long search, we came close to signing a lease on a place that would have ultimately been a disaster. While we were fortunate to have pulled out at the last minute, we'd wasted months working with this would-be landlord, knowing all along that there were far too many red flags. When we pulled out and went back to square one, we felt defeated.

It appeared to be a massive failure at the time, but in hindsight it wasn't a huge deal. We eventually found a new office, and then a third after that. I have mostly forgotten about the ordeal with that would-be landlord all those years ago.

While we meandered the aisles of Costco, we discussed broad concepts that, years later, would make up the principles that we use to make strategic decisions for the agency. The first of which is to *make bad good bets.* A good bet is a good bet, but some good bets are bad—and that's OK. For example, since 2003, the New England Patriots have won their division in every year but one. The exception was 2008, when Tom Brady suffered a season-ending injury on opening day. If you were to bet on the Patriots to win the AFC East in each of the last 20 seasons, no one would argue that it would have been a bad bet—

even if you lost money in 2008. On the contrary, if you happened to win money on the Miami Dolphins in 2008, I wouldn't say that you made a good bet, I'd say that you got lucky. And you can't build a great business by making *lucky bad bets.*

Similar to *making bad good bets* is the realization that *failures are cauterized, while success ripples outwards.* The failure we experienced by over-investing our time with the would-be landlord is cemented in time and has since been forgotten. However, the success of the Udemy course still has a positive impact on our business nearly six years later.

By the time we were finally loading all of our Costco goodies into his car, he had worked out a few action items, or *good bets,* that he wanted me to take the lead on.

He wanted me to learn how to design landing pages on Webflow, a CMS tool that he had recently learned about. He felt that other landing page tools available at the time were too simplistic and would not be an effective value-add for our clients. He predicted that landing page development would become a cornerstone service that we would eventually offer to all our clients.

He also wanted me to write an AdWords Script. It would have to be unique and valuable; he would only accept it if I could prove that it solved a problem that no one else was able to solve. There were other agencies making a name for themselves by publishing useful scripts at the time, and he felt that we could legitimize our thought-leadership by contributing to this fad.

I viewed the former task as an interesting side project; I viewed the latter as a nearly impossible marching order. I didn't understand the first thing about Google AdWords scripts or even the JavaScript coding language. I also had no idea what problem I would attempt to solve.

The irony is that Isaac was incorrect on both predictions, but they were both *good bets.* Most clients today do not require new landing pages, so landing page development has not exactly become a cornerstone service of ours. However, the process of learning Webflow was invaluable. This was the beginning of our journey with UX, heuristics, and design education that would eventually turn into our

Conversion Rate Optimization (CRO) expertise. Today, CRO is baked into every client relationship, and we have several team members on staff who are specifically dedicated to running CRO experiments and analyses. What's more, our website, *adventureppc.com*, was rebuilt on Webflow, a decision that had an immediate positive impact on our own conversion rates.

The script, though, was a long and lonely endeavor. I eventually concluded that I should develop a bid-management script that would automatically make bid adjustments to shopping campaigns based on recent ROAS performance. Nothing like this had previously existed, and for good reason. The AdWords API did not allow you to directly pull ROAS data, so I needed to build three separate programs that could interact with one another. It was a headache for the end user to set up and manage the script; but it was functional, and I was proud of it.

On October 26th of that year, eight months after I received my marching orders in the parking lot of Costco, I emailed my new, fully functional *Shopping ROAS Bidding* script to the AdVenture Media team. I was proud of this accomplishment, but too busy at the time to officially release it to the world. A few days later, Isaac, Danny Tawil, and I would be spending an entire week in Boston for HubSpot's INBOUND 2016 conference—an experience that would ultimately lead me to realize that my new shiny AdWords script (along with many other aspects of my job) would be soon rendered obsolete.

New technology—rather, better technology—was about to drastically turn the marketing world on its head: *Automation.*

I originally promised Isaac that I'd publish the script, and in keeping with that promise, you can get a copy of the script at *joinordiebook.com.* However, if I've taught you anything, you should realize that Smart Shopping and other automated bidding solutions are far superior.

INBOUND 2016

If you're a marketer and have never experienced INBOUND, I urge you to attend the conference at least once. The folks at HubSpot do an incredible job making this a productive, inspiring, and fun event. But they did, however, make one crucial mistake when planning their 2016 conference: It would kick off on Tuesday, November 8th, 2016, the day of the 2016 presidential election.

Gary Vaynerchuck delivered the keynote speech on the opening night. Of all the topics he covered, one quote stuck out in particular: "If you are not actively trying to put yourself out of business, someone else will do that for you."

This stuck with me throughout the remainder of the conference and beyond. As I sat in that massive convention center, it was hard to imagine that my job and our company would ever become irrelevant. However, that's the same irresponsible thinking that led to the downfall of Blockbuster, JC Penney, and taxi companies throughout the world.

We've adopted this mindset, and you should too. As a marketer, you should embrace the fact that your job, as it exists today, will be irrelevant within two to five years.

This is true for nearly every other industry and job function, but the time-range may vary. The current job description of a natural gas engineer likely has a longer shelf life than that of a digital marketer but will ultimately be replaced by a job description that includes experience with technology that has yet to be developed. Even the job description of an NFL quarterback changes over time. Patrick Mahomes, the QB of the Kansas City Chiefs and MVP of Super Bowl LIV, has a completely different set of primary skills than did the likes of John Elway, Troy Aikman, and even Tom Brady. Technology and advanced analytics are major components of Mahomes's training regimen.

When I say that a job function is going to become *irrelevant,* I am not suggesting that these roles won't exist. Ten years from now we'll still have marketers, natural gas engineers, and NFL quarterbacks, but the skill sets and the day-to-day tasks that these individuals carry out are going to be completely different from what they look like today.

The job that I was hired for at AdVenture Media in 2015 doesn't exist anymore. It has been replaced, but thankfully, it was replaced by me. My current job will likely be replaced in another three years.

Hopefully, I will be just as lucky the next time around. I need to continue to reinvent myself and learn new skills. It's not easy, but it's necessary for survival.

After Gary Vee's speech, the grand ballroom emptied out into a massive, cocktail-infused networking event. Few people networked; most just stood in front of the large screens projecting CNN's coverage of the election. It seemed as if the entire crowd immediately forgot the lessons from the keynote.

Over the next few days we attended breakout sessions from some of the top thought leaders in marketing, including Purna Virji of Microsoft, Oli Gardner of Unbounce, Rand Fishkin of Moz (now of SparkToro), Larry Kim of Wordstream (now of MobileMonkey), and Paul Roetzer of PR 2020. All the topics had an underlying theme: AI and machine learning are going to disrupt the marketing industry unlike anything we've ever seen. It will be even more disruptive than the introduction and mass adoption of smartphones.

Paul Roetzer would soon after launch the *Marketing AI Institute,* a resource center designed to make artificial intelligence more approachable and actionable for marketers.[41]

Four years later, if you were to ask the 35K INBOUND 2016 attendees what they remember as the key takeaway from that conference, I would bet that the vast majority will incorrectly cite topics much less essential than AI. I blame the election.*

As I reflected on the coming wave of AI and machine learning, I first thought I'd be ahead of the game. We were already using scripts to automate tasks inside and out of Google AdWords, and I was about to publish a script of my own!

But there was a key difference between these scripts and the machine learning tech I had demoed at INBOUND—Scripts aren't *smart.* Tech that is backed by machine learning continues to get better, without human input, whereas my script needed to be consistently tweaked over time.

---

* INBOUND was the second time that one of Isaac's fans approached him in public, after that first awkward burger bar encounter in Soho. This one was just as uncomfortable for me to witness.

Scripts were just a tool that allowed you to reach the same bidding conclusion that you would have if you manually completed the task yourself. This was not new technology; it was just a trick.

The *Bid to Position* Script

The Bid to Position script is well known and celebrated throughout the PPC community. The goal of the script is to raise or lower keyword bids to achieve a desired average position in the auction. Many say that this script acts in *real time,* but that is a farce. It only runs once an hour.

The advertiser is tasked with manually assigning labels at the keyword level and declaring a desired average position for that keyword. For a branded keyword, you might want an average position of 1.0, but for a TOF keyword, you might want to average a 2.5.

The script will raise or lower bids by 20 percent every hour, until you've averaged your desired position. If my experience in writing a script taught me anything, it's that the logic most scripts run on is incredibly simple. It boils down to this:

For *Keyword A:*

- If *average position* in the last hour is greater than *desired average position,* raise the bid by 20 percent
- Else, lower bid

For *Keyword B:*

- If *average position* in the last hour is greater than *desired average position,* raise the bid by 20 percent
- Else, lower bid

And so on.

You are effectively training a monkey to make your bid changes for you. This works well in a vacuum, but not if there are any outside factors to be taken into consideration.

In an earlier example I explained how Isaac is a fanatical Spindrift seltzer drinker. If he performed a search for *order spindrift online,* a retailer would want to bid more aggressively and therefore earn a higher ad position for this search—as he is likely to bulk order as many cases as he can possibly afford in that one sitting. If I perform that same search, however, a smart retailer wouldn't want to be so aggressive.

It is based on *average* position, not actual position! A desired average position of 2.0 will receive actual placements scattered throughout the Google SERP.

The *Bid To Position* script, or any other script that allows you to automate the process of adjusting bids in a manual CPC campaign, is a time-consuming method of achieving the exact same result.*

However, beyond that small bit of time saved, these scripts provide no value in terms of actual performance compared to if a person was making those bid changes on their own.

If we're being honest, the main reason that the PPC community loves the Bid o Position script is because it fills the Change History tool with tons of changes per day. Your clients can never complain that you are neglecting the account when you are able to export a list of bid changes that you "made" last night at 3 a.m. —even if in reality you haven't checked the account in weeks. However, these bid changes do nothing to improve performance. They are a smoke screen, used by agencies to impress their clients. I am certain that, of the agencies that push back against automation, many do so because they are fearful of what would be logged in a Change History tool once they adopt Smart Campaigns. The best agencies do not allow a Change History tool to represent the value that they deliver to their clients.

Regarding the broader concepts of scripts: They are merely models that do nothing aside from expediting the manual, human optimization process. Scripts are not true automation—that is a title reserved for the work performed by machine learning algorithms.

---

* *Google has since removed the Average Position metric, thus making this script obsolete altogether.*

In the end, I was proud of the fact that I had written a functioning AdWords script, but the real value that came out of that experience was not time savings or improved performance. It was the realization that scripts are incredibly flawed and do not offer a solution to help us deliver profitable growth for our clients.

Below is a screenshot from the client account we inherited in 2017 that I mentioned in the Introduction to this book.

As you can see from the *change history* tool, about 20K changes were made (approximately 300 per week) over a fourteen-month period, but this account did not realize any improvement in revenue or profitability over that period. They were simply paying their agency to make changes in an account, and they were distracted by arbitrary KPI targets regarding Quality Score, Average Position, Search Impression Share, and Average CPC.

Here is an updated screenshot, with the dotted line showing the month in which our team took over the account management.

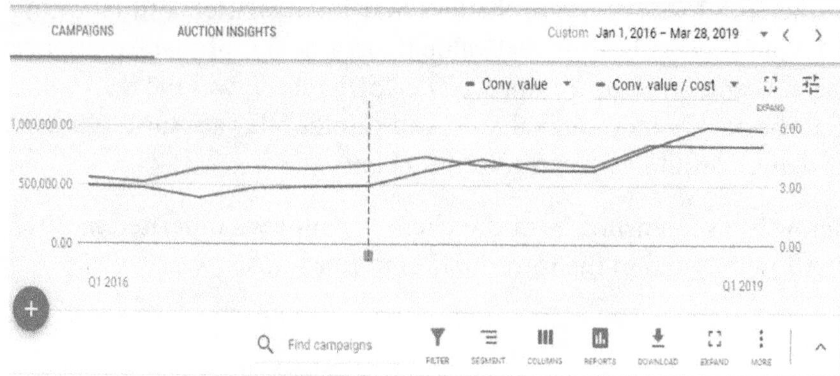

A properly implemented automation strategy was a significant factor in helping this client achieve a 47 percent increase in year-over-year revenue and a 17 percent increase in year-over-year ROAS.

The Cliché Chess Comparison

For a long time, Chess Grandmaster Garry Kasparov was anti-automation in regard to chess. He once claimed that a computer would never be able to outperform human grandmasters in the game of chess. IBM's Watson eventually proved him wrong, and he adjusted his belief to say that machines could be valuable for training purposes but should not interfere with the sanctity of competition between human chess players.

Kasparov is one of the greatest chess players that has ever lived, and theoretically, we could program every decision that Kasparov would make in a chess game into a model. However, this model would never get *smarter* unless the logic inside was changed by a human. If the decision tree that helped the model choose the best move in a given scenario needed to be updated, a person would first have to make that realization on their own and then adjust the model (script) to change the way it makes decisions. The intelligence of the machine would always be limited to the intelligence of the person operating it.

Machine learning algorithms have proven to outperform individuals acting on their own accord, both in chess and elsewhere. A machine learning algorithm taught to play chess will continue to test strategies that have never been attempted by human players. The chess universe has since been turned on its head by radical opening moves and other in-game decisions that have proven to increase the likelihood of victory more than a human grandmaster could have ever dreamed of.

Kasparov has since changed his opinion again and is now an advocate for a new sport of human/machine hybrid chess teams that compete against one another. The chess community has since discovered that humans operating on top of a machine learning algorithm can consistently beat an algorithm playing on its own. But these hybrid teams only work when the person driving the machine has a deep understanding of the pros and cons of the technology itself.

This is exactly the opportunity that smart PPC agencies should embrace in the age of automation. You, by yourself, will never be better or more efficient than an algorithm at making certain decisions. However, an algorithm will never be able to completely manage your client's advertising efforts for them. You need to join forces.

If you learn the pros and cons of the technology that drives ad platforms and cultivate an awareness of your own personal pros and cons, you can have a healthy relationship with automated technology that will allow you to drive profitable growth in a way that you've never dreamed of.

Therefore, the opportunity to provide value to your clients is now greater than it has ever been.

In early 2017, we realized that our next *good bet* was to embrace automation. We were correct, and the success of that bet has had an outward ripple effect that I could have never imagined.

Section 2

Managing Automation

"If somebody describes to you the world of the mid-21st century and it doesn't sound like science fiction, then it is certainly false. Change itself is the only certainty."

Yuval Noah Harari, *21 Lessons for the 21st Century*

---

10 The Evolution of Machine Learning

Many years from now, marketing historians will likely look back on the age of automation and break it down into several distinct categories. The first era will be known as Automation 1.0, in which marketers finally chose to embrace automation, learned the fundamentals of machine learning, and began to explore modern technology with an open mind.

If you've reached this point in the book, you've probably chosen to join the movement (as opposed to choosing the latter option, as is printed on the cover of this book). You are likely in the early stages of the Automation 1.0 era, a truly exciting time for wide-eyed marketers. This period will be defined as the time when marketers stopped referring to machine learning as if it were some buzzword and instead spoke about these concepts with a level of sophisticated intelligence and perspective. The academics that emerge from this time will be able to rattle off the basic constructs of Bayes Theorem in the same way that traditional marketing professors have cited Maslow's Hierarchy of Needs.

In the Automation 2.0 era, marketers will begin finding uses for automation that have never even been considered. Marketers will know how to unlock the golden nuggets of data that can be used to train algorithms to meet their goals under any circumstances. The primary value derived from agencies will be the proper use of data inputs and creative strategy. Marketers living during Automation 2.0

will look back on the current era with the same inquisitive perspective that you and I look back on the *Mad Men* days.

Did the Don Drapers of the world actually leave the office at noon to get drunk with their clients?

Did those Google AdWords agencies really spend all that time making manual keyword bid adjustments in SKAG-segmented campaigns?

In *The Master Algorithm,* Pedro Domingos describes the various schools of thought that surround machine learning, different use cases for each school of thought, and how they might be used together to develop an all-powerful, perfect machine learning solution.

Domingos writes with a semblance of science fiction. There may never be such an all-powerful solution, but striving for perfection is the motivational factor that has driven progress throughout our history.[42]

The machine learning algorithms that drive the primary digital advertising platforms are not simple, although I will attempt to simplify their constructs and capabilities over the next few chapters. Do not be fooled by my examples; the actual machines are advanced beyond comprehension. For example, traditional machine learning algorithms typically fell into one of five classes. Today, the bidding algorithm that drives your Target CPA campaign likely combines elements from all these fields.

Moore's Law

Moore's Law is a concept derived from the semiconductor industry of the 1960s, and it's often cited in regard to the evolution of machine learning. Gordon Moore, former CEO of Intel, observed that the number of transistors in a dense circuit had doubled nearly every two years. He noted that:

> Transistors have not only become smaller, but also faster and more energy-efficient such that a chip now offers at least twice the performance at roughly the same dollar and power budgets.[43]

The transistor is the original building block for modern technological progress, and the exponential increase in transistor capacity is the reason that the size requirements for computer hardware have shrunk over time. Forget about iPhones: a standard Nokia cell phone would never have been possible if not for the phenomenon that Moore observed.

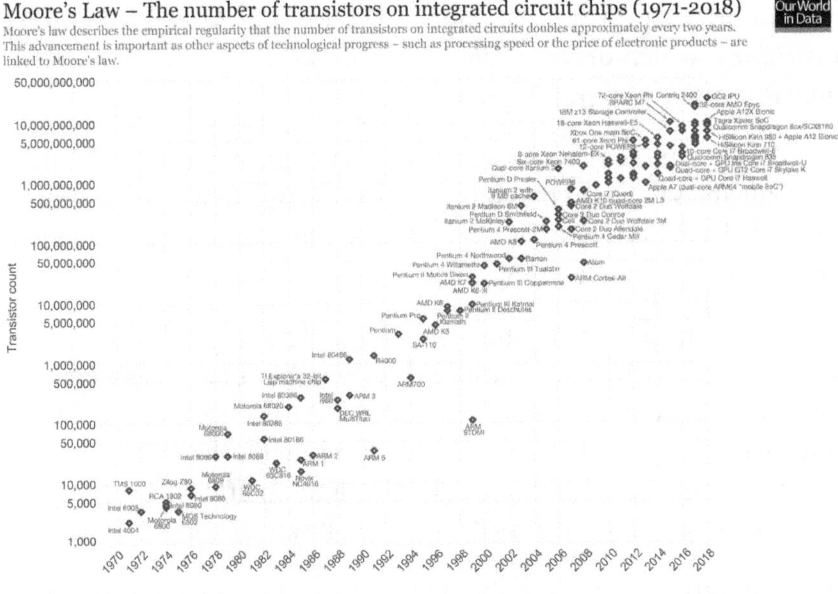

Source: Max Roser and Hannah Ritchie, "Technological Progress," *Our World in Data.org*, 2013, https://ourworldindata.org/technological-progress. Data taken from "Transistor_count," Wikipedia.org.

Moore's Law remained constant for nearly fifty years but began to taper off around 2005. This period is defined as when the electronics industry began to bring modern tech to the masses in the form of mobile phones. The demand for existing hardware skyrocketed around this time, and the motivation to continue to innovate stagnated as a result.

A decade later, the explosion of the machine learning industry has jump-started Moore's law once again. Over the last five years, we've had access to nearly endless amounts of data and programmers who have the ability to develop more advanced algorithms. What we lacked was the hardware systems with the capacity to manage these massive calculations in a reasonable amount of time.

Medium editor Azeem described this problem in his 2017 article, "If We Want to Get to Real Time AI, We've Got to Build Another iPhone Industry. Five Times Over." He notes that, if we want to accomplish something as significant as self-driving cars, three factors need to continue to evolve: Processing power (hardware), better algorithms (software), and higher demand for data, and he illustrates this concept by claiming that *More Processing Power* enables *More Demanding Algorithms,* which drives *Higher Demand for Data,* which requires *More Processing Power*, and so on.[44]

In 2020, we can see that Moore's Law is once again back in full force. The companies that lead the charge by developing innovative electronic hardware have been hard at work, setting the stage for the computer scientists developing learning algorithms to perfect their craft.

As a marketer, I am optimistic that machine learning will continue to get exponentially better. Consider this thought: It has been eighteen months since Smart Shopping campaigns were first introduced. These campaigns were a huge success for nearly all clients that received early access, and now, due to Moore's Law, that same Smart Shopping engine is nearly twice as powerful as it was when it was first introduced.

As we attempt to speculate about the future, it is necessary for us to understand the basic components of the technology that brought us to where we are today.

The Five Classes of Learners

According to Domingos, a learning algorithm is just a scientist in computer form. The computer looks at data, formulates hypotheses to explain the data, tests those hypotheses against more data, refines or discards the hypotheses, and then starts the whole process over again.[45] Continuing until it is confident that it has a good theory about the phenomenon it is studying. The key words here are *confident* and *good,* as opposed to *conclusive* and *perfect.*

It is the scientific method at work, only it's being conducted by computers instead of humans.

The five paradigms of machine learning are inspired by ideas in different fields: those of evolution, neuroscience, psychology, philosophy, and statistics.

Connectionist Algorithms

The first class of machine learning, **connectionism**, emulates learning in the same way that the human brain learns—by strengthening the bond between neurons (data points).

Alan Turing, a connectionist computer scientist, observed:

> Instead of trying to produce a program to simulate the adult mind, why not rather try to produce one which simulates the child's? If this were then subjected to an appropriate course of education, one would obtain the adult brain.[46]

This concept, generally referred to as **Deep Learning**, is one of the methods that drives Google search results or the content that fills a Facebook news feed. The hypothesis in this case would be that a certain series of search results would deliver the best experience for a user on Google. The algorithm then receives the results of the user's experience, which is determined by factors like Click-Through-Rate, and *back propagates* that data to strengthen or weaken the connected bonds (confidence) within the neural network.

In an article titled "Symbolic vs. Connectionist AI" Josef Bajada describes this class as such:

> The key aspect of [connectionist] techniques is that the [programmer] does not specify the rules of the domain being modelled. The network discovers the rules from training data. The user provides input data and sample output data (the larger and more diverse the data set, the better).[47]

Compare this to the learning process of a child, in the event that they pick up on foul language from their environment. A parent, upon witnessing their kid's gleeful repetition of some unsavory new phrase, will generally receive a blank stare from the child when they yell

"WHERE DID YOU LEARN THAT?" A flaw in connectionism is that it is often difficult to ascertain *how* or *why* something was learned.

Bajada continues:

> These algorithms do not need a model of the world. They just need enough sample data from which the model of the world can be inferred statistically. This is a very powerful characteristic, but also a weakness. The input features have to be very carefully selected.
>
> Data driven algorithms implicitly assume that the model of the world they are capturing is relatively stable. This makes them very effective for problems where the rules of the game are not changing significantly, or changing at a rate that is slow enough to allow sufficient new data samples to be collected for retraining and adaptation to the new reality. Image recognition is the textbook success story [of deep learning algorithms].[48]

It is no coincidence that Google's **Data Driven Attribution Solution** is named just that. It is a dynamic attribution model that uses deep learning to reinforce the accuracy of the model as it captures more data.

Evolutionist Algorithms

Evolutionist learners make up a second class. Evolutionists believe that while it is useful to train an algorithm to learn in the same way the human brain does, this principle is limited. They feel that since evolution created the brain and is responsible for the biological advancements that have taken place across all species, computer science should mirror that and use the theory of natural selection to guide machine learning.

Evolutionary algorithms are built on genetic programming, which mates and evolves computer programs in the same way that nature mates and evolves organisms. The Terminator is an extreme example of evolutionist machine learning at work. A less terrifying example includes 3D printers that are able to print new, better versions of themselves.

Chris Nicolson, of pathmind.com, uses an example of a scatterplot to describe evolutionist learners and how they can be used to predict given outcomes based on **fitness**:

> Fitness is a measure of how well an algorithm performs against its predictive goal. Let's say you want to predict house prices based on square footage. Your input is the number of square feet in the house and the output is a dollar amount, the slope of your line is A and the Y-axis intercept is B: dollar_amount = A x square_feet + b.

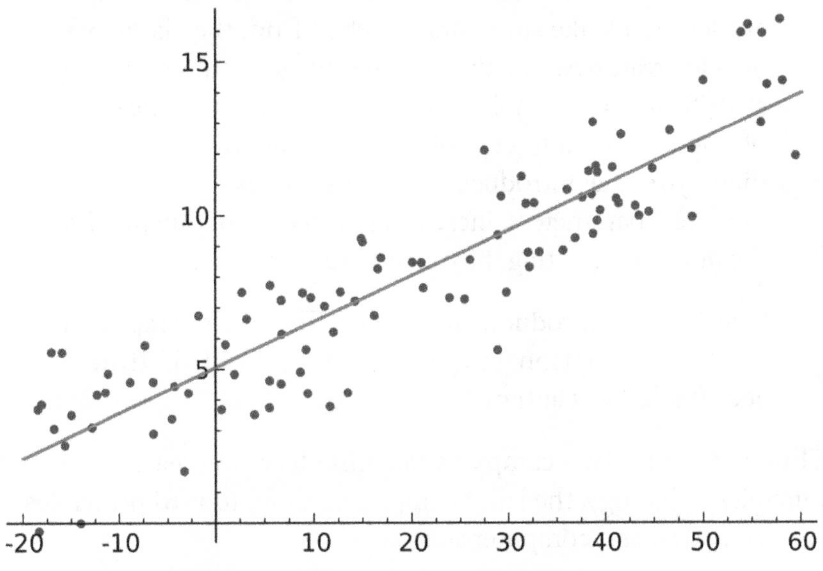

Source: Chris Nicholson, "A Beginner's Guide to Genetic and Evolutionary Algorithms," Pathmind.

> Different combinations of a and b are going to give you different lines pointing up, down, and sideways, and some of those lines will "fit" the data better than others. Fitness, in this case, minimizes the distance between the data points and the line. Some lines will cut through the scatter plot very far from most of the points (imagine a vertical line through one edge of the dots). The line you see slices the cloud of dots through the center, minimizing the aggregate distance of all dots from the closest points on the line.

> Now let's say you want a separate, meta-algorithm to find the right function, the fittest slope and intercept for those dots. Since many problems are too complicated to eyeball, you want to computationally seek the best function. That's where genetic and evolutionary algorithms come in.
>
> A genetic algorithm would begin by randomly generating a group of linear regression functions, with slopes and intercepts that are clearly unsuited to the data at hand. Those randomly generated lines are then measured against the data to calculate their total error. And the lines with the least error are selected—like survivors snatched from the gladiator's pit—to create new functions for the next test. Those winning algorithms are recombined; that is, you might take the slope of one and the intercept of another. And with several of them, you may introduce mutations; that is, variations on the fittest parameters, increasing or decreasing them with the purpose of testing the mutated variety.
>
> Spawn, cull, reproduce, and mutate: That cycle is repeated until the function surpasses a threshold of fitness acceptable to its author.[49]

While these first two camps of machine learning lean heavily on principles of biology, the latter camps lean more toward principles of logic, statistics, and computer science.

Bayesian Algorithms

Bayes Theorem is a mathematical rule dating back to the early 1700s. It's used for updating our degree of belief in a new hypothesis when new data is entered into the mix.[50] As we see more data, the hypotheses that are consistent with that data become more likely, and the hypotheses that are inconsistent become less likely.

We could use our existing neural networks to generate a strong hypothesis about the probability that the sun will rise tomorrow. In any experiment, if $n=0$, meaning there is no historical data to consider, we must conclude that the probability between two outcomes is 50 percent. As *n* increases with each daily sunrise, our confidence in the sun rising the following day increases as well. It will never be 100 percent, as we are never completely certain, but it can come close.

In addition to the strong historical evidence that supports the probability that the sun will rise tomorrow, there are other signals that help us determine the probability of the sun rising. That is, we shouldn't base this prediction solely on the idea that the sun has risen each day before. The prediction will become stronger if we can add other elements that help support our hypothesis.

For example, in the hours just before the sun rises each day, the stars will begin to fade, and we will begin to see streaks of light peak across the horizon. If we were to be suddenly dropped on a strange planet in the middle of the night and had no prior evidence about sun rises on this particular planet, the occurrence of fading stars and streaks of light would strengthen our belief that we will soon see a sunrise.

While Bayesian learning is extremely powerful, it's computationally expensive. Thanks to *Bayesian Networks,* an invention by UCLA professor Judae Pearl, it is now much simpler to implement these types of learners at scale.* A Bayesian Network is a graphical model that can efficiently encode the interactions between millions of variables. It is ideal for taking an event that occurred and predicting that the likelihood of any one of several possible known causes was the contributing factor. The technology behind self-driving cars is heavily influenced by Bayesian Networks.

Symbolist Algorithms

This subset of machine learners operates on the idea that general purpose learning algorithms need the ability to freely combine rules. They discover these rules by filling in the gaps of deductive reasoning. For example, if we know that Socrates is human, what else do we need to know to conclude that Socrates is mortal? The missing gap in this

---

* Judae Pearl received the Turing Award, the highest distinction in computer science, for his work on Bayesian Networks in 2011.

equation is that *all humans are mortal.* Once a machine has learned this rule, it can use this to make other deductions about other humans.

Symbolist systems use tools such as decision trees to deduce conclusions from the input data. A basic symbolist model can be used to quickly determine the best move in a game of tic-tac-toe, for example.[51]

In 2009, researchers at the University of Manchester developed *Adam,* a robot scientist known to be the first machine to autonomously discover new scientific knowledge. *Eve,* the successor to *Adam,* took autonomous discovery to the next level by using symbolist learning models to develop advancements in drug discovery.

In 2015, *Eve* discovered a link between triclosan, a popular antifungal ingredient most commonly found in toothpaste, and its ability to fight malaria.[52] This was a major accomplishment for both the pharmaceutical industry and for machine learning, as malaria affects hundreds of millions of people and is responsible for killing millions of people each year, yet solutions to prevent or cure malaria have traditionally been underfunded and under-researched.

According to Professor Ross King, of the University of Manchester:

> "The cost and speed of drug discovery [to treat malaria] and the economic return make them unattractive to the pharmaceutical industry ... *Eve* reduces the costs, uncertainty, and time involved in drug screening, and has the potential to improve the lives of millions of people worldwide."[53]

In this case, machines have stepped in and completed tasks that are meaningful but very costly for human participants. This is also the case when it comes to digital advertising concepts like setting auction bids and A/B split testing creative.

Analogist Algorithms

Domingos compares analogizer learners to that of a lazy child who doesn't study for exams and improvises the answers.[54] When faced with a new patient to diagnose, analogy-based learners find someone in their files with similar symptoms and assume that the diagnosis will be the same. While this seems naive, analogizer algorithms have proven mathematically that they can learn anything if given enough data. Facebook Lookalike Audiences and Amazon's product recommendation engines are fueled by analogy-based machine learning.

So, what kind of algorithm fuels Google Ad campaigns? I have no way of knowing, and I would imagine that very few people within Google even have the slightest idea. However, I would imagine that a combination of all five classes of algorithms are used at once to run your Smart campaigns. Each of the following scenarios is possible:

- Symbolist learners could help Google understand links between broad match keywords and close-variant search terms.
- Connectionist learners could help Google understand which of your Shopping Feed Products to serve to various audiences, using back-propagation of metrics like CTR and Conversion Rate to strengthen neural bonds.
- Analogist learners could help Google understand which audience trends are more likely to convert on your site.
- Evolutionist learners could help Google understand trends across your campaigns, using the best insights from your Search and Display campaigns to drive success when you first launch a YouTube campaign
- Bayesian Networks could be used to effectively drive your smart campaign automation, using insights learned from the four other categories to find the right audience and ideal ad placement and determine the right bid and creative.

While we can't know for sure if Google actually uses learners in these ways, the important takeaway is an understanding of the massive capabilities of these learners and an awareness of how they might be layered to create even more advanced algorithms. Then, ultimately, to convince you that there is no possible way that a human advertiser setting manual bids could ever outperform smart campaigns. *Join or die.*

In *The Master Algorithm,* Pedro Domingos writes:

> The second goal of this book is thus to enable you to invent the Master Algorithm. You'd think this would require heavy-duty mathematics and severe theoretical work. On the contrary, what it requires is stepping back from the mathematical arcana to see the overarching pattern of learning phenomena.[55]

I agree. The PPC advertiser does not necessarily need to know how to decode a deep learning algorithm, in the same way that a NASCAR driver does not need to understand how to build a car engine. Rather, an understanding of the overarching patterns within these learning phenomena will allow you to become a better driver of automated campaigns, opening doors for creative problem solving and ultimately resulting in profitable campaign growth for your clients.

11

The Premium Auction

The **premium auction** is used to describe the fact that higher-priced ad auctions are more valuable than lower-priced ad auctions, due to the laws of supply and demand.

The premium auction concept proves that CPC is not a KPI. That is, you should not specifically optimize for CPC, and it should only be used to infer other conclusions about campaign performance. In fact, due to the premium auction, an increase in average CPC could be a result of your ads targeting higher value placements: something that we all desire.

The primary goal of an automated bidding algorithm is to predict the probability that an ad click will result in a conversion and then work backward to determine a bid. As we discussed in Section 1, if the probability of conversion is greater than 0.00 percent, it is *technically* worth bidding on. The key is to make sure that the math checks out on the backend to ensure profitability.

In previous examples, we've outlined how lower value placements should not be automatically excluded. A display campaign, for example, can be a key asset to our digital advertising performance so long as automation can help determine the true value of an individual auction and ensure that we remain profitable.

In this chapter, we will explore the opposite end of the spectrum—how expensive and/or premium placements are also extremely valuable.

If you knew, for example, that a given ad click was guaranteed to result in a conversion worth $100 in profit, what is the maximum that you should be willing to pay for that click? $100. If a second ad click was had a 50 percent chance of converting into $100 in profit, we should bid $50 in that auction. The key here is that we are not relying on average Max, CPC bids, or average CPCs; we are specifically honed in on individual auctions.

This very well might be an ecommerce store with an average conversion rate of 2 percent. If we relied on averages to set our bids, we would never want to pay more than $2 per click. An unknowing client would have a panic attack if they found that you were paying $50 or $100 to acquire an individual click!

But the math checks out, and automation can manage this at scale.

Not only should you be open to the idea that quality traffic can be acquired for varying costs, the laws of supply and demand suggest that, in a vacuum, you would be better off by reserving your budget to exclusively bid on higher-cost clicks.

When data is ubiquitous your competitors have access to the same information and keyword research that you do. When a given auction is deemed to be *more valuable* to you and your competitors, the *market price* for that ad click will naturally increase. You should be willing to increase your bid to increase your chances of winning that ad click.

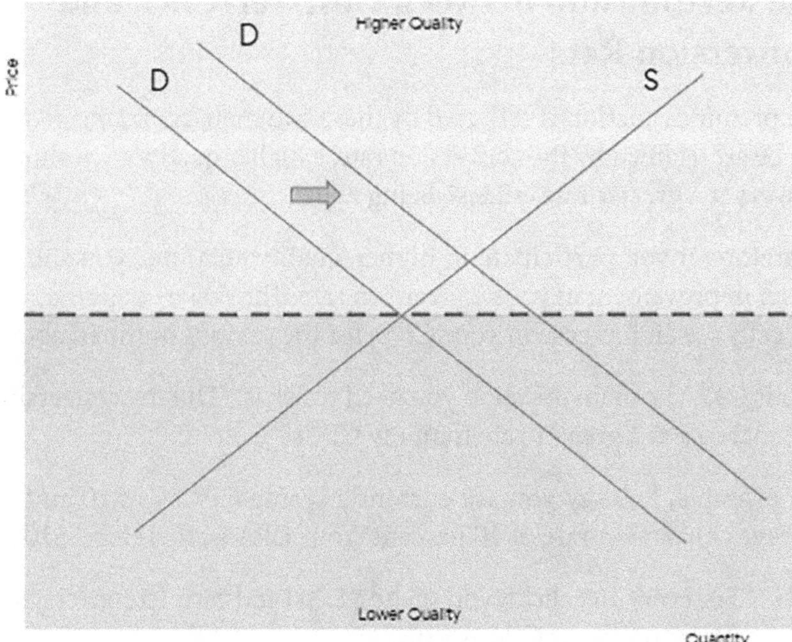

Source: Mark Donnelly and Leon Franco, Google.

If you don't capture the high-value traffic, your competitors will and leave you the low-value, crap-traffic that falls below the dotted line on the diagram above.

Advertising is the marketing equivalent of investing in the market, with CPC being as arbitrary as *stock price.* A year ago, a single share of Shopify stock was priced at about $300, a premium price compared to many other companies available on U.S. stock exchanges. Meanwhile, a share of Macy's stock could be purchased for $17 a year ago and he Cheesecake Factory for $35. Macy's has had to raise $4.5 billion in funding to survive the COVID-19 pandemic, and The Cheesecake Factory has told their landlords that they won't be paying rent next month. Their stock prices are down 65 percent and 35 percent compared to last year. Shopify is up 175 percent.

On the advertising side, if you are stubborn enough to believe that a premium click is not worth your investment, then your campaigns will end up sending you a ton of Cheesecake Factory traffic, and you might be the next business owner that is unable to pay rent next month.

The Relationship between Cost-Per-Click and Conversion Rate

The premium auction is reflected by these two metrics. Traffic *quality* can be ascertained by the conversion rate: a higher quality click should convert at a greater rate, all else being equal.

Therefore, if you participate in higher-quality auctions, you should see an improvement in your conversion rate. The downside is that you typically see an increase in your CPC, for the reasons outlined above.

This is OK! The main question you need to ask is, "Did my conversion rate increase at a greater rate than my CPCs?"

For example, let's say you are currently seeing CPCs of $10 and an average conversion rate of 10 percent. Your CPA is, therefore, $100.

- For every 100 clicks, you spend $1,000 and earn 10 conversions. Therefore, your CPA is $10.

If your CPC increases by 20 percent to $12, but your Conversion Rate increases by 25 percent to 12.5 percent, your CPA drops to $96.

- For every 100 clicks, you spend $1,200 and earn 12.5 conversions. Therefore, your CPA is $96.

Some marketers would see a 20 percent increase in CPC and panic, others would see a 25 percent increase in conversions and a 4 percent decrease in CPA and realize that this was a job well done.

Key Takeaway: If your conversion rate increases by a larger margin than your CPCs increase, you will win more conversions at a lower CPA.

A Premium Auction Case Study

In April 2019, one of our clients asked us to find a way to prove that the premium auction actually held true. We agreed that the concept made sense in theory, but we had yet to find conclusive evidence. After all, Google reports on *average* cost-per-click and sum-total impression metrics, making it nearly impossible to analyze individual auctions at scale.

This data was particularly relevant to this client: a SaaS company in a competitive enterprise software market where CPCs could range from $20 to more than $300.

I made it my personal mission to find a way to prove this, but at the same time, I was open to the possibility of finding data that proved me wrong. I certainly didn't want to be the guy that convinced his clients to be OK with increasing CPCs, only to find out that I was harming their bank accounts in the process.

To run this test, I would need to find results from individual ad auctions. I would not be able to look at the keyword or even the search term level and use Average CPCs and Conversion Rates to prove my hypothesis. If one search term generated 100 clicks and was showing an Average CPC of $10, it is entirely possible that we could have paid $20 for one of those clicks and $1 for the next.

The only way to determine the results of an actual auction was to find search terms that only accumulated one click; the average CPC column would reflect the cost that we paid to acquire that specific click and would not actually be an average of many.

I collected nearly 5,000 individual auction performance statistics for one bottom-funnel keyword and combined this data into one large spreadsheet to find adjusted averages based on standard deviations. The overall average CPC for this data was $56.89, and the average conversion rate was 4.10 percent.

Then I segmented the auctions that were at least one standard deviation away from the CPC average in either direction. Clicks that cost more than one positive standard deviation from the mean were considered *premium,* while clicks that cost less than the mean were considered *Low Quality.* I'd henceforth refer to these audiences as PAA (Premium Auction Audiences) and LQAA (Low Quality Auction Audiences).

These search terms were generated from similar queries. Here are the results:

- Average CPC for the entire data set is $56.89
- Average Conversion Rate for the entire data is 4.10 percent

Cost Per Click:

- For Premium Auctions (PAA), where the CPC was greater than average, the CPC was $103.39
- For low-quality auctions (LQAA), where the CPC was lower than average, CPC was $22.66
- Percent change here is 356 percent. That is, PAA CPCs were 356 percent greater than LQAA CPCs

Conversion Rate:

- PAA conversion rate was 7.66 percent
- LQAA conversion rate was 1.48 percent
- Percent change here is 418 percent

Cost Per Conversion:

- PAA CPA was $1349.61
- LQAA CPA was $1526.48
- Percent change here is 11.60 percent

Key Metric:

- PAA represented 79 percent of our conversions in this data set

This was a massive finding for our team and for our client. To summarize: the traffic that cost more than $56/click represented nearly 80 percent of total conversions, and the CPA for these individual conversions was lower than average.

It should be noted that **premium auction** is just a concept used to describe a relative phenomenon. It might be natural to see the data above and ask if we can reserve our budget to exclusively bid on premium auctions, but that's not how it works. We also don't want to block out any traffic that is acquired for less than $56. The value of this exercise merely represents the idea that higher-quality traffic often costs more to acquire, and we should be OK with that.

I began to run this same analysis in other accounts, and the results were eye-opening. **Across every account, there was always a direct correlation between CPC and conversion rate.** That is, I consistently found that, when CPCs increased, Conversion Rate increased as well. This is excellent news, as it supports my entire thesis about how the market price varies depending on value.

In some cases, though, the Conversion Rare did not increase by a greater margin than CPC. The PAA had a higher CPA, making them *less profitable* than the LQAA. In these instances, we identified that further changes would need to be made to the landing pages, keyword structure, or data-feedback mechanisms to ensure improved outcomes.

The Yin And Yang of Premium Auctions & Liquidity

The Problem with Averages

When we describe the premium auction concept to a client, they often raise their eyebrows and ask if this just means that we expect their costs (CPCs, generally) to continue to rise over time. "Surely, we can't just assume that our conversion rates will continue to increase ..."

That is true. The problem here is that we are all so brainwashed by the law of averages.

In theory, any click that has a predicted conversion rate above 0.00 percent is *worth* bidding on, and basic math can help you determine that worth in terms of what you are willing to bid for that click. Oftentimes, it is worth acquiring lower-cost traffic from Display or YouTube, but just at a lower cost than you would have for a Bottom-Funnel search click. But we will return to this concept shortly.

Averages fail to tell the whole story. It is a waste of our time to measure success or the probability of success by using sweeping averages. Averages fail to recognize that every Google search, every individual, and every customer is unique—even when Customer A searches for the same keyword and buys the same product as Customer B.

We have always defaulted to averages because humans have limited computational capacities. For example, an ecommerce brand doesn't have the time or patience to memorize the individual profit margins of every single product listed in their store, so they determine their average profit margin, and they create all of their marketing goals around that number.

The same goes for keyword bidding. The first fifteen years of PPC were defined by the idea that you should take your profit margins and work backward through your conversion rates to determine the maximum that you'd be willing to pay for an ad click. This is such a wonderful, novel concept that millions of business owners were able to easily understand.

It was also elementary.

Let's say our client is an online university, hoping to use paid search to drive leads and eventual enrollments for a new MBA degree they are offering. The average customer lifetime revenue we will earn from our enrollments is $20,000, and our target profit margin is 50 percent, which results in an ROAS goal of 200 percent and/or a Target Cost Per Enrollment at $10,000.

After a bit of research, we can determine that Bottom-Funnel search keywords should average a 2 percent click-to-lead conversion rate on the site. However, a student is not officially enrolled the moment that they submit a form on our website; rather, we have a sales process with steps that need to be factored into our equation.

Once a prospective student submits a form on our website, a salesperson reaches out to them for an initial discussion. We've estimated that our sales team can successfully reach 80 percent of leads by phone. So, on average, we have an 80 percent lead-to-call rate.

We've also determined that, on average, 10 percent of calls turn into successful enrollments.

If we do the math on our overall conversion rate and factor in our goal of a $10,000 cost-per-enrollment, it becomes clear that **we have a target Average CPC of $16.**

While a $16 bid would be a correct *average* bid, it is almost always the incorrect bid to maximize profit and business outcomes. We are not bidding on groups of people; we are bidding on individuals.

Take three prospective students, all performing a search for "Online MBA Programs."

Jennifer has traveled by plane four times in the last six months. She often shops for luxury brands, and her search history indicates that she is in the market for higher education.

Sarah has recently visited four different university websites and is currently performing this search between 6 p.m. and 9 p.m., which is when she has historically completed the most advertising-related conversion events (as gathered by her habits in online shopping, signing up for a new streaming service and gym membership, and downloading new apps to her phone).

John is performing this search on a Saturday. He is a parent and likes to work on cars in his free time, as gleaned from his YouTube history.

Despite searching for the same keyword, all three have different expected outcomes:

Jennifer:

- Predicted click-to-lead conversion rate: 2 percent
- Predicted lead-to-call rate: 80 percent
- Predicted call-to-enrollment rate: 15 percent
- Expected lifetime revenue, if enrolled: $20,000
- Breakeven CPC: $48
- Desired ROAS: 200 percent
- Max CPC: $24

Sarah:

- Predicted click-to-lead conversion rate: 6 percent

- Predicted lead-to-call rate: 80 percent
- Predicted call-to-enrollment rate: 15 percent
- Expected lifetime revenue, if enrolled: $20,000
- Breakeven CPC: $144
- Desired ROAS: 200 percent
- Max CPC: $72

John:

- Predicted click-to-lead conversion rate: 0.5 percent
- Predicted lead-to-call rate: 80 percent
- Predicted call-to-enrollment rate: 8 percent
- Expected lifetime revenue, if enrolled: $20,000
- Breakeven CPC: $6.40
- Desired ROAS: 200 percent
- Max CPC: $3.20

If you were to bid $16 in any of these auctions, you'd either be drastically overpaying (for John's click), or your bid will be too low to remain competitive, eliminating your chances at winning Jennifer or Sarah's click.

Averages and the traditional methods of determining our bids are the primary reason why PPC managers have failed to grow their clients over the last ten years.

The example above was used to determine the average bid for a Bottom-Funnel search keyword, but that model can also be used to determine bids for any type of ad auction. When you run those numbers for display traffic, the averages almost always conclude that this traffic can never be profitable. As a result, advertisers have failed to embrace upper-funnel channels like display, video, and even broad match search keywords—they assume it can *never* work.

We can all agree that a Bottom-Funnel search click is more valuable than a click on a display ad, but that does not mean we should swear off display forever. We must always consider the role that supply and demand plays in setting the market value for traffic.

For the same MBA program, we could run the numbers and determine that our average conversion rate from display traffic would be 0.0125 percent (low, but still not 0.00 percent!). **In this case, our bid should be $0.15.**

That's great, but what if the market value for quality display traffic, the people who are actually considering enrolling in an online MBA program, is $0.75?

In this event, one of two things are going to happen:

1. Your ads will not receive any impressions, as your bid is far below the Ad Rank Threshold set by Google (see Chapter 4 for more on Ad Rank Thresholds).

2. You will receive impressions, but for the lowest quality traffic that is available.

When you buy lower-quality traffic, your average conversion rate will not hold constant. Therefore, your $0.15 bid will acquire traffic that converts below 0.0125 percent, making the entire venture unprofitable.

Outraged PPC managers will claim that display traffic is primarily bots and cannot ever be profitable, so they'll steer their clients away from it altogether.

The reality is that much of this traffic is valuable, so long as you can determine the optimal cost at the time of the auction, which is exactly why automation is so valuable.

Click Totals and Experimental Probability

I opened this chapter with a question we often get from clients: *Does the premium auction mean our CPCs will just continue to increase?*

If you continue to exclusively target Bottom-Funnel searches and do not allow automated, smart campaigns to explore other mediums of traffic acquisition, then the answer to this question is, yes, your CPCs will rise.

However, if you are also embracing liquidity, then that won't always be the case. Your average CPCs might increase; they might decrease; or they might stay the same. Regardless of what happens to your average CPCs, you must understand that it does not matter.

A liquid environment, where you are less stringent on ad placements and other variables, will provide a natural balance to your digital advertising campaigns. Stubborn PPC managers who understand the concept of the premium auction but fail to embrace liquidity in their campaigns will first see a decline in their total website traffic and eventually in total performance.

A liquid environment provides the opportunity to acquire quality traffic from individual auctions that have a large variance in cost. If you exclusively run Bottom-Funnel search campaigns, embrace automation, and are willing to enter premium auctions, then the natural outcome will be increased CPCs and fewer overall clicks. That is, if your budget remains unchanged, an increase in CPC will reduce the number of clicks that you can buy in a given day.

While we don't necessarily believe that *total website traffic* is a KPI, PPC managers need to be aware of the potential downsides of declining rates of traffic. There is a serious benefit to generating higher traffic levels from your campaigns.

Again, let's make it clear that a click acquired from a Bottom-Funnel search is *better*, albeit more expensive than a click acquired from display. This time, though, we'll use a different example.

Let's assume that we're using averages to determine our CPC bids, as we did in our previous example. We have determined that our bid for a Bottom-Funnel search campaign should be $1, and our bid for a display campaign should be $0.10. This suggests that a click on search is 10x more likely to convert than a click on a display ad, and we've adjusted our bids to reflect this.

Here is the question: If you only had $1 to spend on advertising, would you choose to spend it on a single Bottom-Funnel search ad click ($1), or spread it out across 10 display ad clicks ($0.10)?

The math suggests that this is a wash. If you factor in your average conversion rates, you have an equal chance of success with both options. However, that is the problem with averages.

Let's put it another way: If I was flipping a coin, would you be willing to bet that the next flip would result in tails? Or would you prefer to bet me that 5 out of the next 10 flips would result in tails?

This again appears to be a wash, with 50 percent chance of winning the bet in each scenario, but statisticians would argue otherwise, citing the difference between **theoretical probability** (what should happen) and **experimental probability** (what actually happens). As you increase the sample size of an experiment, the gap between these two concepts gets smaller.

While a coin flip has a theoretical 50 percent chance of landing on tails, this can never be the final result of your experiment if you only flip the coin once. A coin either lands on heads, or it lands on tails. It does not land 50 percent on either side. After this first experiment, the *experimental* outcome will either be 100 percent tails, or 0 percent tails, not 50 percent, as theoretical probability would suggest.

As you increase the number of flips in the experiment, you will reach an *experimental probability* that is closer to your *theoretical probability* of 50 percent.

Let's return to our question: Would you rather spend $1 on a single Bottom-Funnel search click, or spread that $1 across 10 display ad clicks? An experimental statistician would argue that you should choose the latter, as this will give you the greatest chance of achieving your predicted outcome.

It's a numbers game. There is a benefit to acquiring a higher volume of clicks.

This does not mean that you should turn off your search campaigns and dedicate 100 percent of your digital advertising budget to display. The optimal digital advertising strategy includes a balance between these channels, and automation is the only way to achieve this balance at scale.

Yin & Yang: Finding a Balance

To visualize the impact of liquidity and balance, we can use a four-quadrant matrix, with *Expected Conversion Rate (CVR)* on the Y-Axis and *Click Volume* on the X-Axis.

In the top left corner, we will see the channels that have a high conversion rate but low volume. Due to supply and demand, these clicks will be the most expensive to acquire.

In the bottom right corner, we'll see the channels with the most amount of potential volume but relatively low conversion rates. These clicks will be the cheapest to acquire.

The bottom left is represented by channels with lower volume and lower relative conversion rates, and the top right is represented by channels with higher volume and higher relative conversion rates. These quadrants both have mid-tier costs.

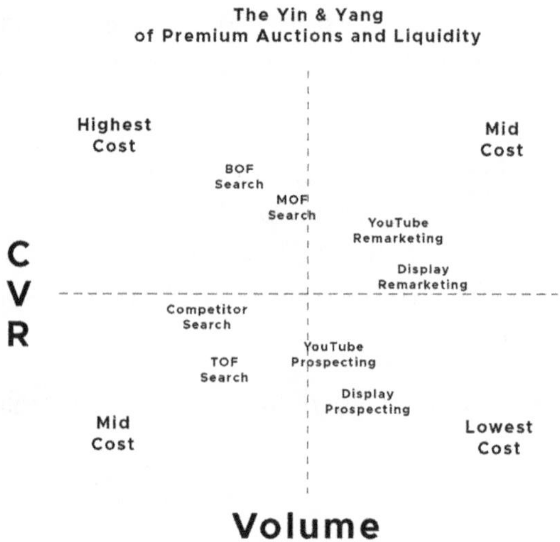

These channels are all worth exploring, as all of them have a conversion rate that is above 0.00 percent. We can lean on machine learning to find individual auctions that are *worth* bidding on, and others that are *worth* a premium bid.

A liquid environment allows the machine to make these decisions in real time, optimizing all of these channels to drive the highest returns. The components of this matrix can be grouped together to reflect a Yin & Yang balance—the Chinese symbol representing seemingly opposite forces that are interdependent and complement one another.

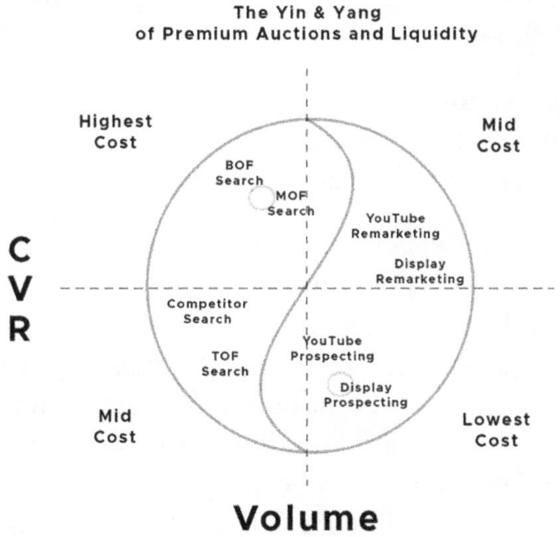

The matrix represents the idea that an average CPC is not our goal, nor is our goal to exclusively bid in premium auctions. Our goal is to find a balance that eliminates as many restrictions from the machine's learning as possible.

Yin & Yang Case Study: Smart Shopping

Smart Shopping campaigns are a perfect example of a liquid environment benefiting from the Yin & Yang balance.

As discussed in Chapter 5, Smart Shopping Campaigns (SSCs) will serve shopping ads across all of Google's networks, including traditional search results page, the shopping tab on google.com, Gmail ads, YouTube ads, and display ads served through the Google Display Network. It is an almost entirely automated solution.

Shopping campaigns have been heavily criticized by the PPC community due to their lack of transparency. You do not see the search terms, for example, that triggered your SSC ads.

It is my belief that PPC managers do not have their preferred level of access to insights and data from the SSCs because Google does not trust them to interpret the data correctly. The fear is that PPC managers would make manual adjustments based on incomplete data that would negatively impact performance. Few marketers understand liquidity as well as the premium auction. Even fewer understand concepts like *The Breakdown Effect,* which will be outlined in a later chapter on Facebook advertising and explains exactly why manual optimizations to a liquid, automated campaign can be dangerous.

As I've made clear, Smart Shopping Campaigns have been the single most important driver of profitable growth for our ecommerce clients over the last two years. The reason these campaigns are so successful is due to their liquid nature.

Below is a screenshot from an ecommerce account I've been involved with for more than four years. We began implementing Smart Shopping campaigns in October 2018, and since then, we have turned over every campaign (Search, Shopping, Video, Display) to automated bidding solutions.

Most PPC marketers would assume that, given our complete adoption of automation, our CPCs would have skyrocketed, and we would have received fewer overall clicks.

The opposite was true. This data was collected over an 18-month period, with $1.5M in spend and more than 1.3M clicks.

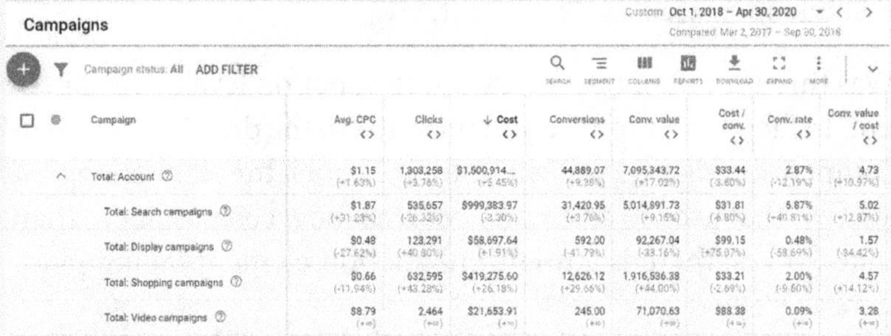

Campaigns

Custom Oct 1, 2018 – Apr 30, 2020
Compared: Mar 2, 2017 – Sep 30, 2018

Campaign status: All ADD FILTER

Campaign	Avg. CPC	Clicks	Cost	Conversions	Conv. value	Cost / conv.	Conv. rate	Conv. value / cost
Total: Account	$1.15 (+1.63%)	1,303,258 (+3.76%)	$1,500,914... (+5.45%)	44,889.07 (+9.38%)	7,095,343.72 (+17.02%)	$33.44 (-3.60%)	2.87% (-12.19%)	4.73 (+10.97%)
Total: Search campaigns	$1.87 (+31.23%)	535,657 (-26.32%)	$999,383.97 (-2.30%)	31,420.95 (+3.76%)	5,014,891.73 (+9.15%)	$31.81 (-6.80%)	5.87% (+40.81%)	5.02 (+12.87%)
Total: Display campaigns	$0.48 (-27.62%)	123,291 (+40.80%)	$58,697.64 (+1.91%)	592.00 (-41.79%)	92,267.04 (-33.16%)	$99.15 (+75.07%)	0.48% (-58.69%)	1.57 (-34.42%)
Total: Shopping campaigns	$0.66 (-11.94%)	632,595 (+43.28%)	$419,275.60 (+26.18%)	12,626.12 (+29.66%)	1,916,536.38 (+44.00%)	$33.21 (-2.69%)	2.00% (-9.60%)	4.57 (+14.12%)
Total: Video campaigns	$8.79 (+∞)	2,464 (+∞)	$21,653.91 (+∞)	245.00 (+∞)	71,070.63 (+∞)	$88.38 (+∞)	0.09% (+∞)	3.28 (+∞)

The key here is to compare the performance between our Search campaigns, a traditionally illiquid campaign type, to that of our Smart Shopping campaigns, the pinnacle of a liquid environment. Both campaign types saw an increase in overall performance but in different ways.

The results of our Search campaigns prove the benefits of automation and the premium auction. CPC is up 31 percent, but conversion rate has increased by a margin of 40 percent, resulting in more overall profit. This is realized by a 12.8 percent increase in ROAS and a 9 percent increase in revenue.

Total clicks have decreased by 26 percent, which was expected due to the fact that search campaigns do not provide the kind of liquid environment offered by Smart Shopping.

The fact that revenue has increased by 9 percent is good news, but it's not ideal. We want this client to be growing by much larger percentages than that. However, there is a finite quantity of search traffic that can ultimately be bought, so at some point, we need to rely on additional channels.

What about Smart Shopping? Should we expect CPCs to increase at the same rate? Many new competitors have entered the shopping space over the last two years. As a result, some might expect CPCs to increase at an even greater rate. That is not the case. The average CPC in shopping was down nearly 12 percent. At the same time, ROAS increased by 14 percent, and revenue increased by 44 percent.

Was this a result of lower CPCs at the auction level? Absolutely not. In fact, I can promise you that, due to the drastic increase in competition that we've seen in this channel, the same shopping auction that used to cost us $1 per click now costs far more than that. So yes, there is a premium auction element taking place here as well.

The overall increase in revenue is a result of us participating in auctions that we previously would have ignored. We are now profitably acquiring shopping traffic from display ads, Gmail ads, and YouTube ads, all of which cost relatively less per click than their search counterparts. The SSC was free to make these auction decisions in real-time, allowing us to drastically increase revenue over this period.

A final takeaway is that, while the Average CPC column is showing a decrease here, that will not always be the case. The averages may go up, or they may go down, but we should not let that distract us from the fact that automation can drive better results on an auction-by-auction level if we remove the barriers and allow it to find the optimal balance of ad placements to achieve our goals.

13 The Modern Google Ads' Ecosystem

Much has been written about Google Ads account structure over the last ten years. Much of this content suggests an account structure that should help improve Quality Score or mitigate risk through restrictive barriers (negative keywords, etc.).

Traditionalist PPC managers need to let go of these outdated habits, as success is not determined by your Quality Score, number of negative keywords, or quantity of landing pages that you've developed. Real success is found when you can successfully train Google's algorithms to make better, real-time decisions on your behalf, allowing you to step away from the minutia and focus your attention on larger marketing problems.

Forget everything you think you know about Google Ads' account structure best practices. Automation can succeed under any account structure. Ultimately, the decisions that lead to your automated strategies will determine your success.

A *simplified* account structure could make your workflow easier and allow you more time to invest in your overall automation strategy, but the structure itself will not make you any more or less profitable. For example, single keyword ad groups (SKAG) implementation is a waste of your time because they won't directly impact profit.

If you wish to make the right decisions for your account structure, we must reevaluate the traditional PPC keyword funnel while being mindful of Google's most recent updates to their auction process.

The Reality of Search Intent

Unfortunately (and to my interminable frustration), search marketers still believe search queries that include *best* and *for sale* need separate ad groups.

I recently had to order a new golf club. I accidentally let go of a wedge during my follow-through and sent the club sailing into a lake. The club flew further than the ball.

I had no interest in experiencing the sensation or giving the onlookers the pleasure of viewing me diving to the bottom of a lake fully clothed. So that night, I performed a Google search for a *52-degree wedge* on my phone. Google served me a Shopping ad from Wilson, showcasing a wedge in my price range. I bought it in three clicks.

Here's what's important: I didn't perform a search for *best 52-degree wedge*. My search was not long-tail, nor did it contain a specific brand or model number. Does that mean that my search wasn't considered to be of high value by Google or its advertisers? No.

Whether I like it or not, Google knows that I play golf often and that I'm a sucker for impulsive golf-related purchases. Google probably knew I played earlier that day because I used Google Maps to get to and from the course. I'm not sure if golfers tend to have a higher conversion rate on golf-related purchases within twenty-four hours of finishing a round, but if that trend exists, I'm sure Google's algorithms factor that into their predicted conversion rate analysis.

The team running the ad campaigns for Wilson Golf was willing to bid on my broad search because they were following modern best practices. As a reward, they won my business.

Advertisers who follow best practices of account structure and automation will win the best traffic, regardless of the search query.

The Traditional PPC Marketing Funnel

Many PPC accounts were traditionally set up using the following marketing funnel approach. This hypothetical funnel was used to assume purchase-intent based on what users were physically typing into Google.

In the graphic below, CVR represents Expected Conversion Rate. If a user's search query were more specific, we assumed a higher conversion rate, and we would manually bid more aggressively on that search.

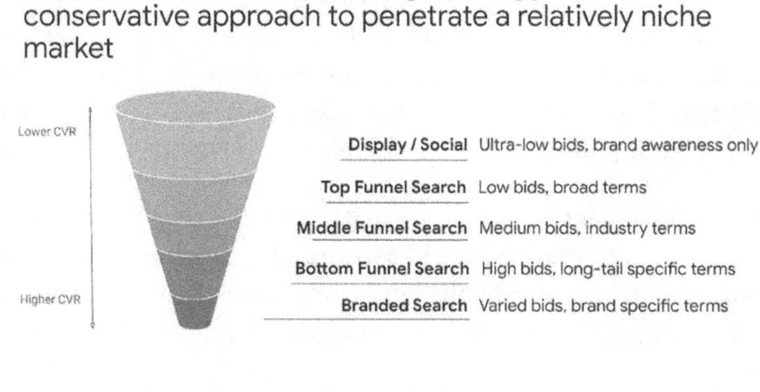

If you were an ecommerce business that sold golf clubs, here's how your campaigns may have been structured:

Top Funnel (TOF) Search Campaign

- Smallest budget
- Example keyword: golf clubs

Middle Funnel (MOF) Search Campaign

- Second largest budget
- Example keyword: "52-degree wedge"

Bottom-Funnel (BOF) Search Campaign

- Largest budget
- Example keyword: [TaylorMade M2 2017 52-degree wedge]

All three of these example keywords are targeting users who are likely in the market for the kinds of products that you sell. As you travel down the funnel, the search becomes more descriptive. The BOF keywords are typically more expensive, as your competitors are likely implementing a similar strategy.

The MOF search includes the genre of club we are searching for, while the BOF search includes a genre *and* a specific brand, model, and year.

If we determined expected conversion rate based on the context of the actual search query and nothing else, our bottom-funnel keyword, [TaylorMade M2 2017 52-degree wedge], will always represent a user with the greatest intent to buy—and therefore receive the highest bid.

Intent to buy is synonymous with predicted conversion rate. Traditionalist PPC managers would assume that the conversion rate for a bottom-funnel keyword will always be greater than a top-funnel keyword, holding other variables like location and device constant.

It is completely foolish to operate by that principle. Who are we to predict relative conversion rates based on nothing except the context of the search query?

My search for *52-degree wedge* might be considered a middle-funnel keyword, but my intent to buy was through the roof due to variables not made clear in my search query.

That said, this traditional funnel structure is still a safe bet for modern marketers. If profitable ROAS is your only goal, then this strategy will likely help you achieve it. If growth is your goal, you would need to find a way to profitably scale beyond this core set of BOF keywords.

ROAS vs. Revenue Growth: Can I Have Both?

There is a finite amount of BOF inventory available. To achieve profitable growth, we will ultimately have to expand into MOF and TOF keywords—and other broader targeted campaigns such as Display and Video.

We would deduct that it will never be profitable to aggressively bid on *all users who* perform TOF searches for "golf clubs," but if you leverage Google automation to find the desperate souls performing that search, just hours after they've accidentally chucked a wedge into a lake, then you've found your competitive edge.

The traditional funnel methodology limits the size of your potential market. Without automation, you will never be able to profitably scale your campaigns beyond bottom-funnel search. A primary benefit of automation technology is its ability to predict conversion likelihood for a specific ad auction with greater accuracy than humans can, regardless of the search query.

Not all top-funnel searches for *golf clubs* are worth bidding on, and automation will be able to make that call. If your goal is profit *and* revenue growth, then automation is for you.

The Modern Google Ads Auction

Google has the power to consider millions of data points to determine the likelihood of a conversion. Search Query is just one of these signals. Beyond search query, Google will consider information not just about the user performing the search, but also specific conditions of the moment in which the search is taking place. This includes signals such as device, location, operating system, audience parameters, and historical data that would only be relevant to a specific auction taking place.[56]

Advertisers previously had the ability to create manual bid adjustments based on entire categories (device, for example), but these bid adjustments ignored the reality that each auction is completely unique. It is illogical, for example, to assume that users performing keyword searches at 2 p.m. are more valuable than users performing searches at 10 p.m.

It follows that:

1. It is illogical to make any assumptions about our audience.
2. It is unnecessary to aggressively segment our ad campaigns based on incomplete assumptions about intent.
3. The majority of your budget should not be dedicated to exact match, bottom-funnel, long-tail keywords that are likely more expensive to bid on than broader terms.

As mentioned in Chapter 10, Sridhar Ramaswamy, Google's Senior VP of advertising and commerce, introduced the concept of the *micro-moment* in 2015. I remember streaming the Google AdWords Performance Summit to the conference room TV in our old office in 2016. Ramaswamy used the term so many times that I wrote a blog post poking fun at all of it. I was skeptical. The micro-moment seemed like a tall tale: great on paper but impractical and out of reach for most advertisers.

Four years later, I stand corrected. Automation helps our clients reach millions of micro-moments every day, and profitably convert those users into customers.

Making Smarter Decisions across Campaigns

Google's algorithms now use **account-level signal data** when making decisions. Your performance data is no longer just tied to the specific keyword or campaign where it is attributed.

For example, if a user converts after performing a branded search, Google will register the signal data related to that conversion and use that information to make smarter decisions for future auctions across the account.

In this example, the branded search query is just one of many signals that Google strips down and analyzes. This is data that you are feeding into the algorithm, in the same way that you would upload your customer list to develop similar audiences.

Additional signal information from that branded conversion, including the demographics and interests of users who've converted are also stripped out and will now be used by the system to predict conversion likelihoods of any other auction taking place in your account. Previous Google search history, device, YouTube history, and other factors are accounted for.

This branded conversion helps Google to accurately bid on other campaigns; including non-branded search campaigns, Smart Shopping campaigns, YouTube campaigns, and more.

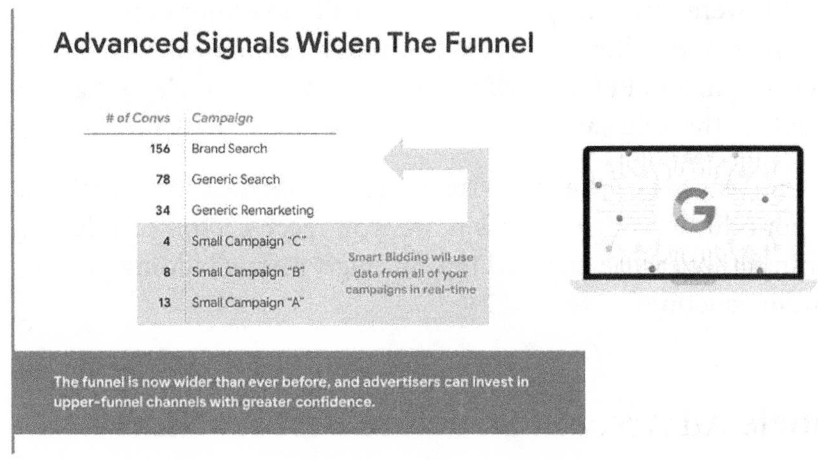

Source: Adam McDaniel, Google

Should I Bid on Branded Search?

For the reasons outlined above, yes. Wilson Golf likely had thousands of branded conversions that helped the system accurately bid on my auction. For starters, Wilson isn't exactly in the top tier of golf brands like Callaway or TaylorMade, but I am not in the top tier of golfing hobbyists, nor am I the kind of person that would be willing to spend more than $100 on a replacement wedge.

I have a lot in common with others who have purchased this exact golf club, and Google knew it.

My colleague, Ronnie Cardno, often uses a poker analogy to describe the value of branded search. There is a concept in poker referred to as **pot odds,** which is defined as the ratio between the size of the pot and the bet facing you. If the pot (potential winnings) of a given hand is $5, and the current bet (what you need to contribute in order to remain in the hand) is $1, then the pot odds are 5:1.

The larger the pot odds, the more often you should call the bet. If the potential winnings were $1,000, and it would cost you just $1 to remain in the hand, you should probably fork over the dollar. Even if you lose the hand, you'll have paid a small amount to participate, and the odds were worth it. What's more, it will force your opponent to show their cards, allowing you to learn more about their tendencies. Poker is similar to PPC advertising in this way: data and learnings are valuable in the long game.

It often costs very little to participate in branded search auctions. The pot odds are huge. What's more, you receive a ton of valuable learnings that can be factored into the algorithmic bidding process for future auctions.

Google Ad Account Structure Best Practices

The Modern Marketing Framework

Instead of applying the traditional keyword funnel strategy to each Google Ads account, we now structure accounts based on a framework that allows the system to maximize earnings and grow over time.

The framework combines three principles which work in conjunction with one another. We start with ensuring that each account is leveraging the most up-to-date features settings. Then we ensure that the system will receive the best possible data. Finally, we properly layer automation on top of everything we do.

A modern approach for optimal account growth

Implement
Best practices & new features
Give the system **as much data as possible** with new tests and proper implementation of beta features.

Leverage Attribution and Audience signals
Use **Non-last click Attribution and Audience signals** (remarketing, etc.) to feed the machine learning algorithms with better conversion data.

Layer Automation
Leverage **Smart Campaigns** so Google (and other ad platforms) can automatically optimize for success.

Source: Adam McDaniel, Google.

A few examples of these stages:

Best practices and new features:

- For ecommerce, ensure conversion tracking is 100 percent accurate, dynamic remarketing tags are installed properly, and shopping feeds are set up through Google's Content API.
- For lead-gen, ensure conversion tracking is integrated with your CRM, tracking each milestone of the sales process as a conversion action.
- Implement Responsive Search Ads and any beta ad formats, including Discovery Campaigns, Lead Form Ad Extensions, and more.
- Promote liquidity across budgets, placements, audiences, and creative.

Leverage Attribution & Audience Signals:

- Strategically create and implement customer lists, remarketing lists, and similar audiences throughout the account.

- Ensure that your conversion settings, including your conversion window and conversion value, most accurately reflect your sales cycle.
- Use selective optimization to manage various optimization goals, especially for broader (top-funnel) initiatives.

Layer Automation:

- Determine your smart bidding and smart creative strategy based on your goals, budgets, and other variables.
- Utilize seasonality adjustments, portfolio bidding strategies, and other goal settings to influence how aggressive the algorithm should bid.
- Develop hypotheses about the machine's confidence, weighing the risks and rewards of new tests that would send the machine into the learning phase.

The examples provide a current snapshot of 2020. These specific examples are likely to change over time. However, the overall framework themes are likely to remain intact for the foreseeable future.

This framework challenges us to constantly seek larger scale business solutions. It forces us to be methodical in our approach and ensures that we are running the proper tests and making informed decisions based on statistically significant, accurate data.

A Modern Approach to Negative Keywords

With properly implemented automation and account structure, you should be more hands-off with your negative keyword lists. Negative keywords reduce liquidity in an account.

Traditionalist PPC managers used to brag to clients about the number of negative keywords they added to the account. However, negative keyword overload can do more harm than good, as it reduces the system's ability to learn and grow.

If you take more of a hands-off approach to negative keywords, the system will learn which queries don't result in conversions and use those observations to make smarter decisions at scale.

One of our clients manufactures custom picture frames. This is an extremely competitive arena with massive amounts of search volume and lots of opportunities for growth. I've personally been working with this account for several years and have helped it transition, over time, from a traditionalist structure to a modern, automated powerhouse.

A few years back, my colleagues and I dedicated time each week to comb through search term data and look for negative keywords. It was boring work that I dreaded doing, but it was essential to maintaining a positive ROAS at the time.

People search for all kinds of picture frames. I remember sitting in our old office and coming across the search term *Ohio State Buckeyes Picture Frame*. The client doesn't sell Ohio State Buckeye frames—or any gimmicky frame for that matter. So, I added "Ohio State" as a phrase match negative keyword and kept moving down the list.

I then stumbled across the term, *Penn State Picture Frame*. I would assume that the user performing that search is of much greater intelligence—and is probably better looking—than the losers looking for Ohio State Buckeye frames. However, we do not sell these types of frames, either. "Penn State" was added as a negative keyword.

Trying to be a more proactive account manager, I spent the next few hours compiling a list of every major U.S. university, sports team, vacation destination, and holiday that I could think of. My negative keyword lists were bursting at the seams with phrases containing "engagement" and "corgi" and "I love you, Grandma."

There is an unlimited amount of personalized picture frames that people want to buy, which are not sold by this company. There was no way for me to proactively negate all those search terms.

In hindsight, if we had allowed the system to naturally learn about individual search terms and their respective conversion rates, then

Google would have eventually learned that we don't sell any gimmicky, personalized frames.

Traditionalist PPC Managers, particularly those performing account audits in hopes of winning new business, will often highlight *wasted spend.* They will look at all search terms that did not convert or seem irrelevant and claim that the current agency has been negligent, as these terms should all have been added as negative keywords.

This isn't the case anymore. If something is blatantly irrelevant, of course, you should add it as a negative. However, most search terms fall into a gray area. In this case, I'd recommend you allow the system to learn on its own. Just as Edison found 10,000 ways to not invent a light bulb, a machine learning algorithm benefits from learning about the 10,000 auctions that don't result in a conversion.

It is no accident that we cannot add negative keywords to Smart Shopping campaigns, or even have access to the search term data for these types of campaigns. Google doesn't give us access to that information because they don't want us manually tinkering with, and screwing up, the learning process.

It is likely that the trend we have seen with Smart Shopping, in which advertisers do not have the ability to add negative keywords, will eventually take over all other campaign types. I urge you not to panic—partly because your complaints will fall on deaf ears, but also because it will ultimately bring you a better outcome.

Google Ads Account Structure Myths

A search for *Google Ads Account Structure Best Practices* yields 85.7M results (compared to just 13M for a search for Google Ads Smart Bidding). There's a lot of outdated content out there, and most of these hacks have been addressed in updated support docs or other material from Google:

- Quality Score is not used at auction time to determine your ad rank. Rather, QS is a general estimate based on a recent sample of performance. It shouldn't be used to grade performance. There is also no such thing as an ad group quality score, campaign quality score, or account Quality Score, and therefore, it is futile to structure your Google Ads account such that you hope to increase your Quality Score (refer to Section 1 for more information on Quality Score).

- The structure of your account does not impact automation or Google's perception of the quality of your ads.
- SKAGs do not result in a higher Quality Score or lower CPC.
- The exact phrase from a query does not need to be on your landing page, and you should not keyword-stuff your landing pages, as this generally comes at the expense of the user experience.
- You do not need to implement all match-types variations for every keyword. This will not increase your coverage or result in more traffic.

I consulted with members of Google's product team throughout this writing process to ensure accuracy and transparency. Below is a slide borrowed directly from Google's internal training materials, addressing the match-type debate:

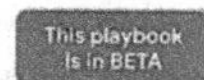

Myth: I need to have **all keywords in all match types** for maximum coverage

Having the same keyword in different match types will not necessarily yield incremental traffic, since:

1) Wider match types (e.g. Broad Match and BMM) will **also trigger for queries that match the exact keyword**
2) Having different match types **do not add any "weight" to the likelihood of a keyword triggering an ad**
3) Having different match types **will not impact the quality score** of an account.

It's also good to remember that Smart Bidding will already optimize for queries with a higher chance of performing better, so **keeping you keyword strategy broad will give our machine learning algorithm more data to work with.**

Google

Source: Adam McDaniel, Google.

Google has also addressed the myth that Dynamic Search ads cannibalize traffic from your other campaigns. Again, here's a slide directly from Google:

This playbook is in BETA

Myth: "DSA will steal traffic from my keyword-based campaigns"

~15% of Google's searches are new, and the main goal of Dynamic Search Ads is to **help you to reach customers that you are not currently reaching only with keyword-based campaigns.** We estimate that 86% of DSA traffic is incremental.

It's also good to keep in mind that whenever DSA and keywords enter the same auctions, they don't cannibalize each other. **Exact match keywords will serve instead of DSA when both are eligible. For other match types, DSA will compete on an even playing field so whichever has a higher bid x Quality Score will serve.**

Google

Source: Adam McDaniel, Google.

The Benefits of Consolidation

A consolidated account structure will not specifically improve performance for automated campaigns. However, if a consolidated account structure makes it more efficient for you to manage, then this will indirectly result in improved performance.

Our team uses as much consolidation as possible. It provides:

- Increased liquidity.
- Better control over budget, allowing you to make more accurate predictions regarding spend and performance trends.
- Simplified reporting, leading to more collaborative conversations with clients.
- More effective implementations of large-scale tests for bid strategies, conversion actions, and creative. (The data will

be cleaner if you have less duplication of keywords, similar campaign types, etc.)

- Risk mitigation. It's easier to spot irregularities, spikes in performance, and other anomalies. Nobody is perfect, and if you have ten thousand ad groups, it's much more likely that you're using outdated ad copy somewhere (or still advertising a promo code from your 2017 Black Friday sale).

With consolidation, we have not forfeited the benefits of segmentation. Google's reporting features are advanced enough that you can find any data or spot any trends that we would have otherwise wanted to see if we were ultra-segmented.

As a rule of thumb, campaigns should be segmented based on budget or geography requirements, and ad groups should be segmented based on what logically makes sense given available ad copy and targeted landing pages. If there is an advantage to be gained with more relevant ad copy or a more targeted landing page, then it makes sense to segment out those keywords. However, as dynamic creative becomes more prevalent, it is becoming less important to segment your ad groups based on ad copy and landing pages.

The Risks of Account Restructuring

While we prefer consolidated accounts, there are times that we inherit an account that has been segmented at a very granular level. In this event, we won't just shut everything off and build it the way we like.

Ultimately, we'd consolidate efforts to take advantage of the benefits listed above, but drastic changes in a short period of time are generally not recommended.

A good rule of thumb for new accounts that are overly segmented:

1. If current performance is bad and conversion tracking was never properly implemented, you can make any changes to the campaign structure that you'd like (after you fix the conversion tracking issues, of course).

2. If current performance is satisfactory and conversion tracking was never properly implemented, set up conversion tracking and let it run as is (with minor optimizations) for anywhere between two weeks and a month before you make any changes to account structure.

3. If current performance is bad and conversion tracking is accurate, begin restructuring with the largest areas of opportunity. Map out your ideal account structure and begin adjusting campaigns that are returning below your account average. Aim to restructure between 25 percent and 50 percent of the total spend, and then make additional changes methodically over time.

4. If current performance is satisfactory and conversion tracking is accurate, begin restructuring, starting with largest areas of opportunity. Map out your ideal account structure and begin adjusting campaigns that are returning below your account average. Aim to restructure less than 30 percent of total account budget within a fourteen-day period.

Case Study: Consolidated Account Structure

Overview

Fig & Bloom is an Australian floral arrangement company. They specialize in high-end, contemporary floral design and deliver across Melbourne and Sydney. Fig & Bloom is a five-star florist with thousands of loyal customers. Their mission is to make ordering flowers online easy and fun.

They came to us looking to develop a playbook for increasing Return on Ad Spend (ROAS) within existing markets, thereby increasing profits which could be reinvested in expansion into new regions.

Challenges

Fig & Bloom operates in a competitive, seasonal market. They benefit significantly from economies of scale, as it's much more cost-effective to ship out one hundred orders than it is to ship out ten. Therefore, they need to take big risks to aggressively capture as much market share as possible. Especially during peak seasons.

The shopping campaigns had traditionally been unprofitable, and the search campaigns were spread too thin. We needed to help by focusing on promoting the products that would yield the highest average order value while increasing our flexibility to capture profitable business throughout different regions.

Strategy

Feed optimization and campaign restructuring helped to dramatically increase the ROAS from our shopping campaigns almost immediately. We ensured that we were only featuring products that were most likely to appeal to our core audience.

This would also train Google's smart bidding algorithms to understand our core audience demographic to see what specific signals related to a search correlate with a higher conversion rate. Training the algorithm to make more confident decisions regarding our best customers is essential in profitably entering new markets.

We then initiated a consolidation strategy within the search campaigns to increase liquidity, a form of freedom and flexibility for the smart bidding algorithms. The previous agency had segmented the search campaigns based on slight differences in keywords: long-tail keywords (keywords that included the name of a city or a specific type of bouquet, for example) received a larger percentage of the budget than did broader keywords such as [flower delivery service].

This is an outdated strategy. Ultimately, Fig & Bloom does not care if a person searches for *flower delivery service* or *flower delivery service Melbourne;* all that matters is if that user converts into a customer under a profitable ROAS.

Assumptions about a given keyword's buyer intent and the decision to structure budget and bids around those assumptions, is one of the largest pitfalls that we see in inherited accounts. Proper implementation of a smart bidding strategy would allow an intelligent algorithm to make more accurate predictions about buyer intent, regardless of the user's search query.

A consolidated account structure allows more freedom for the smart bidding algorithms to profitably capture the low hanging fruit and aggressively go after the traffic that was likely to convert at a higher-than-average order value.

Results

290 percent Increase in Shopping ROAS
27 percent Increase in Search ROAS
25 percent Increase in Shopping Conversion Rate
102 percent Increase in Account-Wide Conversions

A Guide to Google's Smart Bidding Options

14

The Maximize Conversions Bidding Algorithm

Predicted Conversion Rate is the main variable that drives Google bidding algorithms. The differences lie in the end goal and the unintended outputs.

Maximize Conversions is the most basic of the Google Smart Bidding algorithms. As its name suggests, this algorithm works to obtain the largest quantity of conversions and essentially ignores all other outputs such as Cost-Per-Click, Cost-Per-Conversion, ROAS, etc.

It's useful to imagine conversions as something that you need to purchase. All conversions are not created equal, and some conversions are more expensive than others.

By selecting Maximize Conversions as your bidding strategy, you are allowing Google to buy you all kinds of conversions, regardless of their cost.

The conversions you buy will fall along the following line:

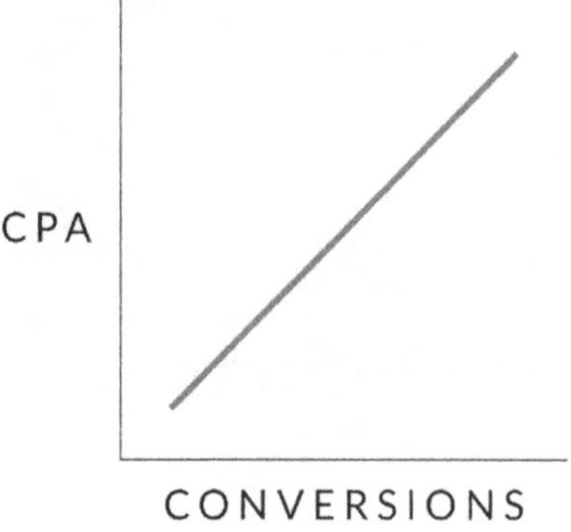

With an unlimited budget, you would continue to purchase more and more expensive conversions and acquire as many as possible in your given market.

Average CPC and CPA would rise, but you'd be able capture the greatest amount of conversions and become a market leader.

While appealing, this is not an economically viable scenario for most advertisers.

Lesson #1: Maximize Conversions is best used in campaigns with a limited budget.

If you limit the amount of budget that can be spent on any given day, it forces the algorithm to focus on the least expensive conversions due to the end goal of acquiring the largest quantity of conversions.

Say, for example, that your potential conversions will range in cost from $1 to $100 per conversion. If your daily budget is $100, the algorithm would not be doing its job if it spent the entire budget on just one $100 conversion.

Instead, the system will work to first acquire as many conversions as possible that cost just $1, and, then, if budget remains, will gradually increase the price in which it's willing to pay for a conversion until the budget is maxed out.

The Target CPA Bidding Algorithm

This algorithm is nearly a clone of the Maximize Conversions algorithm. The primary difference is that tCPA will consider another variable, Cost-Per-Conversion, as part of its goal.

This bidding algorithm still works to achieve the greatest quantity of conversions but will factor the output of Cost-Per-Conversion into its feedback loop.

The distinction here is that CPA only comes after a conversion is acquired. The resulting output is then factored into further hypotheses and tests that the algorithm will run.

Think of it like this:

1. User A is performing a search for your product. The Target CPA bidding algorithm uses predicted conversion rate and other variables to bid on and eventually purchase a conversion from this search. The cost for this conversion was X.*

2. User B is now performing a search for your product. The tCPA algorithm uses predicted conversion rate and other variables, which now include the X cost of acquiring the User A conversion and a hypothesis about similarities between User A and User B to bid on and purchase a conversion from this search. The cost for this conversion is Y.

   The similarity hypothesis between Users is either confirmed or thrown out when this conversion takes place. Either way, the algorithm is now smarter than it was before.

3. When User C performs a search, the algorithm is now able to tie similarities between User A, User B, and User C. With more data, the algorithm can come up with more creative hypotheses and will likely confirm a larger share of those hypotheses over time.

---

* This step is the same for Maximize Conversions. The following steps are where the algorithm becomes more advanced.

This is why your actual CPA will vary over time in these campaigns.

The number that you set as your Target CPA (or ROAS, when using tROAS) should not just be what your end goal is for the campaign. This number is arbitrary and only reflects how aggressive you are allowing the algorithm to bid.

Your end goal might be to consistently acquire conversions at $50, but if your campaign has been consistently earning conversions at $100, then you should not set your Target CPA at $50 from the onset.

The algorithm will not have strong enough hypotheses at that time and you are reducing the amount of positive feedback that would otherwise help confirm new hypotheses.

You should start with a reasonable goal and adjust over time.

Ultimately, the algorithm will be smart enough to purchase conversions that average out around your target. The general time that is considered is about fourteen days, but this may vary for accounts that have significant Time Lag to Conversion.

Consider the impact of a change in your Target CPA, in the sense of buying conversions that vary in price:

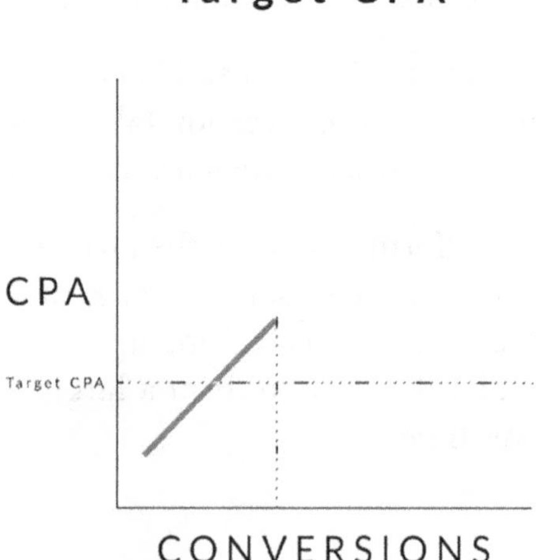

Compare this to if you had a higher, less constrained Target CPA:

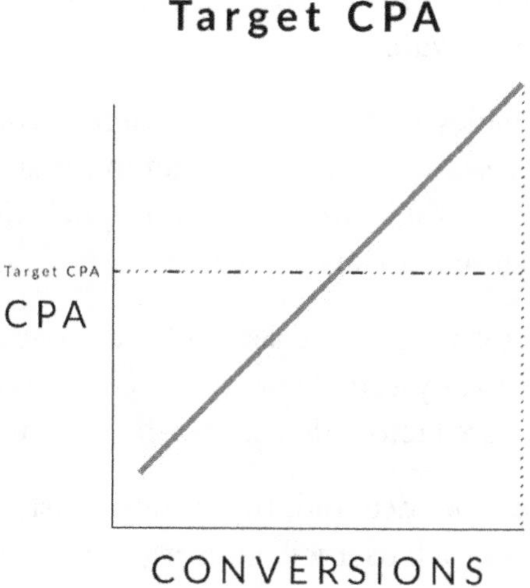

Lesson #2: Google recommends that your Target CPA campaign budget be set at least 10x your target.

This is just a rule of thumb. If you have a massive campaign with ten or more ad groups, then you might need even more budget to allow the algorithm to work for you.

If you have a smaller campaign with lower-volume keywords, then you might be able to get away with 5x budget.

We will cover Target CPA in much more detail in the following chapter.

The Target ROAS Bidding Algorithm

Target Return on Ad Spend is more complex since it has to factor in the *value* that is earned from each conversion.

In this case, you are still buying conversions that come with varying costs, but every conversion comes with a different value, and it cannot be assumed that these two variables are positively correlated. That is, a more expensive conversion does not necessarily guarantee greater conversion value.

In addition to predicted conversion rate, Target ROAS must factor in predicted conversion value.

There are many variables that will be considered when predicting conversion value. The search term or product in the shopping feed is obviously one factor, but there are behavioral signals tied to the user performing the search that are also considered.

Two users might perform the same search for a low-priced product, but User A is looking to buy a single item, and User B is likely to result in a bulk order. These are factors that should be (and are) considered.

In order to determine the ideal bid, the system must compound the rate at which it believes each user will convert, multiplied by the value at which it predicts them to convert.

The result is an algorithm that buys conversions for you, yielding various returns that should average out to your target, with lower returning (i.e., less profitable) conversions on the far right of the chart:

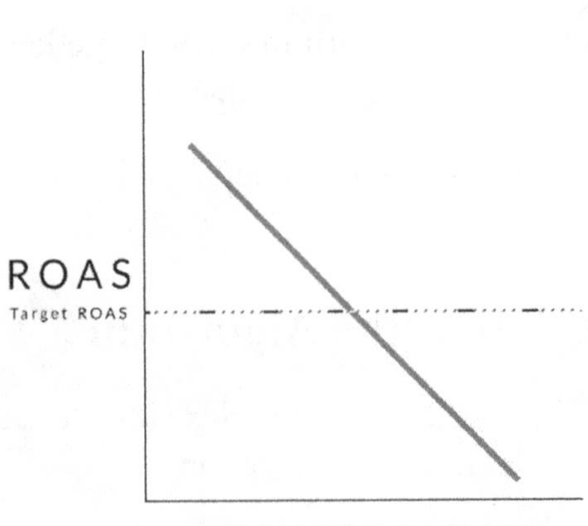

Raising the Target ROAS, and therefore forcing the algorithm to become more conservative, will have a similar effect to what we saw with Target CPA—fewer possible conversions:

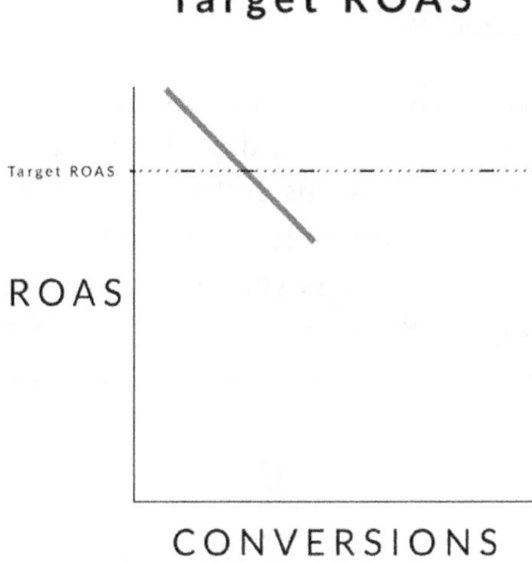

Lesson #3: Target ROAS will only work well when you have a lot of conversion data.

If a campaign does not earn a few dozen conversions per day, you should either proceed with caution or use micro-conversions to add more conversion data into the system.

Seasonality adjustments are advanced settings that allow you to tell your smart campaigns to *expect* a sharp increase or decrease in conversion rate for a given period. While the smart campaigns typically need little guidance, drastic swings in demand as a result of a flash sale, for example, might take a full twenty-four hours to be registered in the system.

That is, if you launch a flash sale on your site, you might expect your conversion rate to immediately increase by 50 percent. Such dramatic swings could take some time before they are officially *learned* by the algorithm. A seasonality adjustment can be used to prime the algorithm to expect certain swings and is, therefore, an extremely powerful tool to help guide the machine.

That said, an increase in conversion rate does not guarantee an increase in conversion value. We often see that a flash sale on a site increases demand for lower-priced items, and as a result, Average-Order-Value (AOV) temporarily decreases.

In this event, you will likely see an increase in conversions, but a decrease in actual ROAS. You should anticipate this and adjust accordingly, depending on your goals. If this sale is likely to continue for several days, the algorithm will learn the new trends over time and should be able to adjust to meet your Target ROAS goals. If not, you might want to temporarily raise your Target ROAS goals to force the algorithm to place more emphasis on auctions with a higher-predicted-conversion-value.*

The Maximize Conversion Value (Revenue) Bidding Algorithm

The Maximize Conversion Value Bidding algorithm works the same way as the Maximize C882onversions algorithm, but it uses *predicted conversion value* as its main goal. This bidding algorithm has fewer constraints (actual ROAS and CPA outputs are not considered), allowing more liquidity and flexibility to scale.

Choosing a Bidding Strategy

Many PPC managers, even some of Traditionalists, will talk about *testing* different bidding strategies with their clients. They might flip a campaign between Maximize Conversion and Target ROAS, hoping to find the strategy that drives the best results.

---

* The following chapter on Target CPA will give you more context as to how this might play out over the course of a conversion window.

Few PPC managers, however, ever attempt to discern *why* a particular strategy might work better than the next. This is a key question that is preventing a lot of advertisers from achieving success through automation. Unfortunately, you'll never really know for sure, but it's still important to ask.

We recently began working with a client who manufactures and sells large containers of hand sanitizer. As COVID-19 ran its course, the demand for this product skyrocketed, as did the competition.

It was a relatively new business that previously had not spent any money on advertising. We kicked off campaigns with a conservative budget, and, based on the best practices outlined above, we opted for Maximize Conversions bidding.

The campaigns were an instant success. We were quickly earning more than 50 conversions per week, with an extremely healthy ROAS. As such, we continued to expand the budget and felt comfortable exploring a Target ROAS bidding option. There was a large variance in order value, so we felt that a value-based bidding solution would force the algorithms to focus on conversions that would yield the highest overall return.

Immediately after we made the switch, performance plummeted. We were left scratching our heads, wondering if this was just a temporary factor of a new learning phase, or if there was actually a difference between these two bidding options that we failed to consider before making the change. We needed to ask the question, *Why is this happening?*

We began brainstorming hypotheses, which led to a deep dive into their actual customer data. A case of this product could be bought for around $30, but we knew that a handful of large orders were being placed by office buildings, school districts, and hospitals. The actual range was between $30 and $10,000. However, the average order value was just $60, suggesting that the vast majority of customers were buying just one or two cases.

Our primary hypothesis became as such: there is simply *too much* variance in these orders, which is creating a confusing learning environment for the Target ROAS algorithm. With enough time, the system will likely be able to figure it out, but we can't afford to wait. However, before making any drastic changes to the strategy, we needed to evaluate the validity of this hypothesis.

Imagine we received 100 individual orders, 99 of which were placed by mothers who would be keeping the hand sanitizer in their homes, but we also received one order from a school district.

The orders placed by mothers ranged from $30 to $90, with an average order value of $60. This accounted for $6,000 in total revenue. The school district placed a single order worth $7,000.

How might these two cohorts of sales impact the bidding process?

To review, Maximize Conversions is a relatively simple bidding algorithm. It cares about one output: conversion volume, and it tries to achieve the highest possible number. It does not care about CPA, ROAS, or Conversion Value.

I would assume, then, that this algorithm places more emphasis on the masses of your customer data: it would place much more emphasis on the signal data gleaned from the ninety-nine mothers than it would the one school district associate. In future auctions, this algorithm is likely to prefer (and aggressively bid on) auctions that are performed by other mothers.

For the sake of simplicity, let's assume that it places 99 percent of its learning weight on the mothers, and just 1 percent on the school district associate.

Target ROAS, on the other hand, is more complex. This is a value-based bidding algorithm that primarily cares about the Conversion Value metric, although I cannot say whether it ignores other metrics like conversion volume.

Let's assume for a second that Target ROAS does, in fact, ignore total conversions and specifically optimizes toward Conversion Value. In this example, 54 percent of our Conversion Value was earned from the school district and the remaining 46 percent of revenue earned from mothers. This is probably a confusing learning environment for a bidding algorithm.

In reality, I doubt that Target ROAS is actually this extreme. That is, I'm sure that conversion quantity carries some level of weight in the learning process. But how much? Personally, I'd prefer the algorithm ignore the school district conversion altogether. This is an outlier that I would not want to be a distraction. Instead, I'd prefer the algorithm to dive deeper into the nuances between the cohort of mothers who converted, with the goal of finding the nuances that led to one mother buying $90 worth of product, compared to those that bought just $30 worth of product.

This comes back to a fundamental principle of marketing: do not be fooled into thinking that your product is for everybody. Sure, a diverse group of customers could ultimately buy your products, but you should focus your attention, and your algorithms' attention, on your primary target audience.

We've determined that this hypothesis holds weight and that we want to guide the machine to optimize for our core audience of mothers. The next step includes a plan of action to achieve that goal, including advanced conversion tracking and new product pages on the site that can help divide our core audience from bulk order customers like school districts.

In the meantime, Maximize Conversions will remain as the bidding strategy of choice.

Case Study: The Impact of Smart Bidding on Campaign-Level Metrics

Most accounts will use a combination of these bidding strategies. There are many strategies that surround campaign structure, where various bid strategies can be implemented to maximize your goals.

Below is an example of an account of ours that has heavily transitioned toward automation over the last few months. You'll see a lot of these concepts in action:

Campaign	Bid strategy type	Avg. CPC	Cost	Conv. value	Cost / conv.	Conv. rate	Conv. value / cost	Search impr. share	Search lost IS (rank)
[illegible]	Target ROAS	$3.23 (+14.27%)	$56,492.41 (+57.53%)	205,893.70 (+65.71%)	$47.67 (-12.46%)	6.77% (+30.53%)	3.64 (+19.80%)	30.99% (-21.69%)	68.83% (+13.91%)
[illegible]	Target ROAS	$1.52 (+23.60%)	$27,254.81 (-27.81%)	112,155.84 (-17.45%)	$38.33 (-7.18%)	3.97% (+33.16%)	4.12 (+14.36%)	61.04% (-29.29%)	38.73% (+183.24%)
[illegible]	Maximize conversions	$1.86 (-8.73%)	$43,902.88 (-6.05%)	164,484.38 (+11.37%)	$38.73 (-11.87%)	4.81% (+3.57%)	3.75 (+18.54%)	30.49% (-41.61%)	57.35% (+68.01%)
[illegible]	Target ROAS	$0.89 (+14.45%)	$43,401.88 (-22.43%)	150,907.71 (-37.31%)	$41.87 (+30.01%)	2.12% (-11.96%)	3.48 (-19.18%)	39.62% (-16.77%)	55.20% (+7.76%)
[illegible]	Target ROAS	$2.08 (+25.83%)	$115,407.99 (-19.87%)	548,542.87 (-6.13%)	$34.48 (-5.69%)	6.02% (+37.81%)	4.75 (+17.14%)	57.76% (+2.17%)	41.62% (-4.24%)
[illegible]	Maximize conversion value	$0.49 (+∞)	$43,522.76 (+∞)	264,261.19 (+∞)	$23.66 (+∞)	2.07% (+∞)	6.07 (+∞)	–	–
[illegible]	Target ROAS	$0.71 (+14.43%)	$80,260.64 (+79.23%)	390,341.89 (+99.12%)	$31.81 (-4.74%)	2.22% (+20.19%)	4.86 (+11.10%)	35.44% (-18.77%)	49.05% (-12.97%)
Total: All enabled campaigns		$1.16 (-3.20%)	$527,387.99 (+11.34%)	2,686,549.13 (+37.63%)	$30.85 (-14.76%)	3.76% (+13.56%)	5.09 (+23.62%)	35.02% (-24.58%)	48.70% (-5.56%)
Total: Account		$1.17 (+1.27%)	$628,689.56 (-12.49%)	3,051,521.27 (+2.24%)	$31.86 (-9.29%)	3.68% (+11.65%)	4.85 (+16.83%)	34.94% (-17.10%)	51.37% (-6.67%)
Total: Search campaigns		$1.81 (+26.99%)	$416,657.63 (-20.50%)	2,111,345.53 (-6.30%)	$31.41 (-9.97%)	5.77% (+41.06%)	5.07 (+17.86%)	32.78% (-18.42%)	51.50% (-8.08%)

Takeaway #1—Search campaign CPC has increased by an astounding 27 percent. This is not an issue, as Conversion Rate has increased by 41 percent. As long as your Conversion Rate increases at a rate greater than your CPC, you will be more profitable. This is illustrated by the 18 percent lift in ROAS (Conv. value / Cost).

Takeaway #2—Search Impression Share has decreased. As I mentioned earlier, SIS is a relative metric and does not indicate the actual size of the market. Previously, this account had been entering into lower-quality ad auctions and winning a larger percentage of impressions. That is no longer the case. We are now entering higher quality auctions (which is proven by our increased CPC and Conversion Rate).

Also, of the 65 percent of auctions that we are entering into and losing, we are losing fewer auctions due to Ad Rank. This indicates that, when a very high-quality search is performed, Google is ensuring that our bid is high enough to win an impression.

Takeaway #3—Only one of the campaigns shown above is using the Maximize Conversions bid strategy. Note that this campaign is the only example that has a decreased CPC over time. This is a result of the limited budget strategy outlined above, where this campaign is working hard to buy the lowest cost conversions before exhausting its budget.

Under the Hood of the Target CPA Bidding Algorithm

In Chapter 2, we stated that machine learning is like a car engine. To drive a car, you just need to know a few basic things, such as how to turn the car on, where the steering wheel and gas pedals are, and the rules of the road.

Unfortunately, a modern PPC manager's job description goes far beyond simple operation. They're required to have the knowledge of an engineer or mechanic. They must be able to diagnose, solve problems, or even reconstruct the engine with spare parts.

This chapter will give you the tools you need to manage your Target CPA engine under any conditions. Once you understand Target CPA, you can apply the same logic to bidding algorithms across Google, Facebook, or any other platform.

My goal is not that you walk away thinking that 10 percent of your budget will always be reserved for learning; that figure is largely arbitrary. My goal is that you build a better understanding of *how and why* a portion of your budget must always be reserved for learning.

Ultimately, the handful of levers at your disposal have serious ramifications regarding the success or failure of your smart-bidding campaigns. Misuse or misunderstanding of these features can have disastrous effects.

Not All Conversions Are Created Equal

Advertising is best described as the act of buying customers at a profit. Customers, or conversions, vary in cost. We can theorize that all probable conversions that could be attained by a given business would create a scatterplot that looks something like this, where the first conversion costs very little to acquire, but the fiftieth conversion costs exponentially more.

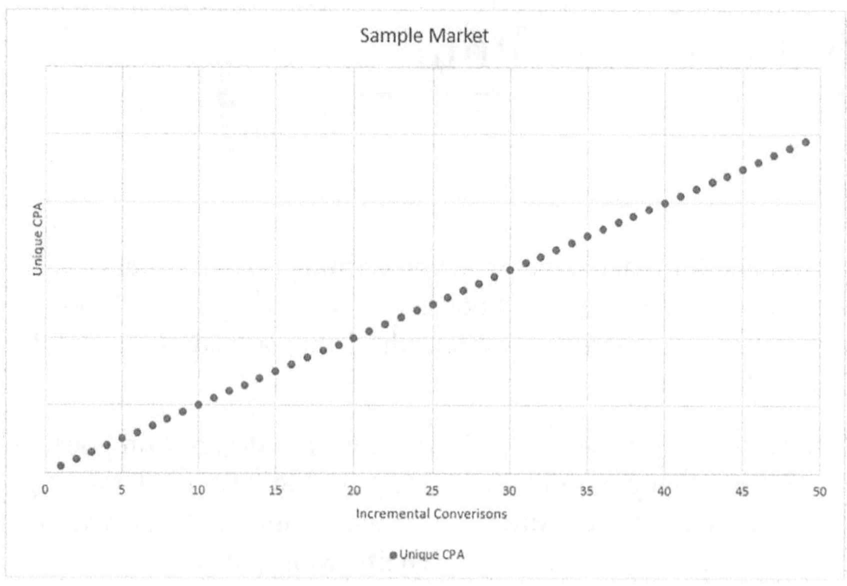

Let's pretend that our client is a custom ping pong table manufacturer. They're a lead generation business that earns $5,000 of profit per sale and has a 10 percent close rate.

Therefore, we can afford to pay $500 on average per conversion if we want to break even.

Theoretically, we could afford to pay $4,000 for a single conversion if we bought ten subsequent conversions for $9.99 each:

($4,900 x 1) + ($9.99 x 10) = $4,999.90 in advertising costs.

The total addressable market for our ping pong business might look like the following, whereby the cheapest customer only costs $75 to acquire, and the most expensive customer costs $925.

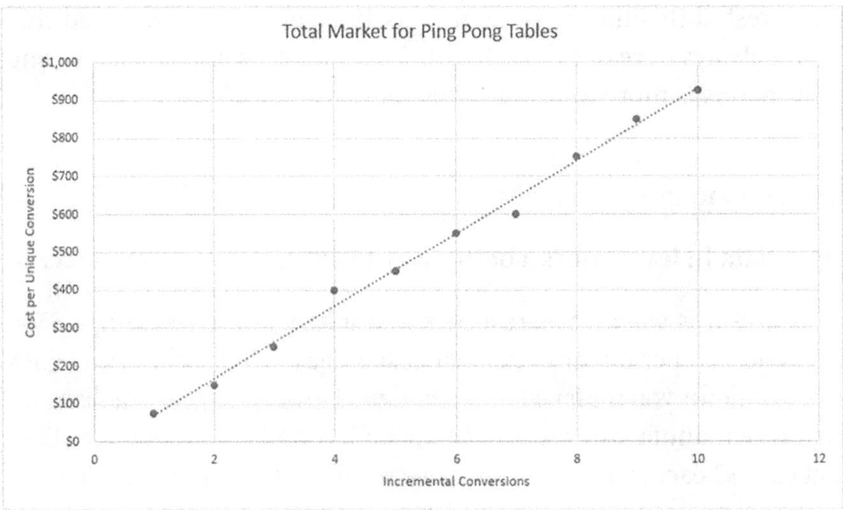

This chart represents the unique conditions of profitability for our specific business. If our competitor has a more efficient Google Ads account or a better website conversion rate, then their addressable market as it relates to the PPC bidding landscape will look slightly different.

If there was a major change in the market or to our own conditions for profitability, then these numbers could change completely. A Target CPA bid strategy could to help us achieve the results we need. But under what conditions?

The Basics of Target CPA Bidding

Google recommends that Target CPA should only be used when you can afford to set your daily budget to at least 10x your Target CPA.[57] They claim that this is the only way to ensure that the system will have enough freedom to run tests and properly learn. This makes perfect sense when you consider how silly it would be for us to set a budget of, say, $600 per day and expect to drive results. In this case, Google would recommend that our daily budget be set to $5,000.

This isn't possible for most clients. Not many ping pong table manufacturers can afford a $150K monthly budget out of the gate. And that's just for one measly search campaign!

We've tested this theory in many accounts and have concluded that it's not always necessary to set a 10x budget. The volume of clicks and conversions is more important than actual spend.*

Keep in mind, you can always set your daily budget to 10x your Target CPA and monitor the results.

More data in less time is a better way to set yourself up for success.

Look at it this way: If you're a personal injury lawyer seeking a $500 CPA and competing for clicks that cost at least $100 each, Target CPA won't work for you under a limited budget. However, if you're a discount furniture manufacturer seeking a $500 CPA and competing for clicks that cost $2 each, you can likely drive results with a smaller budget.

Excluding these outlier scenarios, I'd recommend setting that budget to at least 4x your Target CPA. As a rule of thumb, you should estimate a realistic conversion rate that you can achieve, then factor in the average CPC for the traffic you are targeting. Then determine if you can even afford to receive multiple conversions in a given day.

Conversion Count Minimums

If you cannot afford a budget at least 4x your tCPA, I would recommend starting with Maximize Conversions and keeping your budget tight. Under a limited budget, the Maximize Conversions bidding algorithm will be forced to optimize for the cheapest possible conversions.

Regardless of your smart bidding strategy, you should be realistic about what you expect a conversion to cost and whether you can afford to buy multiple conversions per day.

That is, if you're seeking a $500 CPA, you are setting yourself up for failure if your daily budget is $500 or less for a given campaign. In this

* Google's best practice recommendations typically err on the side of simplicity and are, rightfully so, exaggerated to help manage expectations. For example, Google is better off recommending a budget higher than necessary than if they were to recommend a budget that wouldn't be sufficient to drive results. It's also a simpler rule and requires less math than the example I'll provide below.

event, I would suggest to the client that they outline what they planned to spend over the next six months and spend it all in three months or sooner so that they could run an appropriate test.

One conversion per day, or less than one conversion per day on average, will not give the algorithms the data necessary to drive results and scale. The algorithm would essentially be throwing darts, blindfolded, at a wall and hoping something occasionally lands near bull's-eye.

There is no specific number of conversions that are required on a daily or weekly basis to effectively run Target CPA campaigns. My own personal rule of thumb is that I'd like to see at least thirty conversions per week before completely turning over to Target CPA.*

Thankfully, Google's smart-bidding algorithms consider signals from your entire account when setting bid prices. Conversion data obtained from Campaign A will help guide the algorithm to confidently bidding on behalf of Campaign B.

Therefore, you don't necessarily need thirty conversions per week per campaign to effectively run Target CPA campaigns, so long as you're earning thirty conversions per week from smart campaigns across your account. However, each campaign should still be able to afford at least one conversion per day, or seven per week.

Regarding your actual CPA goals, as an intelligent PPC manager, you may be able to show your client that their actual CPA goals are too aggressive.

Maybe you can help them see that the LTV of their customers is more than what they thought.

Maybe you can help your client see the benefits of breaking even or forgoing profit for the time being, effectively increasing your Target CPA.

Maybe you can help your client optimize their overall business, increasing revenue per customer and subsequently allowing for a higher Target CPA.

---

* This varies by account. Don't hold me to that number, but at least this gives you a place to start.

In other words, don't be in the habit of assuming your client's Target CPA is intransigent. If we had more data on hand, we could likely find that our ping pong table client could afford to spend beyond $500 per conversion.

Having realistic goals and expectations is essential. If you are a personal injury lawyer and see that you're acquiring leads for a $20 CPA, something is not working correctly. Either your conversion tracking is incorrect or you're filling your sales pipeline with junk leads. There is no reality where personal injury lawyers can be acquiring quality leads for that price.

Think of it this way: If I told you that I was selling BMW x7 SUVs for $10,000 each, while they are typically sold for around $70K, would you buy one? Or would you assume that something smelled fishy about this offer and conclude that you would never risk your own and your family's safety on the off chance that you did, in fact, just get extremely lucky?

Your goals should be based on accurate data, and they should be reasonable to achieve.

Using Conversion Rate to Determine Break-Even Point

Let's assume that the average market price for ping pong table keywords is somewhere near $5 per click. We would need a 1 percent average conversion rate to break even.

> *How we got that number:*
>
> $500 CPA / $5 per click = 100 clicks per conversion
>
> 1 conversion / 100 clicks = 1 percent conversion rate

After cross-referencing this data with historical conversion rates that we've seen in Google Analytics and similar accounts, we believe our conversion rate will be better than that. We estimate our conversion rate to be at least 1.5 percent, and we are actively seeking to improve our site conversion rate up to 2 percent over the next three months.

We can estimate that a budget of 4.5x our break-even CPA, $2,500, is an appropriate starting daily budget. We can estimate that we'll achieve around 500 clicks per day.

At 500 clicks per day and 1.5 percent conversion rate, we should generate an average of 7.5 conversions per day, or 52.5 per week.

Again, this is our baseline that helps us determine a daily budget. This may change as we determine our specific goals and other variables.

The key takeaway from this exercise is that we've determined that our daily budget should be at least 4x our tCPA. Now we must figure out what those targets will be.

Determining Your Starting CPA Targets

Here's the next issue: A $500 average CPA would allow us to break even. But we don't want to break even. We want to earn a profit.

So, how should I determine my Target CPA? We know that we'd ideally retain a CPA below $500. But how much profit per conversion should we aim for from the onset?

We used historic conversion rates on the site to predict our baseline budgets and break-even point, but ultimately, smart bidding should optimize for higher conversion rates over time.

While we want to drive as much profit as possible, we also want to be reasonable about what we can achieve in the short term. If we are too conservative from the onset, we might throttle the total amount of learning, and ultimately impede results that we could achieve.

Therefore, choosing a realistic CPA target is important.

A few things to consider:

1. If this is an entirely new campaign, I'd recommend using your own estimation of conversion rate on the site, while factoring in knowledge gained from other areas of the account and/or similar accounts.

But here's the good news: As mentioned above, the algorithm now considers data collected from other campaigns.

If you just created your Google Ads account yesterday and no historical data is available, then Google will pull signals from accounts competing in similar auctions.

2. If this is a new campaign in an account with historical data, Google will consider signals gathered from other campaigns inside of your account. This is a relatively new addition that is extremely helpful.

3. If this is an existing campaign that has been running on manual bidding, I would first check to see Google's recommendation for your Target CPA. Even in this scenario, the system is aware of what it could potentially achieve, given existing data.

   I'm often pleasantly surprised when I uncover an extremely low suggested tCPA.

4. If this is an existing campaign and the results have been nowhere near profitability, then it's even more important to take your budget into consideration when setting your tCPA.

The Importance of the Conversion Window

Conversion Window is an often overlooked component of the conversion settings, but it's just as important as the attribution model you select.

Attribution Modeling Hint #1: Never choose Last-Click attribution when creating your Google Ads conversion actions. Go with Data-Driven if available or Position-Based if you average 2.5+ clicks to conversion. Otherwise, use Time Decay.

Conversion Window is the length of time after an ad click that any conversions will be attributed back to said ad click.[58]

The default conversion window in Google Ads is thirty days. Under this scenario, if a user clicks on your ad on the first of the month but returns on the twenty-ninth, even without clicking on a second Google Ad, a conversion will be attributed back to the original ad click.

It's common practice to extend the conversion window to ninety days so that you can capture as much conversion data as possible. Google prefers this, as do many PPC agencies, because they want to report on as much conversion data as possible. However, this isn't always the best option, especially if you are not using *Data-Driven* attribution.

The goal of the modern PPC manager is to train Google's algorithms to understand their goals while ensuring that the machine is being fed data that will allow it to achieve those goals. As part of this, you want to be realistic and transparent with the algorithm about the nuances of your business.

Imagine you were running a Google Ads campaign on behalf of a local locksmith, and you set up the conversion window to be 90 days with a Position-Based attribution model. On January 1st, a user clicks on one of your ads but does not convert. On March 15th, that same user clicks on a second ad and converts. In this event, 50 percent of that conversion would be credited to the original ad click that took place seventy days prior. Is that fair or reasonable? Of course not, but this is a negligent decision that many PPC managers make every day, and it results in an algorithm that has learned something based on bad data.

You should analyze your Time Lag report to help you make this decision. The longer your average conversion cycle, the longer your conversion window should be. If a significant portion of your revenue comes at least 12 days after first click, then your conversion window should be more than 30 days.

In our chapter on attribution, we discussed the intricacies of the Time Lag report and how ecommerce companies tend to have a longer Time Lag than lead gen. We also saw that, for many ecommerce companies, larger purchases tend to take longer and incur more ad-clicks to convert.

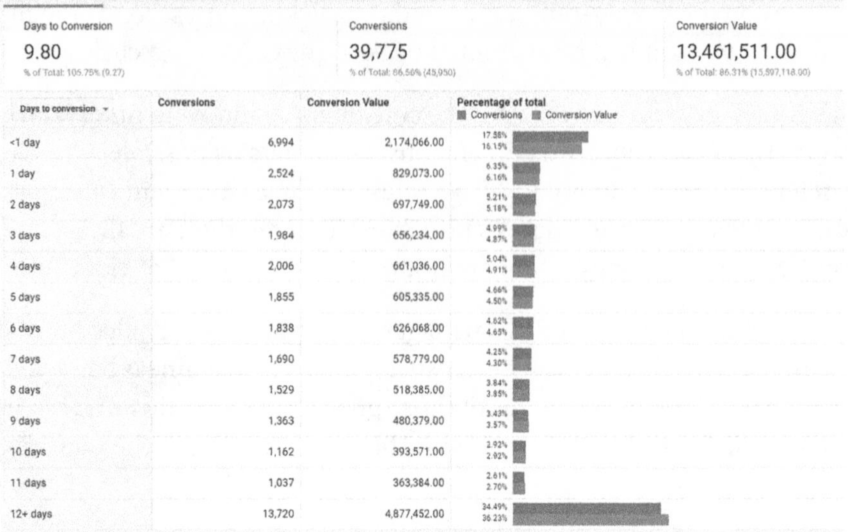

Days to Conversion	Conversions	Conversion Value
9.80	39,775	13,461,511.00
% of Total: 105.75% (9.27)	% of Total: 86.56% (45,950)	% of Total: 86.31% (15,597,118.00)

Days to conversion	Conversions	Conversion Value	Percentage of total: Conversions	Percentage of total: Conversion Value
<1 day	6,994	2,174,066.00	17.58%	16.15%
1 day	2,524	829,073.00	6.35%	6.16%
2 days	2,073	697,749.00	5.21%	5.18%
3 days	1,984	656,234.00	4.99%	4.87%
4 days	2,006	661,036.00	5.04%	4.91%
5 days	1,855	605,335.00	4.66%	4.50%
6 days	1,838	626,068.00	4.62%	4.65%
7 days	1,690	578,779.00	4.25%	4.30%
8 days	1,529	518,385.00	3.84%	3.85%
9 days	1,363	480,379.00	3.43%	3.57%
10 days	1,162	393,571.00	2.92%	2.92%
11 days	1,037	363,384.00	2.61%	2.70%
12+ days	13,720	4,877,452.00	34.49%	36.23%

You should be cognizant of the impact that larger order, which has taken several weeks and many ad clicks to convert, might have on the bidding algorithm's decision-making process. This is similar to the outlier impact that I described with our hand sanitizer client in the previous chapter.

In general, the Target CPA algorithm will attempt to reach your Target CPA over the course of an entire conversion window. If you set a Target CPA of $500 and a conversion window of 90 days, you might see a large variance in actual CPC across one month compared to the next. A dramatic swing in actual CPA might cause you and your client to panic, but it might not be seen as an issue to the bidding algorithm.

Similarly, we often advise clients to not focus too much on the performance of any single day and, instead, measure success from the aggregate of a week, month, or quarter. With a 90-day conversion window, you are telling the algorithm that you care more about the aggregate 90-day results, so you should be prepared to deal with the consequences if there is volatility between individual weeks or months.

When it comes to the conversion window and your chosen attribution model, you are setting the rules of the game. The rules can be changed, but you shouldn't be so quick to blame the algorithm.

Attribution Modeling Hint #2: Position Based attribution modeling will place much more emphasis on outliers. In the event where one user clicked three ads over the course of three months and produced $5,000 in profit, a Position Based attribution model will reward $2,000 in value (40 percent) to the first click, even if it took place 89 days prior. This might be correct and effective for some businesses, but not all.

Optimizing Target CPA Campaigns

Back to the ping pong table example...

Considering all these variables, including the inner workings of the tCPA algorithm and the specifics of the custom ping pong table market, we can summarize our main takeaways:

- Based on our own profitability goals, we've determined that our actual Target CPA should be $400.
- Based on the average we expect to pay-per-click, our daily budget should be at least 4.5x our tCPA. So, at least $1,800.
- Based on our understanding of the ping pong table market, we expect the average customer to convert within seven days of first ad click. That is, if a user does not convert into a lead within seven days, it is very unlikely that they will ever convert. Keep in mind, lead-gen conversion cycles are almost always shorter than ecommerce.

Therefore, our campaign settings become:

Conversion Window: Seven Days

Attribution Model: Data-Driven

Target CPA: $400

Daily Budget: $1,800

We launch our campaign and hope for the best, but we won't fully begin to evaluate results until at least seven days after the launch. It is important to wait until after your conversion window has completed before making decisions about performance.

The daily conversions and actual CPA are measured below:

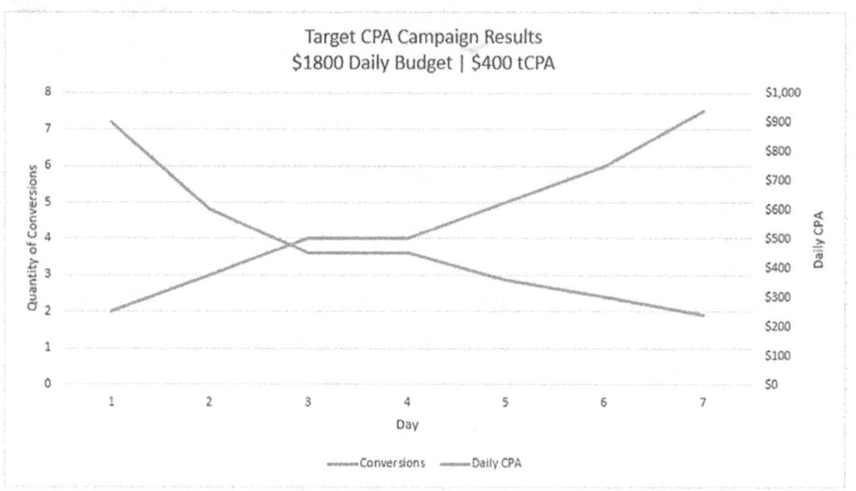

The campaign got off to a rough start, with just two conversions for a $900 CPA after Day 1. However, it improved steadily as the algorithm exited it's learning phase and began making more confident decisions regarding expected conversion rate for Google Ad auctions.

On the final day of the week we earned 7.5 conversions at an astonishing $240 CPA! The totals for the entire conversion window results as such:

Total spend: $12,600

Total Conversions: 31.5

Average CPA: $400

Given a break-even CPA of $500, we've earned $100 in profit per conversion, so:

Total Seven-Day Profit: $3,150

The campaign appeared to be spending nearly all its budget each day, so an increased daily budget would likely result in additional spend and incremental conversions.

After compiling this information and sending it to the client, they agreed to increase spend to $150K a month, more than double their previous spend levels. Adjustments to the budget and tCPA would help us scale spend, but we must first consider the learning phase as part of this process.*

The Learning Phase

The learning phase is the period during which machine learning algorithm is gathering data from initial tests. When a significant change has been presented to an algorithm, the machine must test these new variables until it learns about predicted outcomes with statistical significance.

Most digital advertisers are familiar with this concept, but many do not realize that a portion of a Target CPA budget will always be dedicated to learning, **even after you've exited the original learning phase.**

The Always-Be-Learning construct is a fundamental principle of machine learning and is essential to continued improvement and optimization.

Once you've exited the learning phase, we can technically break down your Target CPA budget into two components: the percent of the budget dedicated to *confidence*, and the percent of the budget dedicated toward *learning*.

Under confidence, the tCPA algorithm can manage your budget in a way that it reasonably believes will help deliver the results that you've outlined (with no guarantees, of course). The algorithm is confident that it understands the primary signals to consider or ignore as part of the bidding process.

---

* It is extremely rare that you will want to set a seven-day conversion window, even for lead gen accounts. However, this example serves to simplify these concepts.

However, the small percentage of the budget dedicated toward learning is always looking beyond confidence to test new variables and hypotheses.

A confident tCPA algorithm might not be evaluating weather patterns as part of its process. However, it may begin testing these signals to determine whether colder temperatures play a role in the demand for ping pong tables.

The algorithm might similarly be testing to see if CEOs of tech firms who are shopping for commercial real estate are more likely to purchase a custom ping pong table and whether they are more likely to be influenced by an early-morning banner ad or an evening YouTube ad.

It's all worth testing, so long as the advertiser still meets their defined CPA goals.

We don't know for sure what percentage of our budget is dedicated toward learning, and I am certain that it changes all the time and is unique for every advertiser. However, let's assume for a minute that at least 10 percent of our budget is reserved for learning.

In this scenario, the tCPA algorithm will need to adjust its actual CPA goals to be 10 percent more conservative than the nominal goal of the advertiser.

That is, if our tCPA is $500 and we set a daily budget of $2,500, 10 percent of which will be reserved for tests that might yield zero results, the algorithm needs to adjust and overcompensate for this potential loss so that it averages out to $500 per conversion at the end of the conversion window.

Looking at it mathematically, we get:

- Daily Budget: $2,500
- Daily Budget Dedicated to Confidence (90 percent of daily budget): $2,250
- Daily Budget Dedicated to Learning (10 percent of daily budget): $250

- Thirty-Day Total Budget (assuming thirty-day conversion window): $75,000
- Thirty-Day Conversion Goal: 150
- Thirty-Day Confidence Budget: $67,500
- Adjusted Target CPA: $450

If Google spends 100 percent of your budget over this thirty-day window, and if every penny invested toward learning is unsuccessful in driving incremental conversions, then Google would need to make up 150 conversions from its confidence budget in order to meet your end goals.

What you see is a $500 tCPA, but Google would be interpreting this as a $450 (and therefore more conservative) tCPA.

Ultimately, you need not worry about Google's interpretation of your Target CPA so long as you are reaching your goals.

The Impact of Increased Budgets & tCPA Adjustments

Any major adjustments to your budgets or Target CPA parameters will have an impact on your learning to confidence ratio.

Let's say, in the previous example, we took our $2,500 daily budget and doubled it to $5,000. Up until this point, Google had been spending $2,250 with confidence, and additional budget won't necessarily increase that number right away.

In this case, you go from a 90:10 confidence-learning ratio to a 45:55 confidence-to-learning ratio, where more than 50 percent of your budget is now in the learning phase.

A massive increase in your Target CPA will cause a similar impact. Either way, your short-term results will likely take a huge hit.

My colleagues at Google and Facebook have stated that budget changes up to 15 percent will not drastically impact the learning phase. While this isn't documented anywhere, Facebook does allude to this in one of their support docs:

> The learning phase will begin when you first launch a Facebook ad or when you make a significant adjustment to a campaign. The learning phase will last for as long as it takes to achieve 50 optimization events. [59]

Any changes you make to your Target CPA campaign, especially if they are greater than 15 percent, should go untouched for at least fourteen days. The algorithm takes time to work itself out.

I cannot promise that you will see the results that you are seeking within 14 days or within your conversion window. However, if you are spending thousands of dollars on a test and making decisions about the outcome *before* the results are conclusive, then you have effectively wasted every single dollar dedicated toward this test.

If your goal is to scale your campaign, but you are afraid to shock the system, here's my recommendation: Increase both your Target CPA and your daily budget, but increase your daily budget by a greater margin than you increase your Target CPA.

Here's why: Think back to my original example of how Google interprets your goals. You say, "I want to spend $2,500 per day and pay $500 per conversion," but what Google hears is "OK, I'll let you spend $75,000 over the next 30 days if you earn 150 conversions."

If you double your budget without adjusting your Target CPA, you are now telling Google, "You can spend $150,000 over the next 30 days if you earn 300 conversions."

Three hundred conversions might be hard to come by in the ping pong table market. It will likely take more time and more money to reach a point where Google is even on the right path of confidence.

So instead, let's raise our budget by 30 percent (to $3,250/day) and our Target CPA by 15 percent (to $575 tCPA).

Google now hears: "You can spend $97,500 over the next thirty days if you earn 169.5 conversions." This is a much more reasonable goal.

As such, the tCPA algorithm will likely be able to exit the learning phase sooner and be on pace to achieve that goal in less time.

Seems like a good deal to me.

What's more, it's important to keep in mind that tCPA goals are somewhat arbitrary. If you raise the tCPA under any condition, you are essentially telling Google that you'd like for the system to be more aggressive. This doesn't necessarily mean that Google will use this as an excuse to increase your costs and drive worse performance.

In addition to allowing the algorithm to be more aggressive, an increase in your Target CPA has another positive impact: increased budget dedicated toward learning.

The Importance of a Learning Budget

Even once you exit the initial learning phase under these new settings, you are still dedicating nearly 10K per month into learning experiments (assuming a 10 percent learning budget, which again, is a number that I am speculating on for the sake of this example).

This additional 10K per month in learning might be exactly what you needed to uncover the breakthrough that completely transforms your market potential. Think of it as R&D for your organization.

Compare this to the impact of a charitable donation. If you care deeply about helping individuals who suffer from a rare disease, where would your donation best be spent? Should you support organizations that help families cover the medical expenses associated with this illness? Or should you support organizations that perform research, with the goal of developing better treatments, drugs, and ultimately a cure for this disease over the next 10 to 20 years?

There's no correct answer to this question, but many would say that it's important to focus on both. Help those that are currently affected while seeking innovative breakthroughs that will have a larger, long-term impact.*

Google has taken the ethics out of this question and decided for us. As an advertiser on Google, a portion of your budget will be spent toward driving short-term results, and the rest will be dedicated toward uncovering major breakthroughs.

Perhaps for our ping pong table client, thanks to the increase in learning budget, Google was finally able to test a hypothesis that married couples who share an interest in wine, are parents of teenagers, and have finished basements have the highest conversion rate compared to any other audience of people who are in the market for ping pong tables.

"Just buy the damn table so that we can enjoy this Cab Sav and watch *Stranger Things* in peace!"

While this may represent a small segment of the market, a confident algorithm would ensure that you bid aggressively in every auction where these conditions are met.

Realized Growth: Unlocked Market Potential

This sort of breakthrough is the whole purpose of machine learning. New knowledge is now added to the algorithm's confidence arsenal and helps improve performance by 20 percent. You have unlocked an entirely new combination of potential customers and the costs required to acquire them!

The chart below illustrates our original market trend line in blue. The orange trend line represents a 20 percent shift, also allowing for an additional two customers who can now be acquired under our new conditions.

---

* *Four Diamonds*, an organization that is based at Penn State Hershey Children's Hospital and my former employer, approaches their mission of conquering childhood cancer by sharing their focus between both areas. Check them out at *fourdiamonds.org*.

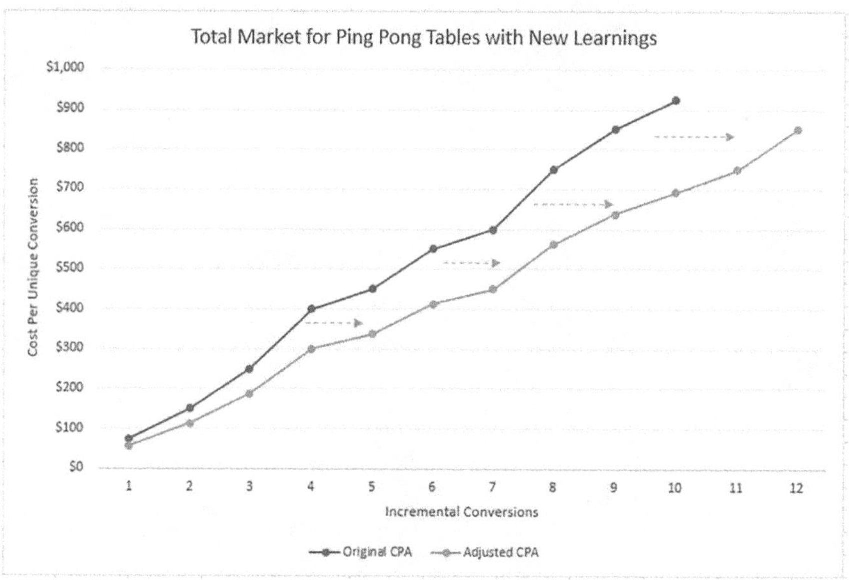

Our original (blue) market conditions earned ten conversions at an average CPA of $500, breaking even on our advertising efforts.

Our new (orange) market conditions can earn twelve conversions at an average CPA of $445, generating $660 in profit.

Once we reevaluate these results, taking a full conversion-window into consideration, we can continue to optimize this campaign for better results or use these profits to invest in completely new initiatives.

16 Automation in Facebook & Instagram Advertising

As I wrote in the book's introduction, these principles do not just apply to the Google Ads ecosystem. Google provides an excellent training ground to learn these principles, which can then be applied to other automated platforms.

I love Facebook advertising. About 85 percent of our clients are running ads on Facebook/Instagram, and in many cases, I prefer to start advertising on Facebook before launching in Google. I personally have not published a lot of Facebook-specific content because Facebook's platform changes so damn rapidly that I fear that any meaningful piece of Facebook-related content will be outdated by the time I hit *publish*. However, this constant evolution is the primary reason that makes Facebook so great!

In many ways, Facebook has been ahead of Google. For example, Facebook was years ahead of Google with *Selective Optimization*.

Despite the ever-changing nature of the Facebook platform, there are a number of best practices and other principles that are unlikely to change any time soon. These best practices, along with your newfound knowledge of how automation works, will allow you to adapt to any future changes to this platform.*

* When I refer to Facebook Ads, I am also referring to Instagram Ads. In fact, many of our clients spend a larger proportion of their budgets on Instagram placements than they do on Facebook placements. But for the sake of simplicity, I will just refer to this entire advertising ecosystem by the name of their parent company, Facebook.

CBO and Automatic Placements

Here is your first lesson in Facebook advertising: All your campaigns should be using *Campaign* Budget Optimization (CBO) and Automatic Placements. Historically, Facebook budgets were set at the *ad set* level. CBO is a budget option that was introduced in 2018, allowing you to set your budget at the campaign level.

This allows for *budget liquidity,* meaning that your entire budget can flow freely between ad sets to achieve the best results. For example, *Ad Set X* might present the best value on January 1st, but *Ad Set Y* might present the best value on January 2nd. It is silly to think that you, a mere mortal human advertiser, should predetermine the budget for each ad set and restrict your campaign from optimizing toward the best results in real-time.

Automatic Placements is a similar concept but related to placements instead of budget. By opting into automatic placements, you are allowing the system to evaluate auctions across Facebook, Instagram, and all other partners to help determine the best value and optimal location to meet your goals.

Here's the second lesson: I've heard many people claim their *target audience isn't on Instagram,* or worse, *my target audience isn't watching Instagram stories.* Stop it. According to Facebook's Global Creative Director Andrew Keller, the average Facebook user scrolls through 300 feet of Facebook content per day. Content which, if printed out, would be as tall as the Statue of Liberty.

So, while it's very likely that your target audience is watching Instagram stories, the point is moot. Facebook's machine learning algorithms are advanced enough to figure that out for you. We should all stop speculating about who and where our target audience is. We should focus, instead, on training our algorithms to do this work for us, effectively and at scale.

Facebook Campaign Types & Goals

The first step of creating a new Facebook campaign is declaring your campaign objective. Unbeknownst to most advertisers, this simple setting has the largest impact on your ad distribution and performance—more than your placements, audience, or even creative.

As of this writing, there are eleven objectives organized into three categories:

- **Awareness**
  - Brand Awareness
  - Reach
- **Consideration**
  - Traffic
  - Engagement
  - App Installs
  - Video Views
  - Lead Generation
  - Messages
- **Conversion**
  - Conversions
  - Catalog Sales
  - Store traffic (Facebook has suspended this campaign type in an effort to prevent the spread of COVID-19)

Conveying direct advice from our lead account strategist at Facebook, there's almost no need to ever opt for *Engagement, Video Views,* or even *Traffic.*

Instead, you will most often be optimizing for *Conversions,* followed closely by *Catalog Sales* (the Facebook equivalent of Google Shopping

Ads) and *Lead Generation* (an ad format that allows a user to fill out a form without having to click through to your site). *App Installs, Messages, Brand Awareness,* and *Reach* all have their place in certain circumstances and with larger budgets.

Many PPC managers like to get cute and test multiple campaign optimization goals when conversions are the goal they are ultimately interested in. This is a waste of time and resources. If conversions are your goal, choose this as your campaign objective and find a more creative and meaningful variable to test.

In early 2018, we were still in the early stages of embracing automation. We were running our own Facebook campaigns with a break-even CPA goal of $38. I wanted to know if it was worth testing these campaign types against one another and convinced Isaac that we should invest our own capital into proving the theory. He reluctantly agreed.

I created four ad sets in our Facebook account, targeting the same audience with the same ads. The differentiating factor of the ad sets was the optimization strategy, as in, the goal of the optimization algorithm.

While the ultimate goal of this account was to drive leads (conversions) below $38, our hypothesis was that perhaps another optimization goal (clicks, impressions, etc.) would be more effective in driving more leads at a lower cost. For example, if *click optimization* allowed us to get more traffic at a lower CPC, perhaps the sheer volume of traffic would generate more overall leads at a lower cost. This is a trap that many marketers fall into.

The four optimization goals included:

- Optimize for link clicks
- Optimize for unique reach
- Optimize for total impressions
- Optimize for lowest cost leads (conversions)

The results were conclusive after six weeks. The different optimization strategies were great at achieving their *individual* goals, but the only strategy that was effective in coming close to our overall goal was the ad set optimizing for *conversions.* The ad set that was optimizing for *impressions* was excellent at achieving a massive amount of those at a low cost, but it wasn't effective in helping us achieve actual leads for less than $38.

Shocking, I know. Who would have predicted that the ad set optimizing for *conversions* would be more effective at driving conversions than ad sets optimizing for *impressions, reach*, and *clicks*?

The results from this test are below, and I've circled the metric that this ad set was optimizing for. Each of these ad sets beat their peers in the respective column that they were optimizing for.

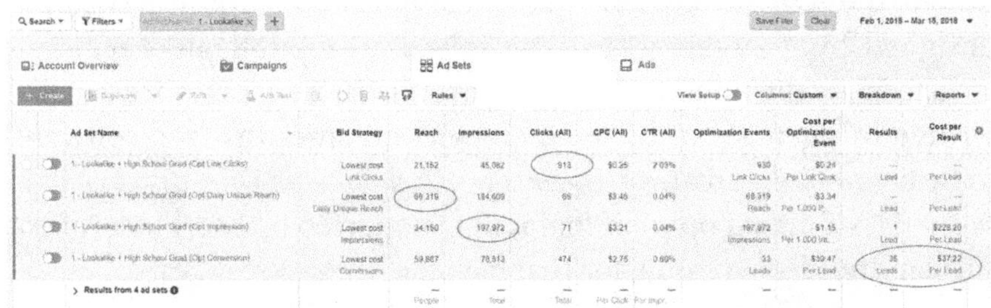

Ad Set Name	Bid Strategy	Reach	Impressions	Clicks (All)	CPC (All)	CTR (All)	Optimization Events	Cost per Optimization Event	Results	Cost per Result
1 - Lookalike + High School Grad (Opt Link Clicks)	Lowest cost Link Clicks	21,152	45,082	913	$0.25	2.03%	930 Link Clicks	$0.24 Per Link Click	— Lead	— Per Lead
1 - Lookalike + High School Grad (Opt Daily Unique Reach)	Lowest cost Daily Unique Reach	68,319	184,609	66	$3.46	0.04%	68,319 Reach	$3.34 Per 1,000 P...	— Lead	— Per Lead
1 - Lookalike + High School Grad (Opt Impression)	Lowest cost Impressions	34,150	197,972	71	$3.21	0.04%	197,972 Impressions	$1.15 Per 1,000 Im...	1 Lead	$228.20 Per Lead
1 - Lookalike + High School Grad (Opt Conversion)	Lowest cost Conversions	59,867	78,513	474	$2.75	0.60%	33 Leads	$39.47 Per Lead	35 Leads	$37.22 Per Lead
Results from 4 ad sets		— People	— Total	— Total	— Per Click	— Per Impr.	—	—	—	—

The ad set optimizing for *conversions* earned us a profit of about $30 during this period ($0.78 in profit x 35 leads), but the overall campaign took a loss. However, the results of this test have helped shape our confidence and understanding of automation, allowing our campaigns and our clients' to flourish in the long run. It was a worthwhile investment—at least, that's what I told Isaac after he received the bill from Facebook.

So, while the lure of lower CPCs and higher CTRs might tempt you to test *Traffic* as your optimization goal, **don't do it**. In the age of automation, you need to be as direct with your algorithms as possible.

The Problem with "Facebook Agencies"

The PPC Paid Social industry has backed itself into a corner. As mentioned, Facebook has always been extremely automated and does not deliver the deep level of data that Google AdWords has always provided. As a result, many agencies have spent the last five years selling their clients on the concept of A/B split testing inside Facebook. Agencies took this to the extreme, citing the importance of testing every single variable from gender to placement to CTA button. This would result in a complicated campaign structure with loads of ad sets, all of which impressed clients and made the agency seem valuable.

You can find countless articles online that claim that this strategy, the Facebook equivalent of the Single Keyword Ad Group (SKAG) strategy, is a best practice. This is not correct. It is just propaganda designed to convince clients that a complicated account structure, designed by an agency that specializes in complicated account structures, is the only way to drive success. These articles are usually written by agencies or by technology companies that sell software to help you *easily create thousands of Facebook ads with the click of a button!* It's a biased opinion that is not supported by Facebook (or by AdVenture Media Group, for that matter).

With a bit of research, you'll find that Facebook has a lot of great content regarding best practices in account structure, and none of it speaks about any of this over-segmentation that you'll see my peers in the industry publish. In fact, a quick glance through Facebook's *Blueprint* training material will help you understand that the exact opposite approach is most recommended. That is, a consolidated account structure, leaning heavily on automation, is primarily recommended by Facebook.[60]

While you should always be running some sort of test within any digital advertising environment, you should be aware of what the automation is doing in the background so that you do not waste your time running trivial tests. It is likely a waste of your time to split out ad sets by gender, for example, as the machine is going to optimize for this on the backend and, over time, understand which ad to serve to which individual.

The Primary Drivers of Facebook Advertising

Marketers who have embraced the age of automation are less concerned with overly segmented account structures and, instead, focus on creative, measurement, trend analysis, and partner support.

Creative includes the actual ads: the images, videos, ad copy, and landing pages that make up your ad campaigns. A quality creative agency will be able to bring much more to the table than just stock imagery with a bit of text layered on top of it.

Measurement includes attribution and testing done within the backend of Facebook's platform. The *Experiments* tab (formerly *Test and Learn)* offers deep insights in the form of multivariate tests, where you can run A/B tests, holdout tests, and brand surveys to measure the real impact of your ads in terms of CPA, conversion lift, and brand lift.

These experiments can be run with any budget, for free!*

Trend Analysis includes layering broader marketing insights into your campaign strategy, often impacting your creative strategy, as well as your landing pages. This is a primary value that agencies can bring to the table, as there is much to be learned by working inside multiple accounts at once and seeing how users' attitudes and behaviors are evolving on the platform. For example, you'd be a fool to not be leveraging video inside of the Facebook ads platform right now, as the market rate for these auctions are at historic lows and so many advertisers have been slow to adapt. What's more, Facebook allows you to create a video slideshow from existing image assets. The tool is built right into the Ads Manager platform and, while the final product likely won't be nominated for an Oscar, it's still a cost-effective short-term solution to your video production dilemmas.

Partner Support includes the support that premium agencies receive from Facebook directly. Similar to the support that Google provides, our Facebook team gets involved with our specific client

---

* Google currently offers a similar Brand Lift study for YouTube campaigns, but advertisers need to commit to a significant spend level before gaining access to this test.

accounts and participates in strategy, reporting, beta-feature access, and troubleshooting. An added value of Facebook's support is their vertical-specific support teams, which typically become available for advertisers with six-figure budgets operating in competitive verticals.

The Breakdown Effect

The breakdown effect is one of the most important concepts to understand if you wish to be successful in the age of automation. The widespread negligence of this concept is the primary reason why so many digital advertising campaigns have failed to achieve profitable growth.

Once again, we return to the fact that advertising is the practice of buying customers, all of which vary in price. The addressable market for a given product could be represented along the following scatterplot, and advertisers that are willing to pay more for a single customer will be able to buy more of them.

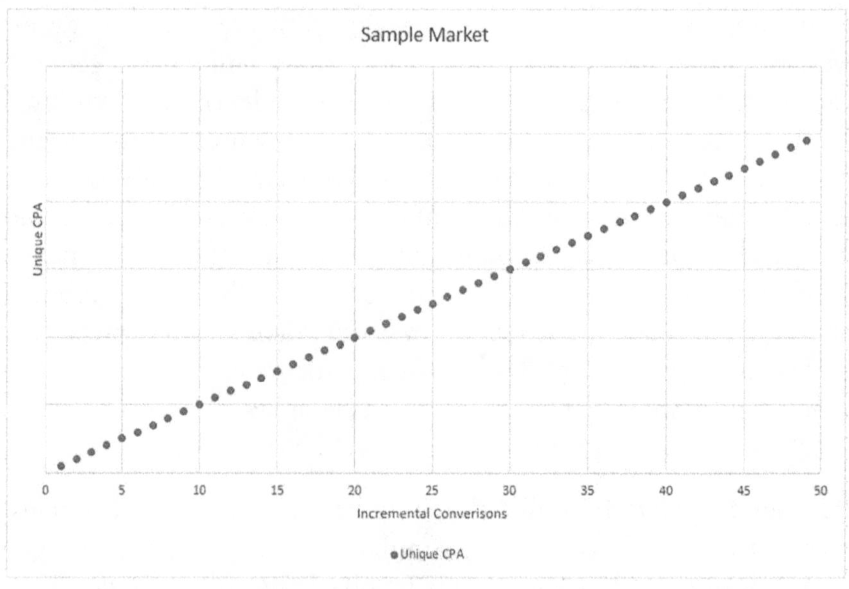

Compare that to how an ad delivery system will work within an automated platform like Facebook. When you declare a budget of $500 and select the *Lowest Cost* bid strategy (the default option, which is most similar to the Maximize Conversions bidding algorithm in Google), you are telling Facebook that you *want* to spend $500 and earn as many conversions as possible. Naturally, the system will have to focus on the lowest possible CPA, as this will allow it to afford the highest quantity of conversions. The important thing to note is that you are telling the system to spend that $500, and it will do so.

The ad delivery system uses both bidding and pacing to distribute that budget. Pacing is the act of stretching the budget throughout the entirety of your budget cycle. This can be for one day, or across the lifetime of your campaign flight period, depending on which option you select. *Discount Pacing* is used by Facebook to help ensure that the system first looks to earn the lowest-cost conversions while also ensuring that you spend your entire budget by the end of the cycle.

Facebook illustrates Discount Pacing with the following graph:

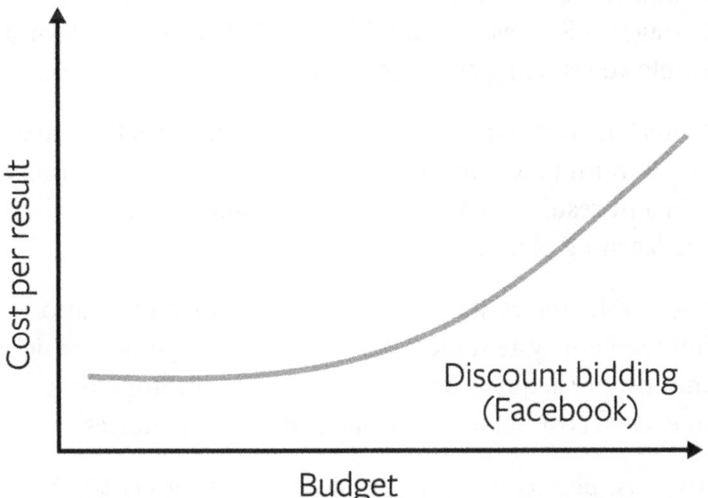

Source: "The Breakdown Effect," Facebook for Business, https://www.facebook.com/business/m/one-sheeters/breakdown-effect.

With a lower budget, Facebook might be able to optimize for the handful of conversions that sit in the lower-left corner of this graph, allowing you to see an astonishingly low average CPA number in your reports. As you increase your budget, Facebook is still optimizing for the lowest-cost conversions available, but you will naturally see your CPA rise over time.

The breakdown effect occurs at the intersection of a discount pacing approach and the machine learning components of the ad platform. Many marketers are confused by their results, where it appears that Facebook shifted impressions and budget over the duration of a campaign into underperforming ad sets, placements, or ads, instead of continuing to increase spend in areas that have shown to have the lowest CPA. In reality, the system is designed to maximize overall results given your selected campaign settings, despite what appears to be the case in your reports. This is a common misunderstanding that typically leads to marketers making changes to their campaigns, which ultimately caps growth.

Facebook uses the following example to describe the breakdown effect:

> Let's say you choose to run a campaign utilizing the conversions objective. You choose two placements to deliver your one creative asset to - Facebook Stories and Instagram Stories. The total budget is $500.00 USD for a single ad set using ad set level budget.
>
> When the campaign begins, our system starts to deliver ads to both placements to see which will drive the most efficient results for your target audience — this is called the learning phase.
>
> Facebook Stories starts out driving cheaper acquisitions, but then our system identified an inflection point at which the cost per acquisition (CPA) on Facebook Stories begins to exceed cost per acquisition on Instagram Stories.
>
> The cost per acquisition on Facebook Stories is $0.35 on the first day, compared to $0.72 on Instagram Stories. However, as the campaign continued Instagram Stories received more budget, even though it still has a higher cost per acquisition. At the end of the campaign, Instagram Stories delivered significantly more budget compared to Facebook Stories, even though Facebook Stories originally had a lower cost per acquisition.

Final results at the end of the campaign:

Placement	CPA	Spend
Instagram Stories	$1.46	$450
Facebook Stories	$1.10	$50

Source: "The Breakdown Effect," Facebook for Business, https://www.facebook.com/business/m/one-sheeters/breakdown-effect.

However, if you break down the daily results and plot them on a chart, you'll see a different story:

Day	Instagram CPA	Facebook CPA
1	$0.72	$0.35
2	$0.78	$0.50
3	$0.88	$0.75
4	$1.02	$1.10
5	$1.20	$1.55
6	$1.42	$2.10
7	$1.68	$2.75
8	$1.98	$3.50
9	$2.32	$4.35
10	$2.70	$5.30

Source: "The Breakdown Effect," Facebook for Business, https://www.facebook.com/business/m/one-sheeters/breakdown-effect.

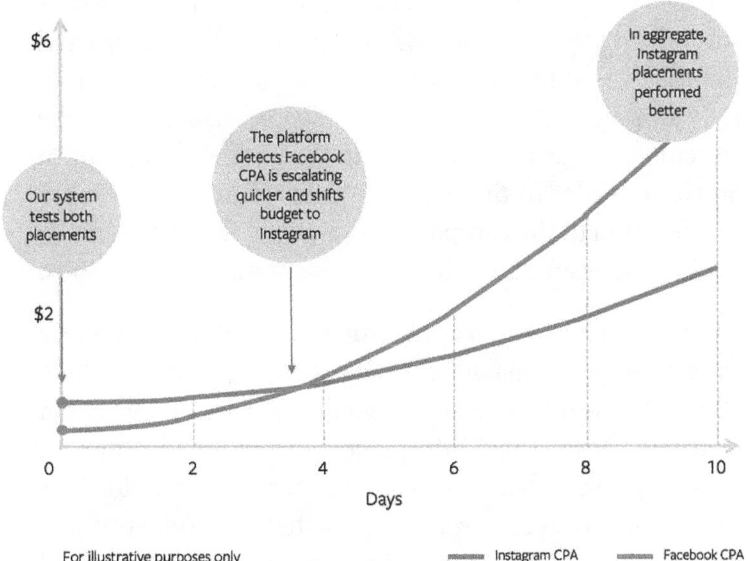

Source: "The Breakdown Effect," Facebook for Business, https://www.facebook.com/business/m/one-sheeters/breakdown-effect.

Prior to the inflection point (where Facebook costs were still lower than Instagram), the system (for example) may spend $50.00 on Facebook Stories and $50.00 on Instagram Stories to test. Since the system can detect that Facebook Stories CPA was rising faster than Instagram Stories, it shifts the remaining budget of $400.00 to Instagram Stories to have a cheaper CPA over the duration of the campaign. In the table, you'll see that prior to Day 4, Facebook Stories achieves a lower CPA; however, the costs would have grown faster than Instagram Stories. As you see above, Facebook Stories reached up to $5.30 by Day 10 while Instagram Stories was delivering at half the cost.

Why Did The System Do This?

At the start of the campaign, the system began delivering ads to both platforms to explore where the lowest cost opportunities were. Early on, the lowest cost results were garnered because the system front loads low-cost results through our discount pacing approach. In the example, the system recognized that although Facebook Stories was driving the most efficient results initially, it predicted the cost was going to increase throughout the duration of the campaign. Based on the anticipated rising costs, the system was able to pivot and shift the budget to Instagram Stories in order to drive a more efficient average CPA for the duration of the campaign. As a result, the system made the right decision and ultimately drove more conversions.

This is where the reporting may not match your expectations. If you had only judged the decision by looking at the CPA in Ads Manager, it would show less budget went to the lower average CPA placement, Facebook Stories. This may be confusing because it appears the decision was incorrect; however, the system pivoted the budget in real time to Instagram Stories which drove more results.

The Breakdown Effect has led to some confusion when interpreting ads manager campaign results. It's a trade-

> off designed to utilize automation and discount bidding. It may seem misguided without context, but ultimately it helps drive significantly more value for folks using our advertising system. The important thing to remember is that it will usually work to your favor when you create flexible campaigns through lowest cost bidding (discount bidding), automatic placements, and campaign budget optimization features that work together to maximize performance.[61]

So if you see that one ad set generated a lower overall average CPA, but the majority of the budget was dedicated to a second ad set, you should realize that Facebook was confident that it had maximized the lower-cost conversions that could be purchased from the first ad set, and the next incremental conversion would have come at a cost exceeding what could have been earned by investing in the second ad set.

You should always evaluate performance in aggregate. Your goal is not to overly segment your campaigns in hopes to strike oil before your competitors do. Your Facebook strategy should not be focused on discovering that *Women between the ages of 25-34 that have an interest in crime podcasts, and favor green ads over blue ads, are our best audience.* If you are looking for this or having these sorts of discussions with your client or agency, you are missing the point entirely.

There are no hidden gems in digital advertising. Instead, the forces of supply and demand are used in real-time to settle the score between competing advertisers looking to buy customers. Success is earned by training an algorithm, then trusting that it is acting in your best interest, and staying out of its way. Not pausing ad sets that you *think* are underperforming.

Facebook Ads Bidding Options

The bidding options available in Facebook today are similar to those that are available in Google, although they use different terminology.

Lowest Cost is the default option and was used in our example to illustrate the breakdown effect above. This bid strategy mirrors

Google's Maximize Conversions bid strategy in that the goal of the strategy is to spend your daily budget on a recurring basis and achieve the highest quantity of conversions. Results vary, but this bidding option forces the system to focus on, as the name suggests, the lowest cost conversions that can be bought. This option is best for advertisers on a limited budget.

Bid Cap is Facebook's version of Manual CPC, and we're far enough into this book to all agree that this is not an effective way to profitably scale your advertising campaigns. This is especially true in an environment where the vast majority of auctions are currently, and have always been, driven by automated bidding. That is, many companies can still get away with manually bidding on Google because of the slow rate of adoption. However, when the vast majority of Facebook campaigns are leveraging *Lowest Cost* or the other automated options, a campaign set to *Bid Cap* will certainly be left with the lowest quality auctions that your competitors couldn't be bothered with.

Target Cost is like Google's Target CPA, but less effective. It only evaluates a tight window of conversions that can be bought that are very similar to your defined cost.

As we discussed in Chapter 11, Google's Target CPA algorithm will look to spend your entire budget, so long as it averages to your defined Target CPA. If your Target CPA is $75, Google is willing to buy a conversion for $100, so long as it buys another for $50 within that same conversion window. Facebook's Target Cost algorithm, however, will only bid on auctions where it believes the actual CPA will be close to $75. It will, therefore, not attempt to buy a conversion for $100, but it will also ignore the conversion that will only cost $50.

Actual spend will vary, depending on how many auctions take place where the expected CPA is in your target range.

I tend to avoid Target Cost, as there are few business models that would benefit from this strategy. This bidding option became available several years ago, and Facebook has since introduced additional options that provide more practical value, including *Cost Cap.*

Cost Cap was introduced in 2018 and makes up for the flaws of its cousin, Target Cost. It is a unique bidding strategy that is more practical for many advertisers than the bidding solutions currently available on Google.

With Cost Cap, you can select the maximum that you're willing to pay to earn a conversion. It is imperative that you understand that this is different from Google's Target CPA option, where you select the *average* that you are willing to pay for a conversion. With Google's Target CPA solution, you might be buying conversions that are technically unprofitable, so long as the system is *also* buying low-cost conversions that allow you to back out at an average close to your target. That is not the case with Cost Cap. This strategy is not considering auctions that are likely to convert above your target.

Unlike Facebook's Target Cost, which will only consider auctions within a tight range of your target, Cost Cap evaluates a broad range of auctions and will first optimize for the lowest-cost conversions that can be bought. As the campaign paces throughout the lifetime of the budget parameters, the system will evaluate more expensive conversions up until it has reached your CPA cost cap.

From Facebook's support documentation:

Cost cap bid strategy allows you to provide us with the cost of the results you care about. This enables us to deliver the maximum number of conversions as we can. The cost you provide us is an average amount we try to stay under by going after the lowest cost events available. As you spend more or increase your budget, your average cost per optimization event might increase.

> We're more likely to go over your cost control during the learning phase. Keep in mind, your costs will stabilize overtime and stay within the cost control after exiting the learning phase.[62]

Cost Cap is a terrific solution for advertisers who have a clear profit margin on their conversions. If you earn $100 in profit per conversion, then a Cost Cap will allow you to buy any and all conversions that can be purchased between $0 and $99.99, allowing you to maximize both revenue and profitability.

Compare this to the many conversations I've had with clients about their ROAS goals or CPA targets. A client might have a 25 percent profit margin, meaning a 4x ROAS on their advertising is required to break even. However, this same client will come to us and say that they have a 10x ROAS goal. While I don't blame the client for wanting to earn a profit, this number is typically pulled out of thin air and not reflective of their actual goals.

Their *real* goal is to earn as much profitable revenue as possible. I will often respond to this situation by asking, "If we could spend $10,000 and earn a 10x ROAS, or $20,000 and earn a 6x ROAS, which would you prefer?"

Any respectable business owner or marketing objective would respond by choosing the latter, as this results in more net profit.

> **Scenario 1:** $10,000 in ad spend + 10x ROAS = $100,000 in revenue
>
> Profit = $22,500 (($100,000—$10,000) x .25)
>
> **Scenario 2:** $20,000 in ad spend + 6x ROAS = $120,000 in revenue
>
> Profit = $25,000 (($120,000—$20,000) x .25)

This client will often roll their eyes at this exercise. *Of course, we'd prefer that!*

But the fact of the matter is that this 10x ROAS goal is a farce, and not enough marketing agencies or client-side decision-makers are bringing this to light and addressing this head-on. In the same way that you should not train an algorithm to optimize with bad data, you should not direct your agency to meet an ROAS goal that might not result in the most amount of actual profit for your business!

I cannot overemphasize the importance of having clear, transparent, and realistic goals. It does no good to have a situation where you will be satisfied with results that come in below your goal. If you have a 25 percent profit margin, an arbitrary 10x ROAS goal, and your agency consistently drives a 9.5x ROAS, should you fire them? Probably not, but we have no way of knowing for sure because actual profit is not mentioned in that conversation.

This is all the say that Cost Cap bidding is a great way to bring these conversations to light. If your average order value is $200, and you have a 25 percent profit margin, then your break-even CPA is $50 and your break-even ROAS is 4x. What would be the ideal bidding strategy to drive profitable revenue?

With a traditional Target ROAS or Target CPA strategy, you could start with your arbitrary 10x ROAS goal and then make adjustments over time to maximize overall profit.

Or you could set a Cost Cap of $50 and trust the system to search for all the profitable conversions that could be bought within that range, allowing you to achieve this goal with much less tinkering.

Facebook currently offers two other bidding options: *Value Optimization with minimum ROAS*, and *Highest Value*, which will work the same way as Google's Target ROAS and Maximize Conversion Value options.

As features and settings, including bidding options, will continue to evolve over time across every ad platform, I would bet that Google introduces a bid strategy similar to *Cost Cap* within the next two years, although it will likely be under the guise of a different name—*Margin Bidding*, perhaps. My goal is that, after reading this book, you will hear of this new bidding strategy and quickly think: *Oh, that's just Cost Cap, but for Google.*

This is the sort of thinking that will determine your own success in the age of automation. It's imperative that you have a deep understanding of the technology that drives your campaigns today so that you can easily adapt to the changes to the technology that will take place tomorrow.

Final Thoughts on Facebook Advertising

Don't get cute. At its core, the Facebook Ads management platform is simple. Too many marketers have made it seem more complicated for the sake of impressing their clients. In the last two years, I have not come across a single account that did not benefit from the basic implementation of these best practices. Facebook's automation is powerful and reliable, but you must be creative in the actions that you take to train Facebook's algorithms to reach your actual business goals. If your goal is conversion oriented, then you shouldn't be keeping that a secret from Facebook. Select *conversions* as your campaign objective, structure your campaign according to the most recent set of best practices, and then focus on testing things that actually matter.

The most underappreciated aspect of Facebook advertising is its measurement capabilities, which can be unlocked through the Facebook Analytics tool and the Experiment tab. See Facebook's robust online training library for more information on these products.[63]

The Breakdown Effect is the single most important takeaway from our experience with Facebook advertising, and it is the primary reason so many Facebook advertisers fail to achieve profitable growth over the long term.

Lastly, *liquidity* is the reason why Campaign Budget Optimization and Automatic Placements are essential aspects of your Facebook strategy.

Facebook Advertising Case Study

Overview

MyWallSt is a fintech / SaaS company with the goal of educating their community on investing principles and sharing insights on their set of hand-picked stocks. The MyWallSt app is a hub of educational content, investment analysis, market updates, and stock picks of the month. It even allows users to invest through the app by connecting their brokerage accounts.

A subscription to MyWallSt allows access to the top 1 percent of investment opportunities that are handpicked by the MyWallSt analyst team and consistently outpace the S&P 500 by more than 50 percent. MyWallSt proves that investing is for everyone, and they will show you how to succeed.

Challenges

Fintech is a competitive industry. MyWallSt is a unique platform that offers content and analysis, thus competing with players like The Motley Fool, but it is also an investing tool, pitting them against the likes of Robinhood and E*trade. Our advertising efforts needed to clearly and effectively articulate the value of MyWallSt to prospective customers in this busy, competitive market.

Embracing a rebrand, MyWallSt was originally founded in 2008 as Rubicoin, but they revamped their brand image in 2019. Every rebrand comes with a unique set of challenges that impact short-term advertising performance. The rebrand also came with changes made to the overall conversion process. We had to recreate every conversion action to ensure we were tracking properly and redefine our target audience to match up with the new brand strategy.

App retention rates are difficult to control when judging performance using app installs. Although we saw a significant amount of app installs, the quality of the install was lacking. The overall conversion rate from download to customer was low.

Strategies

Evolving Goals

When our partnership began, our goal was to drastically increase the number of users on the MyWallSt app, as was the goal they carried over from their previous agency relationship. The bulk of our ad spend was dedicated toward Facebook App Install campaigns, as we felt that was the best channel to drive low-cost app installs.

At the time, our goal was to increase the total amount of app installs given a break-even cost-per-install. The MyWallSt team had determined this cost-per-install based on their average back-end conversion rates.

We achieved those results almost instantly, but over time we realized that very few of these app installs were translating into paying customers. The low install-to-customer conversion rate was just as much our responsibility as it was the client's. We set out to help them improve the app and the conversion funnel within it, but we also knew that our strategy needed to be reworked to help increase back-end conversion rate.

While our original strategy was effective in driving low-cost app installs, it was possible that this strategy was acquiring the wrong kinds of app installs, even if they were acquired at low-cost. We eventually would conclude that cost-per-install was not a metric we should be optimizing for—nor should it be a KPI that we use to evaluate performance. The only KPI that we should focus on is cost per acquired customer.

Technical Adjustments

We implemented a new strategy to be more segmented to our highest quality audience. For example, instead of targeting a lookalike audience of all previous app openers, we created lookalike audiences of the top 1 percent of past purchasers. We wanted to train Facebook's algorithms to understand which of our users not only opened the app but also purchased a premium subscription.

In order to avoid the issue of customer retention, we changed our goals in both Facebook and Google Ads to focus on users who start their trial as opposed to only app installs. This change helped to increase retention rates and generated a significantly better cost-per-start trial than our app install campaigns!

We opted into Facebook's best practices to ensure our campaigns stay efficient, scalable, and are set up for long term success. We heavily invested in video content, creating two versions of our explainer video, one at 30s in length and one at 15s, in order to show on both Facebook and Instagram placements. As a result, video significantly outperformed still images on Facebook. Campaign budget optimization and automatic placements are among Facebook's best practices that have allowed us to expand our reach and increase algorithmic learnings by showing ads to an audience we did not previously identify as our target market.

Creative Overhaul

The previous creative strategy focused heavily on highlighting the individual companies that were included as part of the MyWallSt short list of valuable stock picks, with the goal of showing that MyWallSt was a place to invest in and to stay informed with news surrounding these companies. We later concluded that this strategy was appealing to the wrong audience. These ads were great at driving app installs, but they did not appeal to the savvy investors who would ultimately derive the most amount of value on the app.

We also created a fifteen-second version of the video in order to opt into Instagram placements, which ultimately increased our total amount of free trial signups.

Expanding Reach

By successfully leveraging automation across the Facebook and Google Ads networks, we were able to expand our reach to more potential subscribers. When we began our partnership with MyWallSt, it was believed that the ideal target customers were made up of middle-aged, first-time investors. Through proper implementation of automation and automatic placements, we were able to profitably expand beyond this limited market and acquire customers from different backgrounds. Today, our ad campaigns successfully target investors of all ages and levels of experience.

Results

Better understanding of goals, attribution, and return on ad spend

244 percent Increase in Free Trial Signups
45 percent Increase in New Customers
79 percent Increase in New iOS Subscribers
264 percent Increase in Profitable Average Monthly Ad Spend

17 Advanced Conversion Tracking

Traditional PPC managers often view conversion tracking as an item to check off their to-do list when launching a new client account. The modern PPC manager must take a different approach.

We spend a great deal of time discussing conversion tracking as we think about unique ways to collect and manipulate conversion data to meet our goals. Your conversion data, after all, is the most valuable bit of information that you can feed into a machine learning algorithm.

In Section 1, we discussed how no two users are the same, even if they perform the same search for the same keyword on Google. It is required that marketers seeking to remain relevant understand this basic principle.

As we prepare ourselves for Automation 2.0, the era in which marketers will finally have a sophisticated understanding of machine learning and begin to find creative ways to train algorithms to meet their goals, we must review more fundamental principles:

- Not all conversions are created equal
- Not all leads are created equal
- Not all customers, even if they purchased the exact same item on the exact same day, are created equal

You and I know these principles to be true, but the algorithms in the driver's seat of our digital ad campaigns do not. That is unless we specifically program them to learn about this information.

I have seen too many accounts where multiple conversion actions are set up—actions which have different values to the business but are given equal weight in the *conversion's column.* Novice account managers will track both purchase and email newsletter signup as conversion actions, then assume that the machine is smart enough to realize that purchases are more valuable to the business. This is a disastrous mistake.

Algorithms are brilliant machines and big dumb idiots at the same time. There are many ways in which you can train your algorithm to better understand your goals, and you should always start with the conversion data that you are feeding it.

Conversion Data: An Algorithm's Primary Diet

Let's look at the fictional performance of an online furniture store that offers everything from bedroom sets to living room and outdoor furniture. To radically simplify the example, let's assume that everything in the store costs $100. A bed frame costs $100, as does a dining room table, and each individual dining room chair that you might purchase.

Here's a look at the shopping cart for two different customers who completed checkout on the same day:

- Customer A:
    - 1 Bed Frame ($100)
    - 1 Sofa ($100)
    - Cart Total: $200
- Customer B:
    - 1 Dining Room Table ($100)
    - 4 Dining Room Chairs ($400)
    - Cart Total: $500

Based on traditional conversion tracking standards, we would conclude that Customer B is much more valuable than Customer A, given the fact that their AOV was 2.5x that of Customer A.

Your algorithm will see this data and believe that as well. Over time, the algorithm will favor customers who it perceives are shopping for dining sets, compared to those shopping for bedroom or living room furniture. Within a year, you'll notice that 80 percent of your sales are acquired through paid advertising for dining room sets, and you'll pivot altogether to exclusively selling those products.

Seems like a great story, right?

Before we make any crazy decisions, let's take a step back, think about our customers, and come up with a few hypotheses about who they might be and why they're shopping with us.

Is it possible, for example, that first-time customers who buy a bed frame and a sofa in the same session are likely furnishing a new home and therefore are likely to need additional items on a recurring basis over the next few months?

After brainstorming a few hypotheses, you dig into the CRM data to find that 50 percent of customers whose first purchase included a bed and a sofa returned to the site to order at least $500 worth of additional products over the next 18 months. Whereas no other product combinations, including dining room sets, showed any significant correlation between repeat buyer behavior.

That's incredible! We've discovered that Customer A is, in fact, much more valuable than Customer B!

The question becomes: *how do we alter our strategy to account for this golden nugget of information?* Unfortunately, you cannot just assume that Google's algorithms will pick up on this because most of these subsequent purchases will take place long after the thirty-day conversion window has expired. The best solution includes altering your conversion tracking. This would allow you to optimize for your highest value customers without overhauling your Google Ads account structure.

To determine the nuances of your conversion tracking strategy, you need to first calculate lifetime value, given certain parameters.

Calculating Expected Lifetime Value

In our example, we found that 50 percent of customers who first purchased a bed and a sofa, amounting to $200 in revenue, came back and purchased an additional $500 worth of products. Therefore, for these customers, total lifetime value (LTV) comes to $700.

However, be careful before you assume that *all customers* who purchase a bed and sofa have an expected lifetime value of $700. The data showed that this was only true for 50 percent of that population. After we'd adjusted our calculations, we determined that LTV for *bed and sofa customers* is $450 ($200 + ($500 x 50 percent)).

In order to alter our conversion tracking to reflect this data, we'd simply map out the logic and code this into the backend of the site.

As a customer checks out on the site, the conversion tracking code will have to run a series of if/else statements, including "If cart includes *bed frame* AND *sofa,* THEN increase Google Ads conversion value by 125 percent."

($200 + 125 percent = $450)

This is a simplified version of what would be sent to a developer. The point is that this is both possible and highly valuable. Your algorithms will now be set up to understand the true value of these customers, and even a slight adjustment in strategy could yield massive benefits over the long term.

On the flip side, your reporting is going to have to change, as the values that you see in the *Conversion Value* and *ROAS* columns are going to be inflated, not reflective of actual revenue earned over that period. You will have to figure out a new reporting solution—using Salesforce, Shopify, or even just Google Analytics. But there are much worse problems to have.

I want to emphasize this last point: you should never let reporting guide strategy or account-structure decisions. *Performance* should be the only consideration involved in these decisions. This seems obvious, but it needs to be said. We've received a lot of marching orders from clients regarding campaign structure because the client *likes to see the data a certain way*. This is a slippery slope and should be avoided at all costs.

Selective Optimization

When you have multiple conversion actions in your Google Ads account, you will need to be mindful of which campaigns are *optimizing* for which conversion actions.

Selective Optimization is a new feature that allows you to handpick individual conversion actions for each campaign to optimize. Perhaps I would have wanted a Display campaign to optimize for email signups and sales, but I *only* want my BOF search campaigns to optimize toward sales. In this case, I would adjust the settings at the campaign level. Selective Optimization is one of the most powerful tools at your fingertips.

Advanced Conversion Tracking for Lead Gen

If your business relies on lead generation (phone calls, form submissions, chat features) and you don't have a single, legitimate CRM that automatically creates new contact records and is a central database of all of your sales activity, then you should not be investing a penny into online advertising.

If you have a CRM but have not yet taken the time to integrate a complete feedback loop with your Google Ads account (where a GCLID is captured through a form or phone call, and then offline conversion data is sent back into Google and automatically attributed back to the ad click), then you should *not* be using automated bidding.

I'm serious about this. Stop what you are doing and make sure that you are meeting these criteria. If you are not, then these two tasks should jump to the top of your priority list.

Optimizing for *lead* or *phone call* will not cut it in the age of automation. You need to train your algorithm to optimize for quality leads and closed deals.

In the pre-automation era, every phone call with a lead gen client started the same way:

> *Hey Veronica, how are you? In the account, we're seeing that total leads are up 15 percent, and CPA is down 10 percent compared to last month, but what are you seeing on your end? Are these quality leads? Have any of them closed into deals?*

I used to have bi-weekly calls with one enterprise SaaS client, where we would go day-by-day to discuss the leads, and they would tell me if they were good or bad. We only generated a handful of leads per day, so I would then have to go back into the account and use my best guess to determine if the lead attributed to *Keyword A* was the good lead or the bad lead. This is a terrible use of time and an ineffective way to train an algorithm.

In the automation age, you want your algorithms to receive real-time feedback about leads that turn out to be quality and ultimately close into customers. This, of course, will rely on your sales team to update the CRM contact records as they nurture leads throughout the sales process.

Form Submissions

For a lead that comes through as a form submission on your site, you'll need to edit your forms to include a *hidden field* that captures the Google Click ID (GCLID) and assigns it to the new contact record for this lead. Most CRMs will have a pre-built field for GCLID, but if not, create a custom column and map this field to that column.

As a reminder, each time a user clicks on an ad, a unique Google Click ID is assigned and carried through as part of the URL string.

The URL will include a lot of information, and all of the customized UTM (urchin traffic monitor) data comes after the question mark. For example, an ad click that brings me to *www.mysite.com* might append the URL to look like:

www.mysite.com?utm_source=google&utm_medium=cpc&gclid=CjwKCAjwss

When a user fills out the form, the form will pull the GCLID information from the URL (or from a cookie that your developer will have to install to preserve this information) and then pull it through the form along with the rest of the contact information.

Phone Call Conversions

Solutions like *Callrail*, *Invoca*, and *Call Tracking Metrics* allow you to process GCLID data that results in phone calls. These tools create unique forwarding numbers that carry through the contact record and ultimately make it possible for Google to understand which ad clicks resulted in which phone calls.

I personally prefer Callrail, as I've found the implementation to be rather simple and the support to be fantastic. Call Tracking Metrics is a close second, and Invoca is useful if you have a complicated sales process and expect high call volumes.

On the client side, you need to ensure that the sales team is practicing good *data integrity* and updating contact records as they navigate through the sales process. This goes for both phone calls and form submissions, as this process will break down if your sales team waits until the end of the month to go through the CRM and update deals that may have closed three weeks ago.

Optimizing for Better-Quality Leads

Once you integrate Google Ads with your CRM system, you can create multiple conversion actions for each step of the sales process. Salesforce refers to each *step* as a *milestone*.

For example, let's say your sales process follows four steps:

1. A user submits a form on the website and officially becomes a lead.

2. A salesperson evaluates the basic information and determines whether the lead is qualified. If yes, they are considered a *Marketing Qualified Lead* (MQL).

3. A salesperson reaches out and has a conversation with the lead. The salesperson then deems the lead to be *Sales Qualified* (SQL), and is therefore worthy of proposal.

4. A proposal is sent out and signed by the lead. They are now a customer and have now reached the *Closed/Won* stage of the deal process.

In this case, you would create a unique conversion action for each milestone: *Lead, MQL, SQL,* and *Closed/Won.*

Based on your new knowledge of Google's bidding algorithms (outlined in Chapters 11 and 12), you now understand how these algorithms would learn about lead quality over time.

For example, the Maximize Conversions algorithm is looking to buy as many conversions with your given budget. Over time, the algorithm will learn about auctions that resulted in multiple conversions and place more value on similar auctions.

The algorithm will think: *I can earn as many as FOUR conversions with just this one ad click?? OK!*

Based on our newfound knowledge of premium auctions, we can see that the algorithm will eventually realize that it can afford to pay up to 4x for a click on an ad that is likely to result in a closed deal because it will generate four conversions compared to an ad click that is going to result in form submission and nothing else.

Target CPA will work in a similar way. Each milestone in the sales process will increase the denominator in the Cost/Conversion calculation, therefore teaching the algorithm to favor more valuable auctions.

Theoretically, you could begin to use Target ROAS or Maximize Conversion Value by increasing the value of each conversion action (Lead Gen companies rarely get to take advantage of these bidding options). The value can be completely arbitrary.

For example, you could set up your conversion actions to include the following values:

- Lead: $100 in value
- MQL: $200 in value
- SQL: $500 in value
- Closed/Won: $1000 in value

A Maximize Conversion Value algorithm will learn that a closed deal generates more revenue than a low-quality lead that will never be deemed as an MQL.

The key takeaway here is that a bidding algorithm doesn't understand *good lead* vs. *bad lead.* It understands outputs, like *conversion count* and *conversion value*, and can be trained to learn which actions will yield the highest returns for these goals.

Over time, if you have enough conversion value, you can test removing the lower-value conversion actions from your campaigns altogether. That is, if you use *selective optimization* and optimize for MQL, SQL, and Closed/Won conversion actions, you are effectively telling the algorithm to not waste any time bidding on auctions that will result in a lead and nothing else.

As a best practice, I would recommend implementing this in your display campaigns immediately, as display traffic is known to generate a ton of low-quality leads.

Conversion Tracking Best Practices

Import Option from Google Analytics

We see a lot of accounts that have chosen to import goal data from Google Analytics and count this as a conversion metric. In your Google Ads settings, the source should be listed as *Analytics* and, at least for ecommerce accounts, the conversion action name might be *Transactions (All Website Data).*

Do not rely on this option.

Set up new conversions within the Google Ads dashboard and use this conversion action instead. When you choose to import from Google Analytics, you will only be receiving conversion data from conversions whose last click *was a* Google Ads interaction. Google Analytics uses last-click attribution, and this option will only import goals that are attributed to Google Ads inside the default Google Analytics settings.

If a user clicks on a Google Ad, then returns to the site directly on a second visit and converts on that session, Google Analytics will report that as a *direct* conversion (last-click), and there will be no data for you to import into Google Ads.

This is no way to train an algorithm. Instead, the Google Ads conversion tracking options use a conversion window, ensuring that your conversion data will be sent back into Google Ads so long as the user converts within your predetermined window.

Button-Click Conversions

The traditional method of tracking conversions is to fire a conversion code when a user reaches a *thank you* page. You'd set the conversion action to fire as the page loads, knowing that a user can only reach a *thank you* page after a successful conversion.

This becomes an issue if your site does not redirect users to a thank you page and instead just processes the form and sends a "*Thank You!*"

prompt back to the user, without redirecting them away from the original page.

You might be tempted to take the lazy way out and program the conversion action to fire when the CTA button is clicked. Don't do this. A button click does not guarantee a successful conversion, and your conversion numbers are guaranteed to be inaccurate. That's an extremely dangerous way to train your algorithm.

Instead, you should have to have your developer program the button function to fire an event when a successful submission comes through. Then you will use this new event as your conversion action trigger.

Never take the easy way out. This is the diet that will keep your algorithms healthy and productive. It should be your top priority in all cases.

Final Thought on Conversion Tracking

I strongly recommend that all PPC managers learn JavaScript, which you can do for free at codecademy.com. I also recommend you become proficient with Google Tag Manager. Julian Juenemann, of Measureschool.com, has a ton of free GTM content on YouTube. We often refer to him as *King Julian* around the office, as his videos have helped us through many frustrating conversion issues over the years.

In the age of automation, you will need to be fluent in this language. You don't need to reach the level where you can program these advanced codes yourself, but you will need to be able to speak confidently with the developers who will be doing this programming for you. Most developers do not have a background in marketing and PPC, so you need to take initiative in your own education so that you can reach common ground.

A better understanding of JavaScript will also allow you to brainstorm creative solutions to conversion tracking issues. For example, if you had no idea what a dataLayer is, you would never have reached the outcome outlined in the following case study.

Case Study: Advanced Conversion Tracking

Overview

Exotic Nutrition is an online pet food company that sells over 200 products for pets. They are a family run and owned business that has grown to sell on various platforms and now has its own warehouse production space. Our team manages their digital advertising across multiple platforms, aiming to profitably scale ecommerce revenue.

Challenges

The Exotic Nutrition storefront features a multitude of products, with wide price and profit margins. Without baseline expectations regarding average profit margins or return on ad spend targets, profitably scaling revenue over the course of a large product catalog becomes increasingly difficult. In addition to the goals of our specific ad campaigns, we needed to help the client better understand their internal financials as they grew.

What's more, if we had access to better data regarding actual profits, we could improve the efficacy of the machine learning algorithms that drive the PPC campaigns.

Strategy

A standard ecommerce client tracks revenue as one of its main financial objectives. Sales and top-line revenue typically become the primary conversion actions that drive most marketing efforts.

Unfortunately, traditional conversion tracking methods often obfuscate the bottom-line profit that clients earn as a result of their campaigns.

Let's look at an example:

In Case A, ABC Corp spends $1,000 to produce $5,000 of revenue. In Case B, XYZ Corp spends $1,000 to produce $4,000 of revenue. It is possible that Case B made more profit than Case A. It all depends on the unique variables that contribute to each company's Cost of Goods Sold (COGS). If the COGS in Case A was $2,000 and the COGS in Case B was $1,000, Case B would have had $1,000 more profit than Case A!

As a result, many PPC accounts are optimizing for goals that are based on assumed averages and not on actual profit. At the end of the day, top-line revenue does not pay the bills—profit does.

To solve this issue, we worked with an external development team to create a custom dataLayer variable that calculated the profit margins for each individual product, then pulled this variable through the checkout experience and calculated the sum total of profit on the order confirmation page. We then created a new Google Ads conversion action that pulled profit as the value variable, as opposed to revenue.

The last piece of this puzzle was to implement ongoing quality assurance with the client's internal team to ensure that the profit values were correctly entered into the backend of the website. It is integral that those numbers are accurate as they are now being used to send conversion values back to Google.

After many rounds of edits and dozens of tests, we confirmed that we were accurately calculating profit totals and plugging these numbers back into the Google Ads platform.

We were now reporting on the amount of profit earned as a result of our campaigns, but that wasn't our only goal. We wanted to train Google's algorithms to specifically optimize for earned profit.

As we switched to optimizing for profit, which would replace total revenue in the Conversion Value column, nuanced campaign segmentation became less important. We had previously been required to separate our campaigns based on individual ROAS goals, depending on individual product margins. Now that the dataLayer variable was automatically adjusting for profitability differences on the back-end, we only needed to ensure that nominal ROAS in the Google Ads account exceeded 1.00.

This allowed us to consolidate our campaigns, increasing the ability for the machine learning to capitalize on ad auctions that would yield the highest return.

Results

We finally established a baseline of profitability that the account had earned. After implementing new strategies that specifically optimized for profit, overall bottom-line earned profit increased by 62 percent, relative to the benchmark, in just three months.

Thanks to these efficiencies gained, those profits could be reinvested in scaling revenue. During the same period, we increased top-line revenue by 49 percent.

Topline ROAS also saw an increase of 18 percent over this period, but what's more important is that actual profit on ad spend increased by a far greater number. If not for the true understanding of profitability in the account, we could never have confidently invested in growing overall revenues by such a large percentage.

How to Train Your Algorithm

18

A powerful and productive learner requires two things: quality data and the time to acquire said data.

Unfortunately, many businesses lack one or both.

Data—I've seen large enterprises that lack the most elementary requirements of conversion tracking, customer records, and CRM integrations. I've also worked with executives at ecommerce companies who do not understand their own profit margins and sales executives who cannot even *ballpark* an average close rate or AOV. When a company's leadership lacks this information, it's almost guaranteed that their algorithms, which are deciding how and where to spend their advertising dollars, are operating with incomplete datasets.

If you fall into this category, you can find comfort in the fact that you are not alone. When we bring on a new client, part of our process includes setting a roadmap toward data utopia and outlining all the steps that we will need to take, often over the course of several months, to get those integrations and feedback loops in place. This often requires complicated development processes and forcing stubborn salespeople to adapt new habits. It's generally not something that can be changed overnight.

Time—An algorithm doesn't need time to learn in the way a human might. Rather, data collected as a result of advertising investments generally take an ample amount of time. *How much time* is the million dollar question.

It depends.

As PPC managers, we need to balance two conflicting realities—our algorithms need time (which is directly correlated with an increase in advertising investment), but we also need to ensure that our clients don't go out of business while waiting for an algorithm to learn.

This is one of the areas that causes friction between the advertising platforms and the advertisers that invest in these platforms. Advertisers hate being told by Google that they need to increase their budgets or wait another month before assessing performance, especially when they are tight on cash flow.

How do you strike a balance? You can start by controlling the data inputs.

When discussing account structure in Chapter 13, I discussed the role that negative keywords play in the modern Google Ads ecosystem. In the long term, having fewer negative keywords (restrictions) will allow the system to truly learn more about what drives performance in your account.

You are teaching the algorithm to fish, as the cliché goes. However, in the short term, negative keywords can reduce the amount of testing (and time) required to develop *confidence*. But again, confidence does not equal accuracy; more data will help close this gap.

There are infinite ways in which you can control your algorithmic inputs, and you should start thinking about this now, as negative keywords won't be around forever.

For example, next time you are about to launch a Facebook Ad campaign, ask yourself the following question: Instead of targeting a 1 percent Lookalike Audience of our previous customers, would we be better off if we *only* pulled a list of our *most valuable customers* and used *that* list to generate a 1 percent Lookalike Audience?

Yes, you probably would be better off. If you pulled a list of the top 20 percent of customers in terms of lifetime value, you are training the algorithm to search for signals that are specifically present within that sample.

Survivorship Bias

During WWII, a group of data scientists was given an important task: figure out why so many Allied planes were shot down over enemy territory.

The task force set out to assess damage done to aircraft that had returned from bombing missions. They would analyze trends in the data and then compile recommendations for improving the aircrafts with additional armor.

The data was represented by a diagram of an aircraft, highlighting areas that had received the highest concentration of damage. The diagram showed that the most amount of damage was collected in the wings, around the tail gunner, and down the center of the body of the planes. As per their recommendations, the Navy began increasing the amount of armor in these three regions.

Unfortunately, this did nothing to improve the survival rate of bomber crews. In many cases, the additional armor slowed down planes, making them more susceptible targets.

Andrew Wald, a statistician and member of Columbia University's Statistical Research Group (SRG), was brought on the case and almost immediately realized the error—the recommendations were made based on an incomplete data set.

The planes that were returning home safely weren't the problem. They should have been studying the planes that *did not* return from battle!

Of course, they didn't have access to this data, but they could make some insights based on what they had in front of them. After taking a closer look at the diagram, it became clear that there was one area of the plane that accumulated very few, if any, little red dots—*the engine.*

Wald's recommendations would save the lives of thousands of Allied soldiers. His work would lay the foundation for what is now known as **Survivorship Bias**: a logical error in statistics that occurs as a result of concentrating on data that passed some selection process and overlooks other data that did not.

The Allied statisticians were focusing on the planes that survived when they should have been focusing on the planes that didn't. Marketers fall victim to survivorship bias every day, but the survivors aren't heroes returning from war—they are your customers.

Many of us are guilty of letting existing customers skew our perception of our target market, when we should be focusing on those individuals who *could have become customers* if they hadn't been shot down over competitive territory.

Say, you have an ecommerce store specializing in tools and other hardware. You view yourself as a B2B company with a target customer base of auto mechanics and midsize construction companies. Sure, there is nothing that would stop my father from going to your site and buying a new hammer, but he's not really your target customer, and your marketing efforts should never be built on the premise that your products are for everybody. Instead, there is a specific niche that you are in business to serve, and you should tailor your marketing efforts accordingly.

We have a client who was facing this exact issue, and their previous PPC manager was failing to profitably scale revenue because they fell victim to survivorship bias.

When sifting through the search term report, we found that nearly 50 percent of historical sales came from broad searches, such as *tools*. It didn't even matter that this search term had converted at a profitable ROAS; these were not the kinds of searches that were being performed by auto mechanics or managers of midsize construction companies.

This became apparent after digging through their attribution reports. Their Time Lag and Path Length reports showed that 85 percent of their customers had completed checkout within the first day of visiting the site. Few customers had visited the site multiple times before converting.

You might think that this is great news. A proud marketing manager would likely brag to his CEO that their website was set up to convert customers on their very first visit, and they shouldn't waste money on remarketing!

But does that really make sense? If you've worked on as many accounts as we have over the years, you would understand that this doesn't pass the *smell test*. A B2B ecommerce store selling high ticket items should have a significant Time Lag. These products are not bought impulsively and often require careful consideration before a customer reaches a final purchase decision. The best customers are likely to be considering multiple suppliers, and they should require a bit of courtship, through remarketing, to convince them to choose us.

It's more likely that the lack of remarketing efforts, among other failures in the previous strategy, has been prohibiting their chances of appealing to users who would have converted on subsequent visits. It became clear that the account was set up in a way that neglected their core audience. It was sheer luck that they managed to convert other types of customers, as small as that population may have been.

It's crucial to keep in mind that the sample of data that makes up these attribution reports is exclusive to customers who have converted. These are the planes that returned from battle, despite having taken on some fire, in the way of an imperfect shopping experience. It is extremely likely that, by ignoring the realities of your core target audience's buyer journey, you are allowing potential customers to fall into the hands of your competition.

Being Honest

Throughout all business practices, it's imperative that you be honest with yourself about who you are and what customers you serve. The practice of **brand marketing** is to establish these inner principles. Then to use your marketing messages to train the public to connect these principles with your company name, logo, and products. The best brands realize that they do not exist to serve everybody. Their brand marketing help train the public to understand the principles and characteristics that make them unique.

This also applies to training your PPC algorithms. It would be nice to teach your algorithm to profitably market to everybody, but is that really necessary? If it was, you would need so much time and data to achieve that utopian milestone that you'd likely go out of business long before you got there.

There are four layers of audiences that will be exposed to your marketing:

- Yes/Yes
- Maybe/Yes
- Maybe/No
- No/No

The first, *Yes/Yes*, is the group that will automatically buy from you no matter what. These are the folks that don't really require much attention in your marketing efforts. On the other polar end are the *No/Nos*, the group that is never going to buy from you under any circumstances.

Your marketing efforts should therefore be focused on first converting the *Maybe/Yes* group, as this audience is on the fence but leaning toward *Yes*. As you scale, perhaps you can attempt to convert a portion of the *Maybe/No* group, but this is secondary.

You should be honest with yourself about who you are and what kinds of customers fit into these audiences. Then you should train your algorithms to think this way as well.

You also need to consider those that currently fit into the *Maybe/Yes* or even *Yes/Yes* audience today that aren't key to your business goals over the long term. If they don't, then it might be beneficial to train your algorithm to ignore them altogether, as Ray Kroc did throughout his tenure as the McDonald's CEO.

The McDonalds' Model

In 1954, Ray Kroc knew that the McDonald brothers had developed a game-changing model for running a restaurant. When Kroc opened the first McDonald's franchise location, he wasn't investing in the rights to produce hamburgers. He was investing the rights to produce hamburgers under the McDonald brothers' fast, efficient, and consistent model. He wasn't passionate about hamburgers; he was passionate about the opportunity to serve a market of customers who were desperate for fast and consistent food options, delivered under an efficient business model that could pass the savings back to the customer. He had identified the business model and his target market, and he was honest about it.

Kroc helped ensure that these principles were synonymous with the McDonald's brand. As he eventually bought out the McDonald brothers and began recruiting additional franchisees to open new locations, *consistency* became his top priority. He was even willing to sacrifice short-term revenue opportunities to protect these principles.

The 2016 Michael Keaton film, *The Founder,* depicts Kroc visiting his franchised McDonald's locations and finding them dirty, unkempt, or worse—offering food options that were not included under the original model. Kroc confronts the franchise owner and lambasts him for offering additional items including fried chicken and corn on the cob. The franchisee didn't see the big deal. People loved the fried chicken, and families have appreciated the additional options. The franchisee boasted about these options, stating proudly, "We want to have something for everybody!"

Kroc wouldn't have it. These new menu items put his entire model at risk.

The public's understanding of McDonald's true principles, neurotically protected by Ray Kroc, led to the restaurants long-term success. In the age of automation, you must train your algorithms in the same way that Kroc trained his franchise owners and the general public. Kroc's original model is what ultimately drove their success, and he protected the model by controlling the inputs.

Controlling the Inputs

To train an algorithm, you must think like an algorithm. If you wish to unlock the performance that can be achieved with a powerful master algorithm, you must start by accepting the flaws in the algorithms that you currently have in front of you.

Without good data, your algorithms are dumb. Without perspective, they are stubborn. A naive algorithm will fall victim to survivorship bias—as well as recency bias, confirmation bias, and any other bias that your Psych 100 professor warned you about.

PPC managers need to think proactively about the outcomes that could arise given their conversion inputs, especially as manual controls (negative keywords, search term data) will eventually be removed from the equation altogether.

One of our clients is a leading supplier of digital textbooks and offers more than 4M titles in their library. Their primary target audience is college students who are looking to save money on over-priced print textbooks. Customer LTV is massive, as students are generally happy with the digital textbooks and return to this platform each semester throughout their college career.

In addition to educational textbooks, this library also includes thousands of titles that are not exclusively consumed by our core audience of college students—James Patterson fiction novels, biographies of the British Royal Family, manuals on how to perfectly manicure your lawn—you name it. These titles contributed about 15 percent of annual revenue, and while expanding that audience might seem like a lucrative opportunity, this was no way to train an algorithm.

Instead of being distracted by random consumers downloading the latest Patterson novel, I would rather dedicate 100 percent of my budget toward our target audience. Therefore, it made the most sense to remove those titles from our Smart Shopping campaigns.

Ray Kroc's restaurants were known for consistent and convenient hamburgers. He wasn't interested in being the restaurant that catered to picky eaters who wanted a menu with many options.

In the age of automation, you need to consider the same tradeoff. It might occasionally be worth sacrificing short-term revenue for the sake of training your algorithms to succeed in the long term.

Automation Best Practices

Google will say that many of the suggestions outlined in this section go against their outlined best practices, and that is true. For example, Google would not advise that you shorten your conversion window, or upload an email list of *only* your top 20 percent of customers, or remove products from your shopping feed that might profitably convert. They will say, *the more data, the better,* and *the machine will learn what works best*! This is almost always the case.

You should follow best practices if you are new to digital advertising or have little experience with automation. If you stray from a best practice, do so with extreme caution. You should have a full understanding of the risks and potential outcomes of your automated campaigns. In support of that, your agency should have a way of logging aggressive tests, collaborating across multiple accounts, and ultimately creating a framework for solving complex and varied problems.

As I made clear in the book's introduction, this is not a *how-to* manual. There is no list of instructions that I can hand you that will guarantee campaign success. Rather, I hope that these last few chapters have been informative and help shape your perspective about the digital advertising landscape so that you can find creative solutions to your own complex problem sets.

Section 3

Agencies in the Age of Automation

"Managing an advertising agency isn't all beer and skittles. After fourteen years of it, I have come to the conclusion that the [agency leaders] have one principle responsibility: to provide an atmosphere in which creative mavericks can do useful work.

"In the advertising industry, to be successful you must, of necessity, accumulate a group of creative people. This probably means a fairly high percentage of high-strung, brilliant, eccentric nonconformists.

"Some of the mammoth agencies are now being managed by second-generation caretakers who have floated to the top of their organizations because they were smooth contact men. But courtiers cannot create potent campaigns. Our business needs massive transfusions of talent. And talent, I believe, is most likely to be found among nonconformists, dissenters, and rebels."

David Ogilvy

19

A Change in Culture

We've embraced automation. Now what?

As I wrote in Chapter 1: *Automation will change your job, but it will not replace you. In fact, there is more opportunity to provide value to your clients now than there has ever been before.*

The previous two sections included baseline knowledge that is necessary for developing strategy and setting campaigns up for success in a more automated world. While the breadth of information may seem overwhelming at first, it will eventually become second nature. Access to this information will help you change your way of thinking and your approach to complex problems. The tactics and considerations that I've outlined in the previous chapters are typically discussed and implemented within the first few weeks of client onboarding, after which, our team can dedicate more time to topics that will improve both campaign performance and our client's overall business in the long run.

Culture is what's keeping the broader PPC community from embracing this new way of thinking. Culture contributes to an atmosphere wherein people become comfortable with the status quo and fearful of technology's sweeping change. Culture allows us to cultivate bad habits, like optimizing for Quality Score instead of focusing on the actual business goals.

Culture is not something that can be easily changed. Every person in your organization needs to be bought into your vision, and you will likely need to change everything that you do. You will need to change how and whom you hire, how you structure teams, and how you manage workflows. You might even need to change the kinds of clients you endeavor to work with. Define the principles that will make up your new culture and refuse to make exceptions to those rules. If you do, your culture will suffer, and your team will feel that your vision was never genuine.

The Role of the Marketing Agency

Every agency leader that I've interviewed over the last year has mentioned that they see consultancy as the primary value that agencies will provide in coming years.

Frederick Vallaeys, CEO of Optmyzr (a leading PPC management software company) has added insight into what *consultancy* means for PPC agencies. In *Digital Marketing in an AI World,* Vallaeys describes three roles that PPC agencies fill: doctor, pilot, and teacher.[64]

The agency in the doctor roles diagnoses issues and *prescribes* automation-based strategies to their clients. The pilot will drive the automated systems, similar to a commercial airline pilot that primarily relies on auto-pilot to safely navigate throughout the skies. The teacher is less common but will become more valuable as the automation era unfolds. These agencies will take steps to *teach* the machine. A great teacher has a complete understanding of both the subject matter and their students; a teacher agency needs to understand both the client's business and the inner workings of the machine learning algorithm to properly guide the machine.

Many agencies are already serving in these roles, even though they or their clients might not realize it. Today, clients hire agencies so that they can leverage the agency's experience and collective resources to help them make decisions about how to drive profitable growth. They probably don't view them as consultants; they just want results, and they want to trust someone else to help them drive results.

In the early days, we used to charge clients on an *a la carte* basis. If a client wanted Google AdWords management, there was a specific fee for that. If they also wanted Facebook Ads management and conversion rate optimization, there would be separate fees for each of those services.

We eventually realized that this was a disjointed way to manage client relationships. In this scenario, we were putting the client in the driver's seat to determine whether they should be investing in a given digital advertising channel. Shouldn't *we* be the experts helping them make that decision? I was an account manager, but I felt like a salesperson, having to constantly prove the worth of every small detail that a client was being charged for.

What's more, in this scenario, I might be financially incentivized to keep additional services active *even if they are not in the best interest of the client!*

For example, if we were charging separate fees for Google and Facebook, but I knew that the client would be better off if they dedicated 100 percent of their budget toward Google, then I would either have to *lie* to the client or be honest and suggest that the client stop their Facebook campaigns, effectively reducing the amount of revenue that my agency could earn from that client.

If you ever find that your interests and your client's are not aligned, even in the smallest of circumstances, then you need to reevaluate your agreement. It would be more effective for the client to have an agency that they could trust to manage their ad spend in a way that they believed would deliver the best results.

The PPC manager who embraces the role of consultant is the one with the freedom to make recommendations and guide strategy across a range of digital advertising channels, motivated by nothing but the best interests of the client.

When my industry colleagues refer to consultancy, they are discussing services that are less manual. Instead of doing manual labor, we use our experience to help determine more efficient, cost-effective, or productive solutions. For example, instead of manually doing keyword research, we train an algorithm to do that for us. Instead of manually running an A/B test on a landing page headline, we leverage a tool like Google Optimize to do that for us. Instead of attempting to sync up your Google campaigns with your CRM system, we'll hire an experienced Salesforce developer to do that for us.

Here's why: our primary value comes not from our ability to physically complete any of these tasks. It derives from our ability to stand back as architects of the entire process. To see the big picture as we manage all these projects at once.

This can only be achieved when you graduate from being a *marketer* to the role of *marketing leader.*

Marketing Leadership

Former McKinsey partner Thomas Barta and London School of Business professor Patrick Barwise believe that *doing* marketing is vastly different from *leading* marketing. In their book, *The 12 Powers of a Marketing Leader*, they claim that many marketers are great at *doing* marketing, but the majority are dissatisfied with their career paths.[65] Barta and Barwise's research suggests that marketers' relationships with their CEOs are mixed and concludes that too few CMOs ever make it to CEO level. This is because the skills required to become good at marketing often conflict or otherwise distract marketers from developing the skills that allow them to advance their careers.[66]

> *Leading* marketing isn't just about serving the customer. It's also about increasing and using your knowledge and marketing's influence inside the organization to improve the end-to-end customer experience. It's about mobilizing your boss [or your client], mobilizing your colleagues, your team, and yourself to maximize the overlap between customers' needs and the company's needs.[67]

They refer to the intersection between these two fields as *The V-Zone*, and they assert that a marketing leader not only has to exist in the V-Zone but also focus on activities that expand it.[68]

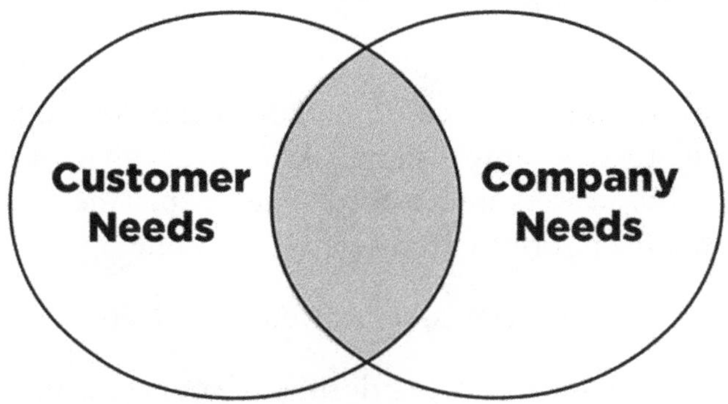

***Source*:** Thomas Barta and Patrick Barwise, *The 12 Powers of a Marketing Leader: How to Succeed by Building Customer and Company Value* (New York: McGraw-Hill, 2016).

This hypothesis led Barta and Barwise to conduct a comprehensive study of chief marketing officers, senior marketing executives, and their peers.

To become a marketing leader, you must find a way to mobilize various stakeholders throughout your organization. This includes your boss, your colleagues, your team, and yourself.

For an agency, the *boss* is often your client. The following three powers will help mobilize your boss and/or client.

- **Power #1: Tackle Only Big Issues**—Make sure that what you work on is inside the V-Zone: it matters for both customers *and* the company (as judged by the CEO). And put a price tag on your work, so people see why what you're doing matters.
- **Power #2: Deliver Returns, No Matter What**—Financial returns should be your priority. Being an effective investor will also help your standing at the top and, ultimately, make more resources available to you.

- **Power #3: Work Only with the Best**—Mobilizing your boss is easier if you work with the best external people who will deliver great work.[69]

In his book, Thomas Barta recalls a time when he provided a leadership workshop for senior marketers of a large U.S. financial institution. To kick things off, he asked the group a series of three questions. The answers are intended to help depict the Venn diagram and identify the priorities that fit into the V-Zone.

1. What are the main issues for your customers?
2. What are the top three priorities of your company, as seen by the CEO, and how does your marketing work overlap with these priorities?
3. For *your* top three marketing priorities, what's their value to the company?[70]

The first question typically energizes a room of marketers, as this is the kind of topic that this population loves to discuss. The second question, however, left many participants scratching their heads. Of those that did have answers, few of them were linked to any responses from the first question. The third question nearly brought the workshop to a screeching halt, as marketers often shy away from accountability and claim that the value of their work is difficult to quantify.[71]

This disjointed mindset will lose you your best clients. Stubborn marketers often lack empathy and fail to understand global business goals and priorities. It's imperative that you align with your clients to ensure that your priorities are consistent throughout their marketing department and top executive team.

20

Building AI-Driven Organizations

Jim Sterne, author of *Artificial Intelligence for Marketing,* spends much of his time helping midsized companies integrate machine learning into their company cultures.[72] Many CEOs or shareholders often assert that they *need more AI,* but few of them know why or what they really want. Some might want to reinvent themselves as an AI-driven company. Those organizations need to start from the top down, with a long-term horizon that will include hiring a team of in-house data scientists.

Other companies are hoping to use AI or machine learning to solve one question at a time. Perhaps they want to build a product-recommendation engine into their ecommerce site, or maybe they want to figure out how to effectively use automation in their digital advertising campaigns. Those organizations can build from the ground up and lean on outside vendors for implementation, strategy, and training.

Our agency currently works with many organizations that fit into this latter camp: eager to embrace automated technology into their culture but wanting to do so one step at a time. Even at the most basic level, an organization that is hoping to test the waters with automation-driven digital advertising campaigns still needs to have certain parameters in place if they wish to be successful. It is often our job to educate clients about what changes they need to make inside their organization to make any of this possible.

Take a SaaS company, for example. Their current marketing and sales process might include capturing leads from bottom-funnel search campaigns, then having a salesperson attempt to reach that lead by phone for an initial conversation. The salesperson would then schedule a product demo and send out a proposal, hoping to close that lead into a deal.

Clients in this camp often come to us without even having a proper CRM system in place. In this event, we'd make a recommendation about which CRM tool might be best for them and assist as their team gets used to the new software. Of those that come to us with a CRM in place, few have even the baseline integrations set up that will allow them to succeed with automation. This is generally where our automation journey begins: working to create a seamless feedback loop of offline conversion data from their CRM back into their Google Ads account.

The next step might include training their sales team to manually score leads on a 1–5 scale. This helps their sales team focus on better opportunities and adds an additional data point that can be used to train our bidding algorithms. Since salespeople are generally reluctant to change their processes, we might also suggest an AI-driven lead scoring solution to automate this process for them.

We might later decide that we want to give prospective customers multiple methods of conversion. This results in onboarding an automation-driven call center (with proper Google Ads data integration, of course) and an AI-enabled chatbot to embed on our landing pages. Then we'd begin exploring top-funnel content development and distribution efforts, all supported by artificial intelligence and machine learning technology. Each new step would require changes to the overall digital advertising strategy.

At the surface, our AI-adoption efforts are exclusive to the digital advertising campaigns. However, the impact creates a ripple effect throughout the company. In the next C-level meeting, the CMO would get to brag about all the innovative tech that the marketing department has adopted. Suddenly the CEO is putting pressure on the rest of the company to think like the CMO does! Within a year, this analog marketing team, and perhaps the entire company, could be completely transformed into an efficient, smart organization.

The Role of the Individual Marketer

In an interview with Sterne, he assured me that, even as automation changes the entire marketing landscape, marketers who don't necessarily come from a data science background can still be valuable.[73] However, a certain degree of *data literacy* is required at every level.[74] He believes that there are four main categories of roles in an automation-driven marketing environment: Business Stakeholders, Analysts, Data Scientists, and Data Engineers.[75]

The **Business Stakeholder** is the decision maker.[76] Speaking on behalf of an agency, this is generally the client. The decision maker will use their domain knowledge about their industry, product, customers, market, competition, and other variables to set top-level business goals, identify business problems, and make business decisions.

What we want, according to Sterne, is for the Business Stakeholders to make these decisions that have been informed by *Analyst Insight.*[77]

The **Analyst** sits in the middle. They must appreciate and understand the business goals that are set by the Business Stakeholder in order to create hypotheses to test.[78]

The Analyst will work with the **Data Scientist** to determine which data might be the most revealing, while accounting for cognitive and innate biases, in order to provide *sound advice* to the Business Stakeholder so that they can then make an informed decision. The Data Scientist will also package this sound advice in the form of data visualizations or other storytelling methods.[79]

The Analyst will be involved with the Business Stakeholder throughout the entire process but will depend on the Data Scientist to choose which methods to use to build models. The Data Scientist will depend on the **Data Engineer** to ensure that the data is trustworthy, valid, and high quality. The Data Engineer has the responsibility to design, build, and manage the data captured by the organization.[80]

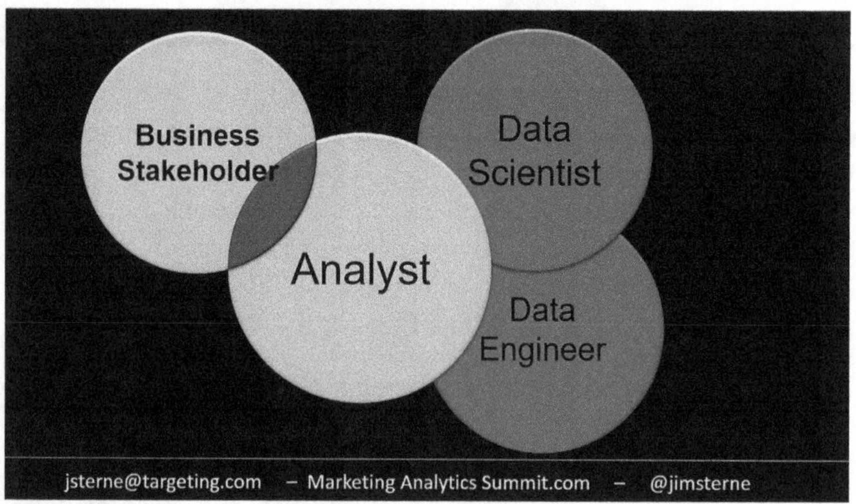

These categories can then be segmented into many specific roles. The Business Stakeholder might be the CEO, the VP of Supply Chain, or the Director of Ecommerce. A Data scientist can include a statistician who uses predictive models to gain insights or a machine learning scientist who develops algorithms.

There are roles that sit outside of these categories but are still crucial to an AI-driven organization. These roles include the Worker Bees, who carry out the remaining manual tasks: including tag implementation, reporting, and presentation development. They also include Managers, Project Managers, Implementation Directors, Planning Executives, Strategists, and Visionaries, all of whom must work together to move an organization forward.

Outside of all of this are the Creatives who handle the design of landing pages, display ads, videos, UX, and copywriting.

Are all these people marketers? Not always, but all of them are essential, in some capacity, to your marketing efforts in the age of automation.

Hiring an Agency vs. an In-House PPC manager

Sterne feels that, for most organizations, the roles of the Analyst, Data Scientist, and Data Engineer *should* be outsourced. During a presentation at the Digital Analytics Forum in 2018, Sterne said:

> If you are Microsoft, IBM, Apple, or Amazon, you should hire these people and compete at an *enormous* expense with your competitors [for that talent]. For the rest of us, these are great roles for outsourcing. If you can find companies that have data scientists and are building these systems: that's where you should go.
>
> You, [the Business Stakeholder], have the unique data set; *they* have the ability to put together the data scientists and the data engineers to help you get it done. So, buy vs. build? I say buy because *you can't afford a data scientist.*

In an *emetrics.org* article titled "The Consulting Pyramid," Stern elaborated on this point, but this time specifically referring to the value that Analysts provide when brought in from the outside:

> Because [Analysts] are not deeply rooted in the culture and history of [your] company, they are free to ask all of those elephant-in-the-room questions that a good, faithful employee has learned not to ask. They have experience from lots of different clients and, honeybee-like, can bring new and fresh ideas to bear on recalcitrant problems and intractable situations. I recommend bringing in outside analysts on a regular basis and benefiting from cross pollination.[81]

Agencies make great analysts. Those that wish to survive in the age of automation must either have their own data scientists and engineers in-house or a network of talent that can be tapped into to solve unique problems. Data literacy, at every level of the agency, is key.

If you are the Business Stakeholder, your goal is to find an agency that is trustworthy and can understand and appreciate your business goals. You need an agency that can develop creative hypotheses to solve your problems and manage the Data Scientists and Data Engineers who will do the rest of the work to solve those problems.

As a member of an agency, my opinion on this matter is obviously biased. However, if this book achieves nothing else, I hope that it helps prove the complexity of this industry. Those who are not entrenched in an environment in which they can constantly learn from highly talented people doing the same work, across multiple accounts and industries, are prone to become obsolete and ineffective within one cycle of *Moore's Law*.

Don't just take it from me: I have a colleague, Nicole, who left her job at a PPC agency to go client-side and manage campaigns in-house for a retail company. She loved it for a short while, but within a year felt that the industry was passing her by. She was not being challenged by the kinds of unique problems that result in learning opportunities, and she was not in an environment that relied on learning to stay relevant. After realizing that she was becoming bored and myopic in her optimizations, she knew that remaining at this company would be detrimental to her career growth.

Nicole has since moved to another company, where she is still client-side. However, her new role includes managing the relationship with their PPC agency. She relies on the agency for day-to-day management so she can focus on other marketing initiatives within her company. She leverages their expertise to help her stay up-to-date with the industry and new technology.

She has told me that the topic of bringing PPC management in-house has come up several times over the last year. The VP of marketing has outlined the short-term cost savings for the department and feels that, given her agency background, Nicole would be well-fit to manage that in-house team. However, she has made it clear that it would be a disastrous decision in the long term, as an in-house team will never be able to stay current and adapt to changes in the digital advertising landscape.

This is great news for agencies, if only more people thought the way Nicole does.

21 Building Your Team

> "The signature move of my career was hiring people who were smarter than me. To pull this off, you need to be humble and respectful. You need to be both a good manager and a leader… and you need to be willing to work harder than everyone else around you."
>
> - Rich Gilbert, Retail Technology Executive and Father

Every heist movie has a scene where the main characters introduce the rest of their eclectic squad. In one of the opening scenes of *Ocean's Eleven,* Reuben Tishkoff learns that Danny Ocean and Rusty Ryan intend to rob three Las Vegas Casinos and offers a bit of advice: He warns that they need to be careful, precise, and well-funded. "You gotta be *nuts* too. And you're gonna need a crew as *nuts* as you are!"

He then pauses and says, "So who've you got in mind?"

This is followed by a montage introduction of the characters who will fill out the rest of their team, each person bringing a specific set of skills to fill a crucial role. There's Frank Catton, the sweet-talking blackjack dealer; Virgil and Turk Malloy, the gearhead drivers; Livingston Dell, the reserved tech and electronics specialist; Basher Tarr, the playful and enthusiastic munitions expert; Linus Caldwell, the analytically-minded pickpocketer; and The Amazing Yen, an acrobatic *grease-man* who can stealthily navigate through a vault without tripping an alarm.

In these movies, the main character narrates this scene in a proud tone that reflects a kind of *you gotta see this person in action* attitude. What's most interesting is that there is not a hierarchy of skill or value. Each individual is both unique and essential. Each of them is the best at what they do. There is a shared respect throughout the entire group.

I'd have no issue writing this scene for a movie about our team. In fact, I dream about the opportunity to do so. Maybe I'll even start asking prospective hires: "In three sentences or less, how might Danny Ocean describe your skills and the value that you bring to our agency?"

Luca Senatore, founder of the UK-based agency Genie Goals and author of: *The Agency: Build, Grow, Repeat,* once told me that he doesn't hire to *fill positions*; he just hires *people.*[82] Once he finds the right people, it is his responsibility to define their role and set that person up for success. As he reflects on how his agency has grown and transitioned over the years, the path has been largely influenced by the people who make up his team.[83] All it takes is one new employee with a unique skill set or passion to be the catalyst for an entirely new business division that could exist five years from now.

When I first joined AdVenture Media Group, *content development* wasn't a part of my job description. But I enjoy it. I would probably do it for free, as a hobby, if I didn't have a role that allowed me to produce it in a professional setting. Isaac identified this early on and gave me the opportunity to explore this passion of mine, and the agency has benefitted from it.

Despite the fact that this is not a new concept, very few companies operate this way. In *Good to Great* (originally published in 2001), Jim Collins outlines the seven key characteristics that are required to take to help transition an average company into a great one. Of them, *First Who, Then What,* is the act of "getting the right people *on the bus,* and then figuring out where you are going."[84]

> You are a bus driver. The bus, your company, is at a standstill, and it's your job to get it going. You have to decide where you're going, how you're going to get there, and who's going with you.
>
> Most people assume that great bus drivers (read: business leaders) immediately start the journey by announcing to the people on the bus where they're going—by setting a new direction or by articulating a fresh corporate vision.
>
> In fact, leaders of companies that go from good to great start not with "where" but with "who." They start by getting the right people on the bus, the wrong people off the bus, and the right people in the right seats. And they stick with that discipline—first the people, then the direction—no matter how dire the circumstances.[85]

The process of getting the right people on, the wrong people off, and the right people in the right seats is key. You cannot afford to have people on the bus who will not find a way to succeed within your organization. What's more, if someone is a poor fit for your organization, it does not mean that they do not possess the ability to be *great* on their own accord. As a leader in your organization, you have a responsibility to each person you hire to help them succeed in their careers, and the reality is that some individuals will be more successful after moving on from your company than they would have been if you stuck them in a dead-end position. It is also your responsibility to ensure that these people can exit with grace and dignity so that the majority of people who have left your bus have positive feelings about your organization.

Regarding roles, it is crucial that you are cognizant of your individual team member's primary set of skills, as well as their passions. Find out what they are good at and what makes them tick. You should be interested in what they find fulfilling. What do they like most about their job? What do they investigate in their free time? What sort of tasks do they find so interesting that they would be willing to do them for *free*. Then pay them to do that.

Growth within your organization can come in a multitude of forms.

Career Growth: Management vs. Individual Contributor Roles

In *Lost and Founder,* Rand Fishkin describes a culture challenge that he experienced while growing his company, Moz: "In May 2012, Moz raised $18 million in a Series B round, and something strange happened: everyone suddenly wanted to be a manager."[86]

Moz needed to fill a large number of roles, and Fishkin recalls that, of Moz's existing forty-ish non-management employees at the time, at least twenty of them made requests to join the management ranks and start hiring their own subordinates.

He goes on to describe *The Peter Principle,* a concept originally developed by Laurence Peter and Raymond Hull in 1969, describing a paradox that exists within career development. The theory behind *The Peter Principle* is that employees are often judged for their next promotion based on their performance in their current role, rather than by their potential aptitude for the work required in a new position. As a result, employees advance to positions that they are not yet prepared to be in and the company grows rife with incompetence at senior levels.[87]

Many companies are structured in such a way that individuals can only advance their career if they take on a management role. However, few people would list common managerial tasks as things that they would do for *free.* Management is not what they are truly passionate about.

Fiskin writes that *management is a skill, not a prize.*[88] After this realization, he dedicated the next several years to building a culture at Moz in which career growth and success can be possible for both managers and *individual contributors,* based on the idea that management should not be the only ladder that you provide for your employees to climb.

Fishkin provides practical advice on this topic in an article titled, "If Management Is the Only Way Up, We're All F'd." The article is currently published on Sparktoro's blog (Fishkin's newest venture):

> Individual contributors have responsibility for themselves and their work. As they get more senior on an IC track, their influence becomes more wide ranging. A good example of this at Moz is someone like Dr. Pete, who recognizes strategic imperatives at the company and pitches in. He assists engineering and big data with reviews, assists marketing with tactical advice and strategic input, publishes incredibly high quality blog posts and guides, and even designs entire projects from the ground up and executes on their creation. His influence is company-wide, cross-team, and as senior as they come. He lets his influence define his role, rather than the other way around.
>
> On the flip side, great people wranglers are responsible for their team's happiness, cohesion, empowerment, reviews, mentoring, and more. The more senior they get, the less "in-the-trenches" they should be. Many times, they 018touch on strategy only to help define the strategic problems. These are then passed to ICs who help define scope, research possible answers, and execute on their implementation. A good example of this at Moz is Samantha Britney. She was an IC for a long time, but has moved into people wrangling, and today helps several ICs on the product team feel empowered about their work, get the tools/resources/help they need to do it well, and provides the mentoring/1:1s/reviews/HR functions a good people wrangler should. She's almost never in the gritty details of her reports but always there to help them drive their projects forward.
>
> Basically, if you love getting stuff done and doing a great job at it, you should be an IC. If you love empowering others and helping them grow and succeed (and you're great at it), you should be a people wrangler.[89]

A culture that allows individuals to perform the tasks that they are passionate about - and allowing for career growth - will result in higher quality work, better employee retention rates, and an improved overall environment.

Our Hiring Process

On a Sunday afternoon in March of 2019, I made my way through security at JFK's international terminal. Isaac and I were flying overnight to London, where I would be speaking at the Google Innovation Summit. As I gathered my belongings, I saw a text from Isaac: "I just got into an Uber." He was late. He's always late. Part of me thinks that he does it on purpose just to drive me nuts.

So, I grabbed a drink and opened my laptop, expecting to go over my presentation notes before boarding the plane. At the top of my inbox sat an email titled: "Recruiting (and other) Principles" that Isaac had sent roughly twenty-five minutes earlier. It was just shy of 9,000 words, which for perspective is much longer than any chapter in this book. It was a valid excuse for being late.

He arrived, panting, around the time I was lining up to board the plane and acted surprised when I told him I had not yet finished reading his novel of an email.

Until this point, we'd never really discussed a framework for making hiring decisions. Instead, we leaned on principles borrowed from Warren Buffett. It sounds silly, but this simple mentality helped us hire the first ten or so superstars who were essential in our growth.

The characteristics that Buffett looks for are *integrity*, *energy*, and *intelligence*.[90]

A strong candidate needs to embody all three of these qualities if they have a chance at succeeding. In fact, having just two out of three of these traits might be more dangerous than possessing none at all. According to Tom Searcy of Money Watch:

- **Low integrity**, high energy, and high intelligence and you have a smart, fast-moving thief.
- **Low energy**, high intelligence, and integrity and you have a shopkeeper, not an engine of growth.
- **Low intelligence**, high energy, and integrity and you have strong functionary, but not a great problem solver or visionary.[91]

The first of these examples is an actual threat to your organization. The second is a threat to your culture. The third is a threat to the progress you can make and the morale of your team.

It is useful to lean on these principles, particularly when you are hiring candidates who don't have specific experience in your field.

I would prefer to hire a candidate with exceptional levels of integrity, energy, and intelligence who has never managed an ad campaign over an experienced PPC manager with red flags in any of these categories. We've learned this the hard way.

We have reworked our hiring process several times over the last few years. Today, candidates start with an initial screening process and introductory call where we can evaluate them using the principles outlined above. If they pass this initial screener, we send them a project to work on and present to us in a second interview. We've compiled a vast number of topics for them to cover in this project, and we select the two or three that are most relevant.

We are on the lookout for a few things, mainly critical thinking and problem-solving skills. We are also analyzing organization skills, the ability to conduct research, communication skills, math proficiency, business acumen, and so on. All projects include a problem that needs to be resolved in Excel or on Google Sheets.

We approach our hiring process in a way that helps us diversify our skill sets, backgrounds, and personalities. As part of this, we ask candidates to complete a Myers-Briggs personality assessment. Of course, all of this should be taken with a grain of salt. It is dubious to assume that any one person would fit neatly into one of sixteen personality categories. However, as we have discussed, *all models are wrong, but some are helpful.*

Even after all of these steps, we often felt uncertain about whether or not to extend an offer. I would end up lying on a couch in Isaac's office, saying, "I don't know. They kind of remind me of *this person,* but different. What do you think?" Isaac would pace back and forth, twirling his hair, then suggest we think about it some more.

This model wasn't sustainable. We needed something better. Something as efficient as an algorithm.

A Model for Making Important Decisions

Isaac's 9,000-word email was the catalyst for dozens of conversations about our decision-making model. Below are some of the highlights that we've expanded upon to make decisions regarding hiring, investing in software, moving offices, and many other big bets that we have made since. This is the much-shortened version of the email that I first read while flying over the Atlantic Ocean, when I should have been catching up on sleep.

> After thinking about this for too many hours, I've developed a greater clarity into some of my own decision-making principles. It's important to me that you understand them, not for the sake of using them as a decision-making *rulebook*, but rather for the sake of using them as a decision-making *framework*.
>
> What follows is an attempt to explain a set overarching decision-making principles, specifically in regards to recruitment.
>
> **Make Bad Good Bets**
>
> With any decision, there's a virtually limitless number of potential permutations for how a decision can play out.
>
> It takes humility to say, "I don't know." And saying, "I don't know" *often*, is a core component in this set of principles.
>
> There are two specific reasons why I've let that principle guide my decision making, by and large, and one reason relates to the chance of failure, and one reason relates to the chance of success.
>
> 1. **(most) Failures are cauterized**
> 2. **(almost all) Successes have a positive, and completely unpredictable positive ripple effect**

I'll elaborate more on both of those ideas in a second, but there's a different idea / concept that comes before that.

Determined Optimism Is Not the Same as Irrational Impulsivity

From the outside looking in, determined optimism (choosing to believe, against the odds, in positive outcomes) can be easily confused for irrational impulsivity (and vice versa), because they can often *look the same.*

When someone makes a decision and the odds are stacked against them, it can be understood as the manifestation of an impulsive personality, or it can be the result of what I usually call "idiotic optimism," but I'll now refer to as "determined optimism," because I don't think it's idiotic at all.

Determined optimism is a psychological mindset, and it can only be manifested once potential positive outcomes have been determined to *at the very least, exist.* That's the important distinction.

Before choosing to believe in the positive outcomes, the potential *for a positive outcome must be at least reasonably established.*

Failures Are Cauterized while Successes Ripple Outward

I believe in determined optimism because failures are cauterized, while successes ripple outward indefinitely.

It's unlikely we'll ever hire anyone who could single-handedly destroy our company. Is it possible? I guess, in some sort of dystopian universe. But it's highly unlikely. It's highly unlikely that we'll ever hire anyone who will have a lasting, long-term negative impact on our company.

It's equally unlikely that any one bad decision, in any domain, will have a lasting, long-term negative effect on the company. None of the bad decisions that we have made over the last five years had long-term negative effects. Those wounds are cauterized.

Bad hires cost you a lot of time and a little bit of money, but those are contained things. The bleeding stops eventually.

Realizing that makes a failure so much more manageable. It also diminishes the natural *agita* associated with the fear of making a bad decision.

It's equally important to recognize the inverse impact of *successful* decisions.

When you make a good decision, the positive impact is almost always unpredictable, and it pays dividends in ways you couldn't have anticipated. Good decisions are the opposite of contained. They are living, breathing organisms, brimming with vitality, continuously generating more positive outcomes as time goes on.

That's what makes good decisions so exciting. They are filled with unexpected opportunity. This goes back to humility. It takes a massive helping of "I don't know" to open yourself up to the great possibilities that accompany good decisions.

I have always made decisions with the awareness that failures are cauterized while successes ripple outward. It's that very idea (the opposing natures of failures and successes) that validates the principle of determined optimism.

The reason I like taking "bad good bets" is because failure will cost relatively little while success will result in enormous good.

My recruiting decisions have been riddled with question marks, uncertainty, and more than reasonable expectations for failure. All those decisions *also* had a reasonable potential for success. When I make a decision to offer a candidate a job, I'm not making a statement that I'm confident the candidate will turn out to be a good hire. I have no idea if the candidate will turn out well or not. My only statement is that I've determined a reasonable

> potential for positive outcomes and that my nature is to wait and see how the story unfolds.
>
> But we're not done. It's one thing to have principles that help guide decision making, but you should also be learning from your mistakes.

Isaac went on to describe several principles that can be used to measure the impact of our decisions as well as learn from our mistakes and improve the overall decision-making algorithm. But I don't want to steal his thunder, nor do I intend to give away all our secrets. Every organization can embrace these principles with the unique set of successes, failures, and lessons that can be built into their own decision-making algorithm.

Embrace determined optimism and be willing to make bad good bets.

The P3X Framework: Systematizing Client Onboarding & Growth

Isaac and I began formulating a framework for making higher level strategic decisions. We soon realized that the entire organization would benefit from similar decision-making models.

As a result, we developed **The P3X Framework**, a model for ensuring the successful onboarding and growth of our clients. The etymology is based on the idea of using this framework to triple profit, as well as labeling the number of phases that make up the framework.*

The framework is broken down into several phases, which are further broken down into smaller stages. Each stage has its own set of questions that we ask ourselves, data that we consider, and deliverables that we use internally or send to our clients for additional collaboration and feedback.

The goal of the first phase is to immerse ourselves in our client's business, their industry, and the historic data available to us. This phase includes any *quick wins* or *Band-Aids* that we need to put in place to improve temporary results as we develop our long-term strategy.

* I largely credit my brilliant colleague, Nechama Tiegman, for spearheading the effort behind the P3X Framework. She worked on this exhaustively over several months, almost exclusively late at night after her children went to bed.

During the second phase, we collect answers and information from the data that we've sourced and use that knowledge to reevaluate client goals and outline the tactical elements of our advertising strategy.

The third phase is about testing, evaluating feedback loops, and brainstorming opportunities for growth.

The framework provides many benefits beyond a formalized process. It has allowed us to increase transparency with our clients and to manage expectations more effectively. For example, we have always charged a one-time setup fee with new clients to cover the additional expenses that we incur in the early stages of a relationship. Several years ago, the additional costs we incurred were related to the time spent building keyword lists, new campaigns, and other manual tasks that have since been largely replaced by automation. Today, that setup fee covers our expenses as we work with our marketing research partners, conduct comprehensive competitive analysis, and other aspects that are clearly outlined in the framework. It might sound redundant, but it is crucial for our clients to be aware of what we are working on and where our priorities lie.

A question we often hear from prospects is, "When will you start working on my account?" This is a lazy question, as the prospect rarely clarifies what they mean by *work* or *account*. To us, working on an account would refer to any task that directly or indirectly benefits a client's business. If I were to spend an hour dissecting your competitors' websites, I would be doing work that benefits your account. However, you obviously won't see that work logged in the Google Ads Change History tool.

I don't blame prospects for asking these unproductive questions. I blame my peers in the industry who continue to convince clients that work means changes logged in an account. This will all change in the age of automation.

Thanks to the framework, we can provide helpful context to this question. The *work* begins right away. If the client is specifically asking about changes to their campaigns, we can point to various stages of the framework to help them understand *when* and *what*.

For example, Stage 1B is an in-depth account audit where we seek to implement best practices and remove anything that is clearly doing damage. We pause any keywords that are unrelated to the business. Then we ensure that Responsive Search Ads are deployed in every ad group and that campaigns are optimizing for the correct conversion actions, and so on.

During this stage, typically a week or two into the relationship, a client should not expect us to deliver a fully fleshed out, long-term strategy. That comes further down the road after we've completed the various steps of research that are conducted throughout Phase One.

The next question we often get is, "When will I start to see results?"

This is another lazy question, which goes back to my point about understanding profit and goals. Prospects often elaborate on the question by asking when they can expect to see stable results near their desired Target CPA or Target ROAS. Again, this is not a complete view of profitability and should not be the deciding factor in whether you hire an agency. What's more, no agency has a magic 8-ball that can predict these things, and anyone who makes strong predictions or guarantees results is probably lying. Those are the folks who are more likely to skew your results or game the numbers to hit benchmarks. Steer clear of them.

Here's a better variation of that question: Do you have a method for evaluating the efficacy of your long-term strategy on an ongoing basis, and are there specific milestones that can help instill confidence in your strategies?

The answer to that question is the beginning of Phase Two, which typically happens around the three-month mark of a client relationship. If a particular strategy has not generated the results that we expected, we have a method for reevaluating our process and either optimizing the strategy or pivoting altogether.

This framework has been essential in creating a structured and consistent process, but also in increasing transparency, collaboration, and trust with our clients. It has also been an excellent tool for our Points of Contact's (POCs) at larger companies. When the CEO asks for an update on the digital advertising campaigns, the VP of marketing can explain whatever stage of the framework we are currently in, increasing transparency and collaboration throughout their entire organization.

The Marketing Flywheel

As we successfully complete the early stages of the P3X Framework, it is natural for us to think about what comes next. On the one hand, if results have not been consistently positive, then we need to go back into the earlier stages and rework our strategy. Our goal is to drive consistent, positive results for a specific initiative, thereby improving the overall advertising engine. Once a campaign or initiative reaches this point, the amount of time required to maintain and optimize it drastically decreases. Then, we need to ask ourselves: *Now what?*

That's when we get to do real marketing! When you zoom out, the P3X Framework is a series of steps that allow us to automate the tasks that used to consume 100 percent of our time. Now that we've graduated a campaign into an ongoing optimization phase, we've freed up time to think about big-picture marketing ideas. This is when we will work on developing content or a video strategy or perhaps launch campaigns on an entirely new platform.

In one client example, we began working with their internal team to help bring an entirely new product line to market. For a different client, we launched a market research initiative that resulted in us recommending and eventually launching an entirely new brand under their parent company's umbrella. We helped them get the new brand off the ground in a matter of weeks, and after just $14K in advertising spend in the first month, the products under the new brand umbrella generated more than $120K in sales. These are the kinds of exciting marketing projects that our team now gets to work on *specifically* because we have a framework for guiding us through initial client challenges.

Rand Fishkin recently published a blog post on the SparkToro blog discussing the idea of a *Marketing Flywheel.*[92] The flywheel is a recurring process, outlined as such:

1. Do a marketing *thing*
2. Boost that *thing's* reach
3. Engage and grow your audience
4. Improve your algorithmic signals
5. Get higher ROI next time [93]

Then the process starts all over again. Fishkin's flywheel diagram relates to any marketing activity, including digital advertising campaigns.

I personally believe that most clients reach out to us between Step 2 and Step 3. Clients have already *done a marketing thing* by launching a project or service. In kicking off their initial campaigns, they've reached at least a portion of their target audience.

As an outside partner, we need our own framework for ensuring that we can jump into an existing digital advertising flywheel without slowing down the process. Regardless of where they are when we are brought into the fold, there will eventually come a time where the initial strategy has been tested—when we need to take a step back and *do a marketing thing.*

The Future of Digital Advertising Platforms

23

In order predict which platforms will emerge and become valuable over the next few years, it's important to consider how the advertising landscape has evolved over time.

The Google and Facebook Duopoly

In February of 2016, Ben Thompson, author of the Stratechery blog, wrote an article titled "The Reality of Missing Out," in which he outlined the events that resulted in a Google & Facebook duopoly on the digital advertising landscape.

Thompson likened these events to what took place in the first half of the twentieth century with newspaper advertising. Traditional advertising was built on the back of newspapers.

> Newspapers are the oldest tool in the advertiser's chest, and were for many years the only one. This wasn't a problem because newspapers had the magical ability to expand or contract based on how much advertising was sold for a particular day; from a business perspective, editorial has always been filler.[94]

When new platforms emerged in the form of television and radio, newspaper advertising continued to grow. This is in spite of the fact that television and radio presented far more compelling mediums than newspapers, particularly when it came to storytelling opportunities and their effectiveness in capturing consumers' attention.

Thompson writes that newspapers' advertising revenues continued to grow for three reasons:

- Because both radio and television were programmed temporally, there was limited advertising inventory; thus, as you would expect in any situation where supply is scarce, prices were significantly higher.
- It was much more expensive to produce an effective radio or television advertising slot relative to a newspaper.
- It was difficult to measure the return-on-investment of radio and television advertising; newspapers weren't that much better, although things like coupons could be tracked more closely.[95]

It became clear, to advertising agencies of the era, that these formats were each valuable in their own way. An advertisement served on one medium served a different function from one on the next.

Thus, the "funnel" concept was born.

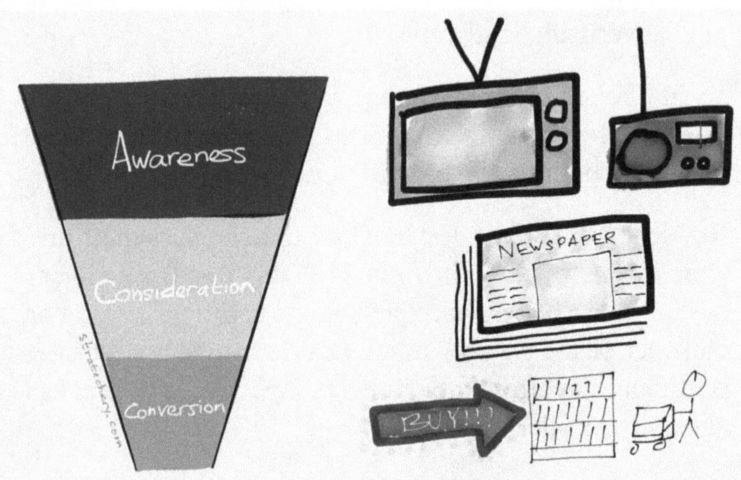

Source**:** Ben Thompson, "The Reality of Missing Out," *Stratechery.com.*

TV and radio were effective at building awareness and brand affinity. Whereas, newspapers played a key role in the consideration stage, which was certainly aided by the use of coupons in such ads. Finally, in-store promotions helped drive the final conversion action.

Digital Advertising 1.0

Thompson refers to Digital Advertising 1.0 as the period that took "square aim at the bottom of the funnel."[96] This was represented by the rise and dominance of Google AdWords. However, efforts to climb up the funnel were largely unsuccessful. Retargeting ads proved mildly effective at reaching a larger audience, but digital advertisers never found a cost-effective way to build awareness and scale with top-funnel efforts.

As per Thompson:

> There were two big problems with brand advertising on the Internet: first, there simply weren't any good ad units. Banner ads were pale imitations of print ads, which themselves were inferior to more immersive media like radio and especially TV. Secondly, given the more speculative nature of brand advertising, it was much more cost effective to spread your bets over the maximum number of customers; in other words, it remained a better idea to spend your money on an immersive TV commercial that could be broadly targeted based on programming to a whole bunch of potential consumers at a single moment as opposed to spending much more time—which is money!—creating a whole bunch of banner ads that could be more finely targeted.[97]

Banner ads were designed to look and feel like traditional newspaper ads, but they were never successful because their roles in the marketing funnel had reversed. An advertisement in the form of a small square image, with a brand logo and short call-to-action, could be effective if it sat in the consideration stage of the marketing funnel, as newspaper ads do. Such an advertisement would be ineffective in the awareness stage, which is often where one encounters banner ads.

My mother still looks forward to the Thursday edition of the local newspaper. Not because she enjoys the news, but because this is the day when her favorite stores advertise their upcoming weekend sales. She's not building an awareness of new brands through this paper. She's using these ads to make a final purchase decision.

Digital Advertising 2.0

The focus on bottom-funnel advertising began to change as Google invested heavily in making their *awareness* and *consideration* stage products, namely YouTube advertising, more effective.* Display ads served on the Google Display Network are following suit. Automation-driven display campaigns are far superior at locating individuals in the *consideration* stage compared to the traditional display campaigns that we would have run on manual bidding circa 2016.

Google has gone so far as to change the name of its platform from *Google AdWords* to *Google Ads* in an effort to encourage the marketing community to view them as more than a bottom-funnel advertising solution.

Facebook, on the other hand, has made even more progress in branding itself as a full-fledged advertising platform. Facebook COO Sheryl Sandberg alluded to this reality during their January 2016 earnings call:

> Leading up to Black Friday, Shop Direct, the UK's second largest online retailer teased upcoming sales with a cinemagraph video to build awareness. They then retargeted people who saw the video with one-day-only deals. On Black Friday, they used our carousel and DPA ads to promote products people had shown interest in. They saw 20 times return on ad spend from this campaign, helping them achieve their biggest Black Friday and their most successful sales day ever.[98]

---

* As I outlined extensively in Chapter 5, I am extremely bullish on YouTube advertising. As of this writing, it is not just a powerful channel with which to reach your target audience in the awareness stage; it is also currently much cheaper than it probably should be. You should act fast and take advantage of this opportunity before the rest of the market wakes up to this realization.

Thompson points to this as proof that Facebook, with its single ad-buying interface, allowed an advertiser to move customers through every part of the marketing funnel. Google is currently attempting a rebrand to help advertisers understand that they are capable of the same.

Thompson concludes:

> Here's the kicker, though, and the big difference from the era of analog advertising: the Facebook and Google platforms turn TV and radio's disadvantages on their head:
>
> - Facebook and Google have the most inventory and are still growing in terms of both users and ad-load; there is no temporal limitation that works to the benefit of other properties (and Facebook in particular is ramping up efforts to advertise using Facebook data on non-Facebook properties)
> - It is cheaper to produce ads for only Facebook and Google instead of making something custom for every potential advertising platform
> - Facebook and Google have the best tracking, extending not only to digital purchases but increasingly to off-line purchases as well.
>
> Both companies, particularly Facebook, have dominant strategic positions; they are superior to other digital platforms on every single vector: effectiveness, reach, and ROI. Small wonder that [other, smaller ad platforms]—LinkedIn, Yelp, Yahoo, Twitter—are all struggling.
>
> Digital advertising is becoming a rather simple proposition: Facebook, Google, or don't bother.[99]

Four months after this article was published, Microsoft acquired LinkedIn for over $26 billion dollars. LinkedIn and other platforms have certainly proven to be valuable, but Facebook and Google remain atop the list, thanks to the *winner-take-all* conditions created by these companies.*

As digital advertising unfolds over the next several years, a significant shift must take place to reduce the influence of this duopoly. The only way for a third or fourth platform to effectively emerge and compete for budget is to pursue aggregator status.

Aggregation Theory

In 2015, Ben Thompson coined the term **aggregation theory** to describe "how platforms (i.e., aggregators) come to dominate the industries in which they compete in a systematic and predictable way."[100]

> The value chain for any given consumer market is divided into three parts: suppliers, distributors, and consumers/users. The best way to make outsize profits in any of these markets is ... to integrate two of the parts such that you have a competitive advantage in delivering a vertical solution.[101]

In the pre-internet era, this depended on controlling **distribution**, as this component sits between the suppliers and the final consumers.

Newspapers are a medium in which editorial content, written by suppliers, is distributed to readers, the final consumers. To increase profits, newspapers integrated backward into content creation, becoming their own suppliers, and earned additional profits through the sale of advertising opportunities. The final consumer became an afterthought for these companies.

The internet has turned the traditional value chain on its head. With the advent of zero distributional and transactional costs, "the most important factor determining success is [now] the user experience: the best distributors/aggregators/market-makers win by providing the best experience, which earns them the most consumers/users, which

* As I write this, Microsoft is also attempting to acquire TikTok—making it clear that they are aggressively attempting to compete with this duopoly. If the TikTok deal falls through, I expect them to pursue another platform, perhaps Pinterest

attracts the most suppliers, which enhances the user experience in a virtuous cycle."[102]

People don't use Bing search because it's not as good as Google. Google's supremacy as a search engine forces suppliers to exist on the platform. Because there are stakeholders joining from both sides, consumers and suppliers, Google receives more data and is in a better position than its competitors to improve the overall experience.

With each passing day, an aggregator increases the value gap between themselves and their competition.

> Because aggregators deal with digital goods, there is an abundance of supply; that means users reap value through discovery and curation, and most aggregators get started by delivering superior discovery.
>
> Then, once an aggregator has gained some number of end users, suppliers will come onto the aggregator's platform on the aggregator's terms.[103]

The entire SEO industry exists because Google has become an aggregator. SEO is simply the act of making changes to your website so that you better comply with Google's systems, even if it comes at the expense of the user experience or your brand image—because you literally have no other option.

> This means that for aggregators, customer acquisition costs decrease over time; marginal customers are attracted to the platform by virtue of the increasing number of suppliers. This further means that aggregators enjoy winner-take-all effects: since the value of an aggregator to end users is continually increasing it is exceedingly difficult for competitors to take away users or win new ones.[104]

In terms of Facebook and Instagram, users generally remain on those platforms because their friends and family are already there. The costs required to convince all of these people to begin using another social media platform are astronomical.

Why does this matter? Three reasons:

1. Google and Facebook are not going away any time soon. Therefore, they'll remain focal points of digital advertising strategy for years to come. These platforms will continue to evolve over time, and advertisers need to keep an open mind toward those changes. They must be willing to learn new skills and change the ways in which they manage campaigns in order to continue providing value to their clients across these platforms.

2. Aggregation theory provides evidence about the value of these two platforms compared to similar advertising mediums. Clients often ask how we feel about other ad platforms, including Twitter, Snapchat, Criteo, Perfect Audience, Adroll, and countless others. These platforms are fine, and many have their place for certain types of creative, messaging, or niche audiences that you want to target. But for the average advertiser, *why bother*?*

   There is a near 100 percent chance that your target audience can be reached between Google and Facebook advertising and likely with a variety of creative formats that will fill out your entire marketing funnel. If that is the case, wouldn't you want to place your bets with the two platforms that have, by far, the most data and the most powerful machine learning capabilities to drive success?

   This is especially true with Google, where the advent of account-level conversion data that is used as part of the machine learning process creates an incentive to spend more on the platform and harvest as much conversion data inside your Google Ads account as possible. Centralizing your conversion data within one platform creates a rising tide that lifts all boats (campaigns).

---

* I am a huge advocate for LinkedIn advertising; however, this platform is only useful under certain conditions. It is largely dependent on your ability to promote quality content, which is easier said than done, as few companies have quality content. The costs involved with producing such content, therefore, makes it easier to reach your target audience on Google or Facebook. That said, LinkedIn ranks #3 in terms of platforms that our clients invest the most into.

There is, of course, an incentive for agencies to encourage their clients to spend on as many platforms as possible. If your agency is managing your budget across a half-dozen ad networks, it's more difficult for you to switch agencies or bring the work in-house. It gives off the impression that the account is more complicated. As a result, the agency has created a moat around themselves and your ad budget. This is no different than agencies that build SKAG campaigns in Google or overly segmented Facebook campaigns—an unnecessary practice that is done with the intention of impressing the client, even at the expense of performance.

If your agency has claimed that Google display advertising does not work and suggests that they manage display through a second network, I'd encourage you to challenge them on *why* Google Display does not work, in their opinion. Perhaps their lack of experience with modern Smart Campaigns has resulted in a couple failed experiments, and they've decided, prematurely, that they don't work. However, it could be because they are financially incentivized to convince you that an additional platform is necessary.

There are certainly exceptions and benefits to spreading your bets across multiple assets. However, you must make these decisions while considering the value that an aggregator platform provides which others simply cannot.

3. Aggregation theory and an understanding of the Google and Facebook duopoly allows us to intelligently bet on which emerging platforms will provide value to our clients in the coming years. For one, we are particularly interested in advertising platforms that are likely to become aggregators themselves. It is clear that ad platforms with the most data—which can be used to fuel powerful automation—are the best equipped to deliver the results that advertisers desire. Aggregator platforms also provide the most opportunities in terms of measurement and attribution, a key factor in whether we will invest our time or our client's resources into a particular platform.

Lastly, we are particularly interested in rising potential aggregators that offer something unique in terms of placement or format. Something that Google and Facebook don't currently offer and are unlikely to compete with in the near future.

Emerging Platforms

There are other elements that we should consider when thinking about emerging ad platforms. We want to find potential aggregators that can offer something unique, and we want to discover the platforms that operate in areas with a large gap between consumer attention and advertising investment.

Part of what contributed to Google and Facebook's success was that the broader advertising industry had been, until recently, over-indexed in legacy media. In 2010, Mary Meeker of Morgan Stanley reported that brands were investing too much in print, radio, and television, as the proportion of spend on these media outpaced actual consumption habits. However, brands were under-investing in internet advertising. Meeker concluded that the delta between internet consumption and internet advertising investment presented a $50B global opportunity for brands.[105]

Brands and their ad agencies eventually woke up to this mass transformation and realized they needed to shift their budgets, to capture the consumer attention that had shifted to digital and mobile. The Facebook and Google duopoly seized this opportunity by making mobile and broader internet advertising more accessible and effective for the average advertiser. By 2019, time spent by Americans on the internet officially surpassed time spent watching television, but we also saw a stabilization in budgets, relative to consumer time and attention.

There are two media channels that currently present a similar opportunity: audio and OTT. By audio, I am referring to both music and the broader podcasting space. OTT, or over-the-top streaming, refers to digital content streamed through a Smart TV. When you stream Netflix through a Smart TV or use a device such as Roku, Apple TV, or an Amazon Firestick to access Netflix on your TV, you are viewing an OTT experience.

At the moment, neither Facebook nor Google has made any attempt to capture the value gap presented in these media. The emerging platforms that I am keeping an eye on are Spotify and Roku. Both platforms offer powerful advertising solutions, but as they inch closer to becoming true aggregators, their potential upside increases exponentially.

Spotify's Advertising Potential

In 2019, I wrote an article for the AdVenture Media blog titled "Why Did Spotify Double Down on Podcasts?" This was largely due to with the overall lack of profitability that can be garnered from the music industry. Podcasts presented a unique opportunity:

> Spotify is largely responsible for saving the music industry. Instead of fighting back against the internet, Spotify embraced the internet and discovered that value could be delivered through convenience.
>
> That is, even though you can still technically pirate music, it's worth a $9.99/month subscription to have a massive music library at your fingertips. And if you're not willing to pay for Spotify premium (as about half of Spotify's user base has decided) an ad-supported platform is still more convenient than the illegal alternative.
>
> Spotify's success has helped initiate revenue growth for the entire music industry, but Spotify itself has not seen the gains that should be associated with such massive disruption.
>
> They are the thankless savior … a dark knight, even.
>
> Spotify has remained a distributor within the music industry and has yet to gain significant influence on supplier activity. They have failed to gain control over multiple levels of the value chain, a hurdle that traditional tech unicorns have overcome on their path to dominance.
>
> The primary investment for most traditional tech unicorns includes fixed costs of R&D, sales, and marketing.

> However, Spotify's primary costs are driven by marginal fees to record labels.
>
> In 2017, Spotify spent an astonishing 3.9B, or *79 percent of their revenue*, on distribution and royalty expenses (via Statista).
>
> As Spotify earns more revenue from users, the record labels earn more revenue from Spotify. It's a cycle that limits long-term potential.
>
> It's unlikely that Spotify will be able to disrupt the supply side of the *music* industry in a way that would remove the constraints from the record labels. However, this constraint does not exist for the *broader audio marketplace*, where a dominant, central figure currently does not exist.

Presently, Spotify ads are exclusive to music streaming. Advertisers are not yet able to programmatically buy ad placements within podcasts, but that is likely to change.

According to a study conducted by the International Advertising Bureau (IAB) and PwC, the podcasting industry generated approximately $479.1 million in revenue in 2018.[106] That same year, the IFPI reported that the global music industry had generated $19.1B in revenue.[107] Forty-seven percent of the revenue earned by the global music industry came from streaming services like Spotify.[108]

Meanwhile in 2018, Spotify reported $614M in earned advertising revenue.[109] That is to say that Spotify earned more ad revenue from free accounts streaming music in 2018 *than the entire podcasting industry* was worth that same year!

We can agree that the music industry should be worth more than the podcast industry, but by this margin? According to Edison Research, in 2018, 26 percent of Americans (73 million people) listen to podcasts monthly, while *48 million Americans claim to listen to podcasts at least on a weekly basis.*[110]

For comparison, approximately 22 million people watch *NFL Sunday Night Football* on NBC: a three- or four-hour viewing experience that consistently ranks as the highest rated, most watched television program.[111] NBC currently pays $950M per year for the right to air these seventeen games.[112]

The podcasting industry attracts more than twice the amount of weekly active customers than does the highest rated television show, and yet this exact show is worth more than twice the entire podcasting industry! What's wrong here?

The IAB predicts that the podcasting industry will be worth $1B in 2021.[113] I still believe this number is low, compared to what it *should* be worth; but either way, you can bet that Spotify is attempting to scoop up as much of that as possible.

The Power of Audio Advertising

Audio, in the form of radio advertising, has been a key driver of brand awareness for nearly 100 years. However, Meeker's analysis published above shows that radio advertising has been declining, relative to consumer attention, for more than a decade. This is due to traditional radio's inability to effectively drive both awareness and consideration with consumers in the modern era, but it does not suggest that audio itself is dead.

Audio remains a powerful medium for brands to increase awareness and tell stories. A 2017 Nielsen Media Lab study found that, compared to traditional display ads, audio ads are 28 percent more informative, receive 24 percent more *ad recall,* and are more than 2x more persuasive.[114]

I can personally attest to this. Perhaps it is because I work in advertising and probably pay more attention to ads than a traditional consumer, but I can rattle off twenty different brands that have reached me via podcasts and radio over the last year, but I can't recall with confidence a single brand's display ad that I've seen in the last twenty-four hours.*

The primary difference between modern audio and traditional radio is that traditional radio was primarily consumed during the hours in which people commuted to and from work. That has changed in the modern era. Consumers stream audio content during every aspect of their day: while they are getting ready in the morning, commuting, working, exercising, shopping, cleaning, cooking, vacationing, relaxing, and socializing.

Spotify claims that its users are 3x more likely to stream music while shopping or traveling, thus presenting the same kinds of *micro-moment* opportunities that make Google and Facebook advertising so effective.

Current State of Podcast Advertising

As I write this in 2020, podcast advertising remains analog, exclusive, and far too expensive. Despite the significant upsides of this valuable advertising medium, it is currently a waste of time and resources for most advertisers.

Most podcast reads are negotiated directly between the brand/agency and the owners of the podcast that will feature the ad read. Some media companies act as middlemen to this process, negotiating deals with brands and allowing for access to a large variety of podcasts and audiences under one centralized deal. Midroll is an example of such a gatekeeper, providing access to many popular podcasts, including *Freakonomics, WTF with Mark Marron,* and more. Unfortunately,

* Some podcasters have put in the extra effort to provide a unique experience to the traditional advertising read. Gimlet Media, acquired by Spotify in 2019, has always attempted to connect brand messaging to the context of the podcast show or episode, providing a more relevant and interesting experience. Comedian Bill Burr is the king of this, as he tends to make fun of the brands as he reads the advertisements on *The Monday Morning Podcast.* Do yourself a favor and look up "Bill Burr Shari's Berries." This ad read appeared to go horribly wrong, but the additional exposure that this brand received after this clip went viral is invaluable.

there is an inherent upcharge when negotiating a deal through Midroll that does not exist for platforms like Facebook and Google.

In addition to costs, there are other downsides to the current system, namely:

1. Lack of measurement and attribution. Advertisers have no way of knowing how many people, or what kinds of people, actually heard their ad read.

2. Permanent shelf life / Lack of programmatic abilities. Once an ad read is used for a podcast episode, it exists forever within that audio file. There are countless individual podcast episodes that have stood the test of time. However, the ads within them are outdated. What's more, this prevents the podcaster from earning additional advertising revenue from this episode with more downloads.

3. It's so easy to skip through the ads!

This last concern is particularly troublesome. Even if you can measure downloads, a brand has no idea how many users have actually sat through their ad reads. What's worse, some of the most popular podcasts front-load their ad-reads, thereby training their listeners to know that they can just skip to the six or eight-minute mark immediately after download—Joe Rogan, Tim Ferris, and Mark Marron come to mind.

Yes, I am guilty of doing this, and I don't feel bad about it. It's a bad experience for the listener, and it needs to change. I do feel bad for brands that pay up to $50K for an ad read that is probably being skipped by 90 percent of listeners. I feel worse for the customers who overpay for their products because brands need to increase their margins to justify the massive costs of podcast advertising.

Podcast advertising is certainly effective for products with massive lifetime value. Squarespace is the best example of this. Squarespace has always invested heavily in podcasts because their business model affords them that right. When a new customer signs up to create a website on Squarespace, they are likely to continue paying that monthly subscription fee for many years.

Consumer-packaged goods are not as lucky. I am particularly skeptical of any product that is heavily advertised on podcasts. I can generally assume that the company is either wildly unprofitable, like Blue Apron, or that the product is priced high above the real value. I've never purchased MeUndies briefs, but I seriously doubt that they're worth $24 a pair.

The future of podcast advertising will be defined by the ability to hone in on your target audience via programmatic ads in real-time. Under the current Nielsen model, the original ads are locked into a podcast file forever. Soon, a centralized platform will allow advertisers to programmatically insert their latest messages into predefined ad slots at the moment a listener begins streaming.

We will then be granted the ability to measure the impact of an ad placement as a customer navigates from the awareness stage into consideration, and ultimately conversion. Advertisers will be able to leverage podcasts to effectively reach their target audience without having to overpay for broad awareness efforts. Podcast advertising will be more like YouTube advertising in terms of its value proposition and measurement capabilities, and much less like traditional radio advertising.

All this to say that podcast advertising is currently overpriced and has significant challenges that have prevented its scale. As a result, the typical podcast creator is not currently earning a level of revenue that accurately represents the value that they are providing, presenting a value-gap similar to what Meeker exposed with internet advertising throughout the 2000s and 2010s.

A centralized platform stands to benefit both advertisers and the podcasters who hope to earn a living by producing quality content.

The advertisements themselves will come in the form of 15-, 30-, or 60-second audio files that will be dynamically inserted into various placements within the podcast, or between songs, like we currently have with YouTube. Most ads will be traditional reads, whereby a voice actor will read ad copy aloud. However, creative agencies will occasionally leverage songs, jingles, or other unique twists on the traditional ad read.

The Spotify advertising platform allows you to upload your own audio file or to have one of their professional voice actors read your ad copy *for free*. This is a tremendous offering, as consumers can recognize the difference between a professionally read ad and an amateur.

Spotify ads are also served with a display image that appears on the user's device where you'd typically see an album cover, with the ability to link to a landing page. This is a great feature, but the click-through-rates are incredibly low. Advertisers should not be running ads through Spotify with the goal of gaining direct clicks back to their website. Success will be measured by building brand affinity within their target audience.

Spotify as an Aggregator

I wrote "Why Did Spotify Double Down on Podcasts?" after Spotify acquired Gimlet Media and Anchor in 2019. Spotify began as a *distributor* within the broader audio value chain. These acquisitions made it clear that they were attempting to increase their control over *supply*.

From the article:

> In the not-so-distant future, when the dust settles and Spotify has solidified themselves as the dominant leader in the audio marketplace, most end users won't really notice the difference.
>
> Suppliers, as in the creators of audio content, will have had their world turned upside down.
>
> Traditional incumbents will have been forced to change their ways, either by opting into Spotify's platform or by remaining independent and relying on a small niche of loyal fans to [hopefully] drive revenue.

Spotify will focus on developing their own content, like the Netflix Original Series Collection, but also garner exclusive content that was produced elsewhere.

Tools like Anchor will make it even more lucrative for content creators to burst into the podcasting space. Many content creators will be incentivized (through advertising/ monetary incentives and overall convenience of a centralized platform) to exclusively host their podcasts on Spotify.

Slowly but surely, Spotify will replace Apple as the go-to for hosting and sourcing podcast content and will have developed massive influence over each level of the value-chain.

Similar to how YouTube creators have exploded as a result of increased supply of YouTube advertising revenue, I expect to see the same take place for audio (get ready for your ASMR podcasters that earn millions in revenue ...).

I expect Spotify to acquire a handful of other podcasting platforms, with the goal of leveraging existing technology and user data, but also to eliminate competition. Overcast, for example, would be an interesting acquisition target that would allow them to integrate the Smart Speed technology into their playback functionality.

Other podcast platforms like Stitcher will need to pivot into a niche ("the go-to platform for true-crime podcasts!") or they will become completely irrelevant altogether.

I also expect Spotify to develop technology that inhibits the ability to skip through advertisements, like what we currently have on YouTube. This will be met with massive public backlash, but we'll all get over it (and Spotify will gain more premium subscribers as a result of the change). Advertisers will be much more willing to invest in audio if they can be certain that their ads will be heard.

> **As for Audio Advertising …**
>
> The Spotify self-service advertising platform will become as robust as the Facebook's, complete with retargeting / conversion pixels, interest-based targeting and more—all backed by powerful machine learning algorithms. And any advertiser will be able to bid for a placement on the Bill Simmons or Joe Rogan podcast, regardless of their overall budget.
>
> Audio advertising middlemen, such as Midroll, will either go away altogether or will pivot into offering broader-scope advertising solutions.[115]

Perhaps it was a premonition that I chose Bill Simmons and Joe Rogan as my examples. Within the eighteen months, Spotify had acquired Bill Simmons' media company, The Ringer, for an undisclosed amount and signed an exclusive multiyear deal with Joe Rogan worth $100M.[116]

As of this writing, Spotify has not yet completed their transition to aggregator status, although it seems imminent. The Spotify ad platform is still exclusive to their music content, and they have not released information on how they plan to release a solution for podcasting advertising just yet. What's more, the music advertising solution is somewhat nascent. I am hopeful that they will increase their measurement and audience targeting capabilities over the next year or so.

Roku

There's been a lot of talk about the *streaming wars* between Netflix and, well, everyone that wants to compete with Netflix. A *war* in the traditional sense suggests that there will eventually be a winner, but I don't see that happening here. It is hard to imagine a time when households only subscribed to a single streaming service, whether it's Netflix, Hulu, Disney+, AppleTV, HBO, or another of the plethora of options.

As long as consumers subscribe to multiple streaming services, they will benefit from a centralized platform that allows them to access a variety of content. Roku is one such platform. Roku's advertising platform will finally make high-quality television advertising available to the broader advertising community.

Roku is also currently a *distributor* in the value chain. However, unlike how Spotify first moved backward into controlling supply, Roku is doing the opposite. Roku has invested heavily into gaining access into American households, many of which have never even heard of the company. The sheer number of end users they currently have will force suppliers to continue bringing their content onto Roku's platform, on Roku's terms.

Roku's rise as a platform is largely due to their decision not to compete directly with any of the streaming giants. As the proverbial streaming wars unfold, the diplomatic Roku sits just out of focus. Ready to form alliances with the powers that emerge.

As it happens, the platform was created with the ambition of avoiding competition with streaming companies.

In a December 2019 interview with *Forbes* magazine, Roku CEO Anthony Wood alluded to how the company's future includes a large focus on its advertising capabilities. From the *Forbes* article:

> Wood, 54, is now betting that Roku will be able to move beyond its hardware business into a more lucrative software business: measuring the reach and effectiveness of ads on streaming apps.
>
> "Traditionally, the only way you would measure a TV ad is through Nielsen ratings, which could tell you roughly how many people have watched it," Wood says. "Our measurement is very precise, where we can tell a company that out of everyone who saw your ad, 5 percent went to your website and bought something," he explains. "We're bringing the sort of technology that's already been around for a while on the internet to the TV world." Roku does this with in-house measurement tools, but also with 11 partners including New York-based Nielsen, in order to tell advertisers

> like clients Jaguar Land Rover and Baskin-Robbins how their ad campaigns performed with which demographics.
>
> The shift is paying off. In 2015, 84 percent of Roku's $320 million in revenue came from hardware; 16 percent, or $50 million, came from advertising and content. Now advertising is the fastest-growing segment, and those numbers have nearly flipped. Roku doubled down in October, announcing a $150 million acquisition of dataxu, a Boston-based tech outfit that allows clients to plan and buy video ad campaigns.[117]

This last paragraph is worth particular consideration. Roku was, first and foremost, a hardware company but has since shifted to becoming a platform. This has allowed them to drastically reduce the cost of the actual Roku device, from $100 to less than $30, which has made the Roku platform more affordable to more people. This has fueled its massive expansion over the last five years.

The dataxu acquisition will help create a scalable advertising solution.

As of this writing, Roku is the OTT market leader, with significant market share over Amazon, Apple, Samsung, Google, and other players. Fifty-nine percent of programmatic OTT ads are being run through Roku's platform; Amazon is #2, claiming just 19 percent of this opportunity.[118]

OTT vs. CTV

The term "over-the-top" has been used in broadcasting to describe any content that is delivered through the internet, as opposed to the traditional method of a cable box or satellite provider. Netflix and Hulu are OTT streaming services.

CTV, or *connected-TV*, is the act of viewing your OTT content through an actual television—as opposed to a laptop, tablet, or mobile device. CTV devices include Roku, Amazon Fire TV Stick, Apple TV, and Google Chromecast. It also includes gaming consoles, such as XBox, that allow users to stream OTT services through their system. Smart TVs are also considered CTVs, as they often allow users to directly access the OTT content. Samsung Smart TVs, for example, allow you to access Netflix directly through their Smart TV interface, without requiring an additional device.

From the IAB Tech Lab website:

> In the context of ad tech business, and especially where initiative work is geared toward addressing challenges in one domain or the other, use the most appropriate term:
>
> - Use CTV when you are specifically talking about Smart TVs and streaming devices that are attached to TVs. Mobile and desktop devices are not included under the term CTV.
> - Use OTT when it doesn't matter which devices are included. For example, if you want to talk about "OTT services" (like Hulu or TubiTV), and delivery to a particular device doesn't matter. OTT is still a valid term that distinguishes premium television content from the vast world of online video where user-generated content is commonplace.[119]

This is an important distinction to be aware of, as most brand managers would suggest that an OTT ad that is placed on a CTV is more valuable than another device. I tend to agree. If a video ad is served to me while I am streaming a show on my mobile device, I will subconsciously treat it just like any other video ad that I see on the internet. However, if that same ad is served to me through my television, it becomes a *commercial*, and I might have a different perception of the brand that served me that ad. It's silly, but it's the reality nonetheless.

Thankfully, advertisers can buy both CTV and traditional OTT placements through the same Roku interface. This provides further opportunities for liquidity, premium auctions, and other components of automation to help advertisers reach their goals.

While it might seem that Roku can only reach audiences who connect to OTT services through a Roku device, their reach goes far beyond that. Roku has partnered with several TV manufacturers, allowing the Roku operating system to be the backbone structure of the Smart TV itself. The host of Smart TVs offered by TCL, Sanyo, Phillips, and JVC are all using Roku's technology. As a result, Roku's advertising platform can tap into millions of U.S. households, occupied by people who may have never even heard of Roku.

Roku's Advertising Opportunities

Roku's *One-View* ad platform allows for a host of different ad formats. The most popular are ads served directly into the OTT services themselves. For example, Hulu has an ad-supported subscription, as well as a premium membership that does not include ads. When a user is accessing Hulu through a Roku device or a CTV that uses Roku's operating system, the ads they see can be served through the Roku interface.

In addition to the traditional, ad-supported OTT services that can be accessed via Roku, their customers gain access to *The Roku Channel*, an always-changing selection of free movies, shows, live news, kids' TV, and more. This is similar to an HBO subscription, which provides access to HBO-exclusive content, but also a number of other on-demand or live streaming options. Roku refers to *The Roku Channel* as "the channel for cord cutters," and it's currently ranked as the 3rd highest ad-supported channel through the platform.

Roku claims that consumers streaming *The Roku Channel* will be served half as many ads, compared to other ad-supported streaming channels (such as Hulu). While this may appear to be a disadvantage, it is actually a huge advantage from an advertising perspective.

Roku claims that, while these viewers will see fewer ads per capita, they typically stick around for longer, increasing the total amount of ads that they are exposed to. As a result, *The Roku Channel* is currently the #3 ad-supported channel on all of Roku. This is nothing to scoff at, as it's a medium in which you can effectively reach a massive audience without annoying them. Some might call this *advertising nirvana.*

Google's platform rose above the rest because they prioritized the user experience above all, as evidenced by *Quality Score* and other efforts. Facebook followed suit with *Relevance Score*, and their policy that states that image ads cannot be covered in promotional text. No other company has been willing to sacrifice short-term ad revenue to the extent that these two companies have. This is one of the reasons they've been so successful. Roku certainly has the opportunity to do this as well. Time will tell if they truly care about the end user or if they will let short-term greed and the motivation to impress shareholders at the next quarterly earnings report distract them from this key principle.

Roku Advertising: Beyond OTT

The $150M acquisition of adtech and data platform dataxu is the primary reason why I am bullish on Roku's advertising future. After the news broke of the acquisition in 2019, TechCrunch noted:

> With the addition of dataxu, Roku will be able to provide advertisers with a data-driven solution they can use to plan and buy their ad spend across Roku's platform. The deal will also bring in dataxu's experienced team, which includes talent in software engineering, data science and analytics.[120]

In 2020, when I first received a demo of Roku's OneView ad platform, I was shown a twenty-six-slide presentation. Of those twenty-six slides, fourteen were dedicated to highlighting their measurement and attribution capabilities. This was a notable contrast to other platform presentations I've seen, which focus almost exclusively on audience reach and ad formats. Measurement is either tangentially tacked on, at the very end, or not at all mentioned.

Roku is directly addressing a key challenge that advertisers have struggled with since the introduction of digital: How can we ensure that affinity-based advertising is not just reaching our target audience, but also generating any sort of profit? Roku has invested more than $150M in attempting to answer this question. Today, their platform can leverage data from partners, including Neilsen, Salesforce, Oracle,

LiveRamp, Factual, Tapad, Acxiom, Neustar —as well as your second-party data (retargeting audiences, etc.) to help achieve this.

What's most interesting is that companies like Google and Spotify are among Roku's partners. You can serve audio ads on Spotify or display ads on the Google Display Network exclusively through the Roku OneView platform. This unlocks a host of retargeting and conversion opportunities, all the while ensuring clean attribution.

Roku already claims to reach four out of five households in America. That is not to say that four in five households include a Roku device or even a Roku TV. It is rather that their ad platform has the capability of reaching these folks through their platform directly or partner platforms.

Roku as an Aggregator

Roku recently flexed its aggregator muscles in regard to negotiations with AT&T over the new HBO Max product. Ben Thompson chronicled the event as part of his Stratechery update on June 1st, 2020:

> One might have thought that in the streaming world it would be the content owners that end up with most of the leverage; after all, it is easy enough to get content through any number of channels, whether that be Amazon, Apple TV, Roku, or your smart TV. It turns out, though, that controlling the consumer touchpoint still really matters, and affords a lot of leverage. This is where Roku is the perfect example: by virtue of selling a ton of TVs and cheap set-top boxes Roku is in a position to dictate terms to AT&T (or at least hold out until it gets a deal to its liking). Even when consumers have options, their defaults are still incredibly powerful.

Roku has worked its way into the homes of so many households that content suppliers on the opposite end of the value chain have been forced to comply, or at least negotiate, on Roku's terms. This minor negotiating chip is not anywhere near the level of influence that pure-play aggregators like Google have earned. The entire SEO industry is a result of suppliers attempting to comply with the terms that Google has set. However, it is certainly indicative of what might become the norm if Roku continues to hold such a significant share of the market.

In the end, it does not matter if Roku or Spotify officially reach aggregator status in the traditional sense. However, the steps toward this status, successful or not, are what will define their advertising value in coming years. If either of these platforms is able to attract a massive amount of stakeholders from both sides of the value chain and develop an easy-to-use, self-service advertising platform that makes it easy to reach these end users, and measure the effectiveness of the advertisements themselves, then they will certainly earn their way into the conversation alongside Facebook and Google.

Fast Forward

As exciting as all of this may be, this sort of evolution tends to move at a glacial pace. Many advertisers still don't have the budgets to scale beyond bottom-funnel search. Some are just beginning to test the waters with Facebook and other platforms that have proven valuable for several years. Of the companies that do have the budgets, many of them are restricted by bureaucratic budgeting processes, often left to decision-makers who don't understand a damn thing about modern digital advertising.

Bottom-funnel search will remain a valuable aspect of your marketing strategy, but smart advertisers (and their agencies) will need to realize that this is just the tip of the iceberg to what can be achieved through digital advertising.

By 2024, the brands driving the most profitable growth online will be the ones that have forged forward with an open mind toward change. Google Ads and Facebook Ads will continue to grow more automated, but smart advertisers will realize that this is with the full purpose of making it easier to drive the desired results. We will also see a shift in the goals set by marketing departments and their agencies toward actual profit and other metrics that are more meaningful than arbitrary CPA or ROAS targets.

Agencies will be forced to increase their data literacy at every level of the organization. They will invest in data scientists, of course, but also in the analyst-type individuals who can act as intermediaries between those data scientists and the business-minded stakeholders who set the budget and company goals. Agencies will have to realize that their new value will be found in consultative services and not so much in campaign implementation and keyword research. They will spend more time thinking about how to *train* algorithms, as opposed to imagining up futile ways to beat algorithms.

We might see additional platforms emerge, such as Spotify and Roku, that help provide a more comprehensive omni-channel approach. However, this is completely dependent on these platforms' abilities to provide meaningful measurement and attribution solutions for their advertisers.

None of this can happen if you don't begin to embrace the technology that will inevitably turn this entire industry on its head. In many regards, it already has. But it's not too late. While this might be the first step that you've taken to mastering digital advertising in the age of automation, it is far from over. You will need to continue keeping an open mind and convince yourself that this technology will leave you behind if you don't fight to keep up. It's your only chance of survival, but it's going to be a fun ride.

Join … or die.

24 Onwards

Today is June 9th, 2020. It has been three months since our company has gone remote in response to COVID-19. Yesterday marked the 100th day since the first case was diagnosed in New York City, but yesterday also began Phase One of reopening the city. We should be able to reconvene in our office, with limitations, within the next few weeks.

Not long after this whole thing began, Isaac sent a company-wide email outlining his thoughts and instilling confidence in the team. He confirmed that no one would be at risk of losing their job or being furloughed, even if it meant that the company had to significantly dip into savings and run at a negative cash flow for some time.

Later that day, the two of us had a virtual drink together through Google Hangouts. We confided in one another that we were both terrified of what was to come, but we agreed that we could weather the storm if we hung on to our core principle of *determined optimism* and kept in mind that *short term failures are cauterized while success ripples outwards.*

I thought back to when he sent me that email outlining our principles nearly a year earlier, as we were embarking on our trip to London. I remembered how he almost missed our flight so that he could finish that email. Now I'm incredibly grateful that he did so. It was encouraging to have our principles so eloquently laid out as we entered this unprecedented period, which promised to put them and us to the test.

We stayed positive and did our best to remain strong resources for our clients. We've signed a handful of new clients (without having to sacrifice client quality) and were able to help existing clients profitably increase their budgets or expand into new channels. Within the last month, we've once again started interviewing prospective candidates to join our team.

We've made it through. I can't describe how proud I am of our team for what they've pulled off over the last three months, particularly those with young children at home.

Today I am finishing this book, a project that has consumed almost all my free time over the last 18 months. I am excited to literally, and metaphorically, turn the page on this time period and get back to work.

But first, I want to reflect on what all of this represents.

Meaningful Work

This industry presents endless opportunities for meaningful, fulfilling work. Whether you are working with small businesses that spend only a few dollars in advertising per month or large enterprises with seven-figure ad budgets, there are few career opportunities where your work directly impacts the income that someone else takes home to their family. At times, it feels like an incredible cross to bear. More often, it continues to be the most rewarding experience I could have ever asked for.

Helping to build AdVenture Media over the years has proven to be the project I am most proud of. This has little to do with my position at the company. Every person on our team has played a significant role in our success. My goal is to ensure that *meaningful work* continues to remain available throughout the entire company as we grow.

One of the most significant risks to an agency culture is not addressing the *threat of the hamster wheel.* When you are constantly working on a backlogged pipeline, it can feel like you're not getting anywhere. If not addressed, this creates tension between your sales team and the client services team that carries out client work. This is not good. The entire organization should share in the excitement of signing new business, rather than being stressed about the added workload that new business entails.

The remedy to this is an environment where meaningful work is both produced and acknowledged. Many quality agencies are capable of the former but struggle with the latter.

David Sable, the former CEO of Young and Rubicam, has provided some useful mentorship to our agency over the last year. He recently told us the story of a successful ad campaign that one of his colleagues ran for a German winemaker in the 90s. The agency discovered that many Americans felt intimidated when handed a wine list in a nice restaurant. These wine lists are usually massive, filled with hard-to-pronounce labels that had different pairing notes. Good wine seemed to be reserved for the snobs.

This particular German wine, though, was easy to pronounce, and their ad campaigns spoke to the masses—the non-snobs—about how this wine pairs with anything. The agency recommended that the brand increase their retail price to establish it as a premium selection.

"It was a massive success." Sable said, followed by a laugh: "The best part is that the wine wasn't even that good!"

What an incredible story. It was short and brilliant and even concluded with a punchline. This is not just a terrific example of this agency's capabilities, it is also the kind of story that, no doubt, the agency employees involved take immense pride in.

It is so important, I thought, to work on projects that you can be proud of. To have a quick and easy story to share with your family when they ask about work at Thanksgiving. I realized that it is the responsibility of the leadership team to first ensure that each person in our organization has access to this type of meaningful work. And to ensure that I help my team realize how meaningful their work actually is.

Of course, you first need to build your team. Then you need to find working opportunities that can develop into meaningful projects. The third piece is reflection: finding ways to turn those experiences into stories and anecdotes of praise.

Case studies have been instrumental in helping us reflect on our meaningful work. A case study's primary purpose is related to sales and business development, but the act of writing a case study is often revealing and cathartic. When I sit down with a team member to discuss a possible case study, they are often reluctant to take credit for a client's positive results. If a client saw an increase in conversion rate after we implemented a new landing page headline, the team member who wrote the headline might dismiss it as *one small change*. They are overlooking the months of research and analysis that provided them the ability to make that *one small change*. That's something worth pointing out, and it's something to be proud of.

If not for the case study, that moment of reflection and progress would not have taken place. It would have been dismissed as someone just *doing their job*. But it is often much more than that. Failure to recognize meaningful work, particularly within a hectic agency environment, is bad for the culture and increases employee burnout.

Three years ago, I began hosting a full team meeting every Friday morning. Referred to as the *Weekly Client Rundown,* we first share company updates and then discuss a handful of individual clients.

Over time, an additional benefit to these meetings has been revealed: It is a great opportunity to share positive feedback and to call attention to progress made on a weekly basis. When a client milestone is reached, we take a moment to recognize the team members that were involved in the process. As cheesy as it may sound, there is something special about this act: It is the equivalent to a salesperson ringing a gong after closing a deal and indicates a job well done.*

---

* I owe much of this benefit to Ronnie Cardno, who is always the first to erupt with applause and congratulations throughout these meetings.

Meaningful Relationships

In this book's introduction, I outlined how my search for meaningful work and meaningful relationships helped lead me toward AdVenture Media. I've been fortunate to experience the former and blessed to experience the latter. What might appear to be a long day at the office is so often just a day spent with people I sincerely enjoy being around.

Like my thoughts on meaningful work, *meaningful relationships* are contingent on your culture, which starts with whom you choose to hire. We take our hiring principles very seriously and strongly consider the impact that someone might have on the larger environment. We have made the decision to pass on certain candidates that excelled in all areas but gave off the impression that they would not buy into the collaborative team environment that we've worked so hard to protect.

There are times when one team member might become overwhelmed with a particular project, and we might need everyone else to drop everything and spend the day helping their colleague in need. This might result in a late-night or other work that gets backlogged for a day or two, but these are the kinds of experiences that are the building blocks for long-term, meaningful relationships.

The concept of meaningful relationships extends beyond just your internal team. You should seek to develop meaningful relationships with clients, vendors, and external partners that you work with on a daily basis.

My father made this clear to me at an early age. There are dozens of people whom I have considered to be a part of my extended family for decades but originally came into our lives because they worked with my father. To this day, my parents still host a massive BBQ each summer at their house that is specifically for these people and their families, despite the fact that my father has not actually worked with many of these people for over ten years. It's a day that both he and my mother look forward to for months.

I envy that. It is a result of an entire career focused on doing good by other people, having shared interests, and caring about them personally.

One thing that we preach all the time with our team is to be extremely empathetic to the individual POCs (points of contact) that we work with within a client's larger organization. Sure, everyone wants to meet the marketing goals, but you can't lose sight of the fact that they are also people with goals of their own. We try to find ways to help our POCs look like rock stars to their bosses and encourage them to take all the credit for the work that we do. After all, they're the ones responsible for managing the relationship.

There are a number of milestones that have brought me great joy over the years, many of which have nothing to do with the success of an ad campaign. Seeing our team members grow within our company and develop skills that they never thought they possessed is certainly at the top of the list. Similar to that, few things are as satisfying as when one of our POCs earns a promotion or takes a better job with a different company, as we can often feel that we helped contribute to that milestone in some way.

This mentality helps set the foundation for meaningful relationships within your organization and beyond. It's the reason why one client chose to fly to San Francisco to support Isaac during his very first conference speaking engagement in 2018, and why another client invited us to spend a weekend at her family's lake house one summer. More than that, it's why I get to go to work every day surrounded by a group of wonderfully dysfunctional people who I consider an extension of my family.

It's Time to Build

In the midst of the COVID-19 pandemic, Marc Andreessen of Venture Capital firm Andreessen Horowitz penned an article in response to the lack of basic medical equipment for healthcare workers. He titled the article "It's Time to Build."

> New York City has put out a desperate call for rain ponchos to be used as medical gowns. Rain ponchos! In 2020! In America!

> Why do we not have these things? Medical equipment and financial conduits involve no rocket science whatsoever. At least therapies and vaccines are hard! Making masks and transferring money are not hard. We could have these things but we chose not to—specifically we chose not to have the mechanisms, the factories, the systems to make these things. We chose not to *build*.[121]

According to Andreessen, our society, as a whole, lacks entrepreneurial spirit and moxie. He goes on to suggest that this same *smug complacency* exists in all areas of Western civilization—from education to transportation to manufacturing and construction.

We've become too comfortable with the status quo. Our society is not as technologically advanced as we should be. Andreessen admits *building* isn't easy. But he encourages us all to contribute—to *build*—because we are all capable of contributing to the forward movement of our society.

> Every step of the way, to everyone around us, we should be asking the question, what are you building? What are you building directly, or helping other people to build, or teaching other people to build, or taking care of people who are building?[122]

I've thought about this a lot over the last few months. Is AdVenture Media *building* anything?

I believe we are.

The P3X Framework, our hiring principles, and our model for decision making are all individual building blocks. These cornerstones will help agencies and practitioners develop more successful and profitable digital advertising campaigns in the modern era.

We're building a challenging yet rewarding work environment for our employees. We're building a playbook for business growth—for our clients and for us.

What we've built has enabled our clients to continue to serve their customers throughout an unprecedented global pandemic.

So we've built.

But now we ask ourselves: *Are we helping others build?*

People I meet are always intrigued when they ask me what I do for a living. *Digital advertising? That's exciting! Cutting edge!* They assume digital advertising is overflowing with the adoption of new technology, AI, and futuristic strategies. But it's not.

The smug complacency Andreessen highlights in healthcare exists in our industry, too.

It's time for a transformation, and you are capable of being a part of it. All of us, together.

This book is a transformational roadmap for all the talented people in our industry interested in driving digital success in the age of automation.

It feels damn good to have written it … to have *built* it. I hope you'll build on top of it.

After all, success ripples outwards.

Onwards,
Patrick Gilbert

Acknowledgments

Writing this book has been an incredible journey, and it would never have been possible if not for the many people in my life that have supported me.

Thanks to:

~My father, Richard, for being an incredible role model, a mentor, and a friend. You've taught me so much about business, hard work, leadership, and the importance of keeping family at the center of it all.

~My mother, Kathy, for being my #1 fan and the most interesting person I have ever met. Your ability to tell captivating stories has certainly transpired into your children (and hopefully into this book). Thank you for helping me appreciate all of the wonderful things that life has to offer.

~Aubree, for being my primary support system always, but particularly throughout this writing process. You bring so much happiness to my life, especially when I need it most. Thank you for being by my side throughout the early mornings, late nights, and whenever I am stressed or otherwise need someone to vent to. I couldn't have done this without you.

~Melanie, Sean, Christina; and to Joe, Sarah, Bryan; and the broader Gilbert, Heaphy, Julian, Weiss, Harrs, Humann, Kilduff, Smith, and Cannone families. I am so blessed to be surrounded by so much love and support.

~The team at Jay's Appliances in Levittown, NY, for having taken me under your wing and supporting me for so long.

~Kinjal Mathur and Michael Ringenbach, my two counterparts from my time working at Four Diamonds at Penn State Hershey Children's Hospital. Kinj, you were the first person to ever encourage my writing; Bach, you were the first person to teach me about and spark my interest in, data science. Among many other things that you've both helped me with over the years, these two examples certainly stand out.

~The many Googlers who have helped educate me and our team over the years. Particularly, Annie Tao, Mark Donnelly, Adam McDaniel, Richie Reynolds, Seb Kassegne, Ana Kiguel, and Stepanie Lehmann.

~Amanda Snajder, our primary agency strategist at Facebook who has singlehandedly done more for our agency and our clients than I could possibly describe.

~Luca Senatore, Frederick Vaelleys, and Jim Sterne for their willingness to be interviewed for this book and to collaborate on many of these topics.

~Leigh Green, Cathy McMahen, Teddi Black, and Megan McCullough for the edits, citations, and design of this book. Thanks for helping this dream become a reality.

~Everyone who has advocated for and supported AdVenture Media over the years, particularly Gary Karrass, Ruth Hearn, Elsa Guerrero, Phil Engert, Erik Murnighan, Daniel Rubinstein, Alex Zukovski, David Sable, and so many others.

~The AdVenture Media team. I am so proud of what we have accomplished together, and I am honored to come to work each day and be surrounded by such a talented, passionate, intelligent, and eclectic group of people.

~And of course, to Isaac Rudansky, for being the mentor that I sought after and described in this book's introduction. Thank you for believing in me and coaching me over the years and for always pushing me to do better than my best. This book would not exist if not for your support, your constant feedback, and your inspiration.

There are many others that I am grateful for: my friends, family, and colleagues past and present who stretch far beyond this list. I am so fortunate to have so many incredible people in my life. Thank you.

Endnotes

1 Ray Dalio, *Principles* (New York: Simon & Schuster, 2017).

2 Pedro Domingos, *The Master Algorithm: How the Quest for the Ultimate Learning Machine Will Remake Out World* (New York: Basic Books, 2015).

3 *George Box and Alberto Luceño, Statistical Control: By Monitoring and Feedback Adjustment (New York:* John Wiley & Sons, 1997), 6.

4 Peter McCullagh and John Nelder, *Generalized Linear Models*, 2nd ed. (Boca Raton, FL: Taylor & Francis, 1989).

5 Shivali Best and Joe Pinkstone, "B2B Marketers Are Looking Past Leads and Looking Toward Influencing Accounts," *Daily Mail Online*, December 7, 2017, https://www.dailymail.co.uk/sciencetech/article-5155009/Googles-AI-mastered-chess-four-hours-scratch.html.

6 Malcolm Gladwell, *Outliers: The Story of Success* (New York: Little, Brown and Company, 2008).

7 J. K. Rowling, *Harry Potter and the Sorcerer's Stone* (New York: Scholastic Press, 1997).

8 Bill Taylor, "What Breaking the 4-Minute Mile Taught Us About the Limits of Conventional Thinking," *Harvard Business Review*, March 9, 2018, https://hbr.org/2018/03/what-breaking-the-4-minute-mile-taught-us-about-the-limits-of-conventional-thinking.

9 Nathan Brannen, "Only 1497 Humans Have Ever Broken the 4-Minute Mile—And I'm One of Them," *CBC Sports*, June 27, 2018, https://www.cbc.ca/playersvoice/entry/only-1497-humans-have-ever-broken-the-4-minute-mile-and-im-one-of-them#:~:text=Only%201%2C497%20humans%20have%20ever%20broken%20the%204-minute,that%20race%27%20By%20Nathan%20Brannen%20for%20CBC%20Sports.

10 Kenneth Goodrich et al., "Application of the H-Mode, A Design and Interaction Concept for Highly Automated Vehicles to Aircraft," NASA Technical Reports

Server, August 23, 2013, https://ntrs.nasa.gov/archive/nasa/casi.ntrs.nasa.gov/20060051774.pdf.

11 Ibid.

12 "Understanding Liquidity, How Machine Learning Helps Media Teams Work Smarter," Facebook IQ, May 6, 2019, https://www.iab.com/wp-content/uploads/2019/05/IAB-Member-Research_Facebook_2019-05-06_Understanding-Liquidity.pdf.

13 Ibid.

14 "Optimizing Audience Buying on Facebook and Instagram," Facebook IQ, July 26, 2016, https://www.facebook.com/business/news/insights/optimizing-audience-buying-on-facebook-and-instagram.

15 Andrew McStay, "Micro-Moments, Liquidity, Intimacy and Automation: Developments in Programmatic Ad-tech," in *Commercial Communication in the Digital Age*, ed. Gabriel Siegert, M. Bjorn von Rimscha and Stephanie Grubenmann (Berlin: de Gruyter, 2017), 143-160.

16 Ibid.

17 Sridhar Ramaswamy, "How Micro-Moments Are Changing the Rules," Think with Google, April 2015, https://www.thinkwithgoogle.com/marketing-resources/micro-moments/how-micromoments-are-changing-rules/

18 McStay, "Micro-Moments."

19 Ibid.

20 "About Quality Score," Google Ads Help, accessed April 1, 2020, https://support.google.com/google-ads/answer/7050591?hl=en.

21 "Auction," Google Ads Help, accessed February 1, 2020, https://support.google.com/google-ads/answer/142918.

22 "Actual Cost-Per-Click (CPC): Definition," Google Ads Help, accessed April 29, 2020, https://support.google.com/google-ads/answer/6297?hl=en.

23 "Ad Rank," Google Ads Help, accessed January 10, 2020, https://support.google.com/google-ads/answer/1752122.

24 "Ad-Rank Thresholds: Definition," Google Ads Help, accessed January 15, 2020, https://support.google.com/google-ads/answer/7634668.

25 "About Quality Score," Google Ads Help.

26 "Landing Page Experience: Definition," Google Ads Help, accessed May 1, 2020, https://support.google.com/google-ads/answer/1659694.

27 "Follow Up on Your Quality Score Diagnosis," Google Ads Help, accessed May 10, 2020, https://support.google.com/google-ads/answer/6167116.

28 "Expected Clickthrough Rate: Definition," Google Ads Help, accessed March 9, 2020, https://support.google.com/google-ads/answer/1659696.

29 George Nguyen, "Now, More Than 50% of Google Searches End Without a Click to Other Content, Study Finds," Search Engine Land, August 14, 2019, https://searchengineland.com/now-more-50-of-google-searches-end-without-a-click-to-other-content-study-finds-320574.

30 "About Responsive Search Ads," Google Ads Help, accessed August 29, 2020, https://support.google.com/google-ads/answer/7684791?hl=en.

31 "Gallery Ads (Beta) Available in 11 Languages Globally," Google Ads Help, August 5, 2019, https://support.google.com/google-ads/answer/9430978?hl=en.

32 "Display Network: Definition," Google Ads Help, April 29, 2020, https://support.google.com/google-ads/answer/117120?hl=en.

33 "About Smart Display Campaigns," Google Ads Help, April 10, 2020, https://support.google.com/google-ads/answer/7020281?hl=en.

34 "Title: Definition," Google Merchant Center Help," accessed April 29, 2020, https://support.google.com/merchants/answer/6324415?hl=en.

35 "True View," Think with Google, August 2016, https://www.thinkwithgoogle.com/products/youtube-trueview/.

36 "About Similar Audiences for Search," Google Ads Help, accessed August 29, 2020, https://support.google.com/google-ads/answer/7151628?hl=en.

37 "About Audience Targeting," Google Ads Help, accessed January 30,2020, https://support.google.com/google-ads/answer/2497941?hl=en.

38 "Accrual Accounting," *Entrepreneur*, accessed May 30, 2020, https://www.entrepreneur.com/encyclopedia/accrual-accounting.

39 Box and *Luceño, Statistical Control.*

40 "About Data-Driven Attribution," Google Ads Help, accessed April 10, 2020, https://support.google.com/google-ads/answer/6394265?hl=en.

41 "Build Your Competitive Advantage with Artificial Intelligence," Marketing Artificial Intelligence Institute, accessed August 29, 2020, https://www.marketingaiinstitute.com/

42 Domingos, *The Master Algorithm.*

43 Hans Gunnoo, "Moore's Law Is Dying. Here's How AI Is Bringing It Back to Life!" Towards Data Science, August 15, 2018, https://towardsdatascience.com/moores-law-is-dying-here-s-how-ai-is-bringing-it-back-to-life-c9a469bc7a5a.

44 Azeem, "If We Want to Get to Real Time AI, We've Got to Build Another iPhone Industry. Five Times Over," Medium, July 17, 2017, https://medium.com/s/ai-and-the-future-of-computing/when-moores-law-met-ai-f572585da1b7.

45 Domingos, *The Master Algorithm.*

46 Alan Turing, "Computing Machinery and Intelligence," *Mind* 59, no. 236 (October 1950): 433-460.

47 Josef Bajada, "Symbolic vs. Connectionist AI," Medium, April 8, 2019, https://towardsdatascience.com/symbolic-vs-connectionist-a-i-8cf6b656927.

48 Ibid.

49 Chris Nicholson, "A Beginner's Guide to Genetic and Evolutionary Algorithms," Pathmind, accessed May 31, 2020, https://wiki.pathmind.com/evolutionary-genetic-algorithm.

50 Adam Hayes, "Bayes Theorem Definition," Investopedia, updated June 14, 2020, https://www.investopedia.com/terms/b/bayes-theorem.asp.

51 "Game Tree for Tic-Tac-Toe Game Using MiniMax Algorithm," ResearchGate, accessed May 29, 2020, https://www.researchgate.net/figure/Game-tree-for-Tic-Tac-Toe-game-using MiniMax-algorithm_fig1_262672371.

52 "Robot Scientist 'Eve' Could Boost Search for New Drugs," University of Manchester, February 4, 2015, https://www.manchester.ac.uk/discover/news/robot-scientist-eve-could-boost-search-for-new-drugs/.

53 Veronica Cruz, 'Robot Scientist 'Eve' Discover New Drugs Super Fast and Cheaply," *Market Business News*, February 9, 2015, https://marketbusinessnews.com/robot-scientist-eve-discovers-new-drugs-super-fast-cheaply/47459/.

54 Domingos, *The Master Algorithm.*

55 Ibid.

56 "About Smart Bidding," Google Ads Help, May 1, 2020, https://support.google.com/google-ads/answer/7065882.

57 "About Target CPA Bidding," Google Ads Help, accessed May15, 2020, https://support.google.com/google-ads/answer/6268632?hl=en.

58 "About Conversion Windows," Google Ads Help, accessed May 29, 2020, https://support.google.com/google-ads/answer/3123169?co=ADWORDS.IsAWNCustomer percent3Dfalse&hl=en.

59 Ben Heath, "The Facebook Ads Learning Phase—What You Need to Know," November 12, 2018, https://www.business2community.com/facebook/the-facebook-ads-learning phase-what-you-need-to-know-02138589.

60 "Facebook Blueprint," Facebook for Business, accessed May 29, 2020, https://www.facebook.com/business/learn.

61 "The Breakdown Effect," Facebook for Business, accessed May 29, 2020, https://www.facebook.com/business/m/one-sheeters/breakdown-effect.

62 "About Cost Cap," Facebook for Business, accessed May 29, 2020, https://www.facebook.com/business/help/272336376749096?id=2196356200683573.

63 "Transform Your Business with Smarter Measurement," Facebook for Business, accessed January 10, 2020, https://www.facebook.com/business.

64 Frederick Vallaeys, *Digital Marketing in an AI World: Futureproofing Your PPC Agency* (Marketing Masters, 2019).

65 Thomas Barta and Patrick Barwise, *The 12 Powers of a Marketing Leader: How to Succeed by Building Customer and Company Value* (New York: McGraw-Hill, 2016).

66 Ibid.

67 Ibid.

68 Ibid.

69 Ibid.

70 Ibid.

71 Ibid.

72 Jim Sterne, *Artificial Intelligence for Marketing: Practical Applications* (Hoboken, NJ: Wiley & Sons, 2017).

73 Interview with Jim Sterne, May 11, 2020.

74 Ibid.

75 Ibid.

76 Ibid.

77 Ibid.

78 Ibid.

79 Ibid.

80 Ibid.

81 Jim Sterne, "The Consulting Pyramid," eMetrics Summit, March 31, 2016, https://www.emetrics.org/blog/2016/03/31/the-consulting-pyramid/.

82 Interview with Luca Senatore, April 20, 2020.

83 Ibid.

84 Jim Collins, *Good to Great: Why Some Companies Make the Leap and Others Don't* (New York: HarperCollins, 2001).

85 Jim Collins, "Good to Great," Jim Collins.com, 2001, https://www.jimcollins.com/article_topics/articles/good-to-great.html.

86 Rand Fishkin, *Lost and Founder: A Painfully Honest Field Guide to the Startup World* (New York: Portfolio.Penguin, 2018), 207-218.

87 Laurence Peter and Raymond Hull, *The Peter Principle: Why Things Always Go Wrong* (New York: Harper, 2011).

88 Fishkin, *Lost and Founder*.

89 Rand Fishkin, "If Management is the Only Way Up, We're All F'd," SparkToro, April 26, 2013, https://sparktoro.com/blog/if-management-is-the-only-way-up-were-all-fd/

90 Marcel Schwantes, "Warren Buffet Says Integrity Is the Most Important Trait to Hire For. Ask These 12 Questions to Find It," *INC.* accessed May 31, 2020,

https://www.inc.com/marcel-schwantes/first-90-days-warren-buffetts-advice-for-hiring-based-on-3-traits.html.

91 Ibid.

92 Rand Fishkin, "Why Marketing Flywheels Work," *SparkToro* (blog), May 25, 2020, https://sparktoro.com/blog/why-marketing-flywheels-work/#:~:text=%20Why%20Marketing%20Flywheels%20Work%20%201%20The,tend%20to%20be%20great%20marketing%20flywheel...%20More%20.

93 Ibid.

94 Ben Thompson, "The Reality of Missing Out," *Stratechery* (blog), February 9, 2016, https://stratechery.com/2016/the-reality-of-missing-out/.

95 Ibid.

96 Ibid.

97 Ibid.

98 Sheryl Sandberg quoted in Thompson, "The Reality of Missing Out."

99 Thompson, "The Reality of Missing Out."

100 Ben Thompson, "Aggregation Theory," Stratechery, July 21, 2015, https://stratechery.com/2017/defining aggregators/.

101 Ibid.

102 Ibid.

103 Ibid.

104 Ibid.

105 Mary Meeker, "Mary Meeker's Internet Trends 2010," Slide Presentation Published November 18, 2010, Slideshare, https://www.slideshare.net/marketingfacts/mary-meekers-internet-trends-2010.

106 Ethan Craft, "Revenues from Podcast Advertising Are Projected to Hit $1 Billion by 2021," Ad Age, June 4, 2019, https://adage.com/article/digital/revenues-podcast-advertising-are-projected-hit-1-billion-2021/2174971.

107 "IFPI Global Music Report 2019," IFPI, April 2, 2019, https://new.ifpi.org/ifpi-global-music-report-2019/.

108 Ibid.

109 "Spotify Technology S.A. Announces Financial Results for Fourth Quarter 2018," Spotify Investors, February 6, 2019, https://investors.spotify.com/financials/press-release-details/2019/Spotify-Technology-SA-Announces-Financial-Results-for-Fourth-Quarter-2018/default.aspx.

110 Ginny Marvin, "U.S. Podcast Audiences Keep Growing, 62 Million Listening Weekly," Marketing Land, March 7, 2019, https://marketingland.com/u-s-podcast-audiences-keep-growing-62-million-listening-weekly-258179#:~:text=Half%20of%20the%20U.S.%20has,podcast%2C%20

according%20to%20Edison%20Research.&text=For%20the%20first%20time%2C%20more,have%20listened%20to%20a%20podcast.

111 Marc Berman, "Over 22-Million Viewers for 'Sunday Night Football' Season-Opener on NBC," PI, September 9, 2016, https://programminginsider.com/22-million-viewers-sunday-night-football-season-opener-nbc/.

112 John Ourand, "Sources: NFL Could Create Eight-Game Package Bringing in up to $700M," *Sports Business Daily*, October 24, 2013, https://www.sportsbusinessdaily.com/Daily/Issues/2013/10/24/Media/NFL-Thursday.aspx.

113 Ashley Carman, "The Podcast Industry Expected to create $1 Billion in Annual Revenue by 2021," The Verge, June 3, 2019, https://www.theverge.com/2019/6/3/18650526/podcast-iab-advertising-industry-revenue.

114 Ads Wizz, "It's Time to Help Businesses Find Their Voice on Audio," *The Business Journals*, October 15, 2019, https://www.bizjournals.com/bizjournals/news/2019/10/15/its-time-to-help-businesses-find-their-voice-on.html#:~:text=In%20fact%2C%20according%20to%20a,to%20purchase%20the%20advertised%20product.

115 Patrick Gilbert, "Why Did Spotify Double Down on Podcast?" AdVenture, February 10, 2019, https://adventureppc.com/blog/why-did-spotify-double-down-on-podcasts.

116 Sean Burch, "Joe Rogan Signs Exclusive $100 Million Podcast Deal with Spotify," MSN, May 19, 2020, https://www.msn.com/en-us/tv/news/joe-rogan-signs-exclusive-100-million-podcast-deal-with-spotify/ar-BB14jDHC.

117 Angel Au-Yeung, "How Billionaire Anthony Wood Quit His Netflix Job, Founded Roku—And Then Quadrupled His Fortune in the Past Year," *Forbes*, December 31, 2019, https://www.forbes.com/sites/angelauyeung/2019/12/16/how-billionaire-anthony-wood-quit-his-netflix-job-founded-roku-and-then-quadrupled-his-fortune-in-the-past-year/#2894399f5aea.

118 "Roku Devices Command 59% Programmatic Ad Market Share in 2019," *Pixalate* (blog), May 12, 2020, https://blog.pixalate.com/ott-ctv-programmatic-ad-device-market-share-roku-2019#:~:text=OTT%2FCTV%20advertising%3F-,Roku%20devices%20command%2059%25%20programmatic%20ad%20-market%20share%20in%202019,other%20OTT%2FCTV%20device%20type.

119 "OTT Vs. CTV: What's in a Name?" IAB Tech Lab, May 7, 2020, https://iabtechlab.com/blog/ott-vs-ctv-what-is-in-a-name/.

120 Sarah Perez, Roku Buys Adtech Platform Dataxu for $150 Million, October 22, 2019, https://techcrunch.com/2019/10/22/roku-buys-ad-tech-platform-dataxu-for-150-million/.

121 Marc Andreessen, "It's Time to Build," Andreessen Horowitz, accessed September 1, 2020.

122 Ibid.

CPSIA information can be obtained
at www.ICGtesting.com
Printed in the USA
BVHW080955280722
643232BV00004B/319

9 781632 217684